Women in the Civil War

Women in the Civil War

Extraordinary Stories of Soldiers, Spies, Nurses, Doctors, Crusaders, and Others

LARRY G. EGGLESTON

McFarland & Company, Inc., Publishers

Jefferson, North Carolina, and London

ISBN 0-7864-1493-6 (illustrated case binding : 50# alkaline paper)

Library of Congress cataloguing data are available

British Library cataloguing data are available

*On the front cover: Frances Clayton standing in uniform and sitting in dress.
Boston Public Library/Rare Books Department. Courtesy of the Trustees.*

Manufactured in the United States of America

*McFarland & Company, Inc., Publishers
Box 611, Jefferson, North Carolina 28640
www.mcfarlandpub.com*

Acknowledgments

The assistance of the following people and organizations is gratefully acknowledged. Their courteous help in gathering data and illustrations has contributed greatly in the preparation of this publication.

• Hargrett Rare Book and Manuscript Library, University of Georgia. Athens, Georgia.
• Lake Blackshear Regional Library, Special Collections. Americus, Georgia.
• National Park Service. Andersonville National Historical Site. Andersonville, Georgia.
• The LaPorte County Historical Society Museum. LaPorte, Indiana.
• The LaPorte County Public Library. LaPorte, Indiana.
• The Valparaiso Public Library. Valparaiso, Indiana.
• The Valparaiso University Library. Valparaiso, Indiana.
• The Valparaiso University School of Law Library. Valparaiso, Indiana.
• The Chicago Historical Society. Chicago, Illinois.
• The Chicago Public Library, Special Collections and Preservation Division. Harold Washington Library Center. Chicago, Illinois.
• Betty Estes, Director of Tourism. Pontiac, Illinois.
• Bill Lannon. Saunamin, Illinois.
• The Illinois State Historical Library. Springfield, Illinois.
• The Pontiac Public Library, Historical Collections. Pontiac, Illinois.
• The MINERVA Center. Pasadena, Maryland.
• The Boston Public Library. Boston, Massachusetts.
• The Bentley Historical Library. University of Michigan. Ann Arbor, Michigan.

• The Grand Rapids Public Library, Historical Collections. Grand Rapids, Michigan.

• The State Archives of Michigan. Michigan Library and Historical Center. Lansing, Michigan.

• The New York Historical Society. New York, New York.

• Appalachian State University. Boone, North Carolina.

• Avery County Historical Society. Newland, North Carolina.

• Duke University. Special Collections Library. Durham, North Carolina.

• The University of North Carolina. Southern Historical Collection. Chapel Hill, North Carolina.

• Maggie Marconi. Sandusky Library Follett Museum archives. Sandusky, Ohio.

• The Sandusky Public Library, Archival Collections. Sandusky, Ohio.

• The Western Reserve Historical Society. Cleveland, Ohio.

• Gettysburg National Military Park, Library Archives. Gettysburg, Pennsylvania.

• Leib Image Archives. York, Pennsylvania.

• U.S. Army Military History Institute. Carlisle, Pennsylvania.

• Florence Public Library. Florence, South Carolina.

• Buddy Hughes. Pound, Virginia.

• The Richmond Civil War Visitors Center. National Battlefield Park. Richmond, Virginia.

• The Valentine Museum and Historic Center. Richmond, Virginia.

• The Library of Congress. Washington, D.C.

• National Archives. Washington, D.C.

• The West Virginia State Archives. Charleston, West Virginia.

• Terry Foenander. Toowoomba. QLD, Australia.

Thank you
L.G. Eggleston
January 2003
Wanatah, Indiana

Contents

Contents

Preface

The four-year American Civil War was a period of great suffering and hardship. It was also a period of great heroism and sacrifice, filled with many exciting stories of those who went far beyond the call of duty to do their part for the cause in which they believed. Great heroism and loyalty were displayed by many brave men and women on both sides of the conflict, as normal everyday people rose to the challenge and made extraordinary contributions to their cause.

In studying the Civil War it becomes evident that the great contributions made by many extraordinary women have not been properly recognized. This can be explained as one begins to understand the moral attitudes of the time and the way women were viewed by society. Women were held with respect even though they were considered to be the weaker sex. It was not acceptable for a woman to lower herself by doing what was considered to be men's work or to wear men's clothing. Those women who did were considered odd and thought of poorly by society. This way of thinking seems strange to us, since many women at that time were doing very hard work on the farms as well as in the homes. The nation, being mostly agricultural at the time, saw families working the land side by side. Women participated in the same work as men. Women who worked on the early farms tended the livestock and helped with plowing, planting and harvesting, as well as performing the many duties associated with keeping the home.

Many women broke away from society's traditional view of women when the Civil War began. Those brave women distinguished themselves in many different fields, even though at the time they were looked down upon by society.

Hundreds of women disguised themselves and joined the armies of the North and South as fighting men. Some were quickly discovered because of not being able to hide their feminine characteristics such as how they walked, how they sat, and how they acted. Some recruits who were suspected of being female would be tested with little tricks such as tossing them an apple to see how they would react. Those who held out their shirts to catch the apple as if in an apron were found out. Tricks like this caused many women soldiers to be discovered and subsequently discharged.

Those women who were not discovered usually practiced walking, talking, and acting like men prior to their enlistment. Many took to chewing tobacco or changed their fair complexions to a more rugged look by using some sort of stain. They would make padded vests to hide their breasts and make them appear stout and masculine.

Personal and toilet problems in the company of so many men were additional problems women had to overcome. One would think that women could easily be detected while living in such close proximity with a huge number of men. Their personal needs, it seems, would surely give them away. In some situations this might have been true, but in the Civil War many of the soldiers were very young. Most of these young boys were easily embarrassed and a bit shy. Some could not relieve themselves in front of other soldiers but instead went into the woods or somewhere private to tend to their toilet needs. Therefore the women soldiers could likewise go somewhere private without it seeming strange.

Those young soldiers for the most part had fair, boyish faces and had not yet begun to shave. The women soldiers therefore were not under suspicion for not shaving since it was not considered unusual.

Those women who were not discovered served with honor and endured all the hardships of army life. Some endured great suffering by being captured in battle and sent to prison camps. Many women were killed in battle and buried without their gender being revealed. Many others made it through the war undetected and were granted pensions even after their gender was known. Estimates of the number of women who fought in the Civil War disguised as men range from 400 to 700. Records indicate that approximately 60 women soldiers were known to have been killed or wounded during the Civil War. It is not known how many lie in unknown graves on the many battlefields.

Many women soldiers wanted to stay active and on the move. In order to do so they volunteered for other duties during the long periods between battles. Those other duties included working in the regimental hospital, which usually kept them up late and allowed them to go to bed after all the men were asleep. This lessened the chance of their being found out. Many volunteered as couriers or spies, which kept them out of camp for long periods of time.

The reasons women disguised themselves as fighting men are many. They included running away from pre-arranged marriages, a quest for excitement, a sense of duty and patriotism, a desire to be part of history, wanting to be with a husband or lover, a desire to receive better pay on a steady basis, and wanting to help support their families. For whatever reason these women chose to become soldiers, they all served with courage and dedication and deserve recognition.

Other women served as "daughters of the regiment," a duty that included many different tasks such as nursing, cooking, mending uniforms and being flag bearer.

These courageous women usually carried the flag ahead of the regiment into battle. They marched with and trained with the soldiers and often participated in battle to replace fallen comrades.

Women volunteered to serve as nurses and doctors once the government decided to accept them into those professions. This acceptance was the result of the great need and the lack of available male help. Those women served on the battlefield as well as in the hospitals and regimental aid stations. Their courage and dedication saved thousands of lives.

Women stood up and answered the call when the need arose. Many volunteered as vivandiers, cooks, laundresses, couriers, and spies. Some used their talents to help their cause by writing, teaching, organizing relief agencies, and administering programs to help the soldiers.

Only a handful of those heroic women have been remembered by history. Others are slowly coming to light with diaries, letters, and personal papers being found by descendants as estates pass down to new generations.

The purpose of this book is to give recognition to those extraordinary women and their remarkable contributions to American history.

L.G.E.
Wanatah, Indiana
January 2003

❧ 1 ❧

Women POWs at Andersonville Prison

In early 1861, as the Civil War began, many women felt compelled to serve their country by disguising themselves and enlisting in the Union or Confederate armies as fighting men. Some of these brave women were quickly discovered and discharged, while others served throughout the war undetected.

There are many accounts of women soldiers who were captured on the battlefield and held as prisoners of war in one of the many Civil War prison camps. Some endured the hardships while others were discovered and set free. None, however, revealed themselves in order to be set free. Instead, they stayed with their comrades and endured the hardships and cruel conditions of prison.

One of the most interesting accounts of women POWs is that of the three women incarcerated at Andersonville Prison.

By late 1863, overcrowding was becoming a huge problem in the Confederate prisons. The Confederate government was in need of new facilities to house the increasing number of Union prisoners being captured. They began to search for a suitable location that would be accessible and yet safe from possible Union raids.

In early 1864, an isolated spot for a new prison camp was selected. The new site was south of Atlanta, Georgia near the end of the Southwestern Railroad, at a small town called Andersonville Station. The prison camp was built in an oak and pine forest and was named Camp Sumter. Camp Sumter is commonly referred to as Andersonville Prison.

The 26-acre stockade was hastily constructed and the camp opened prior to any buildings being constructed to house the prisoners. As a result, the prisoners

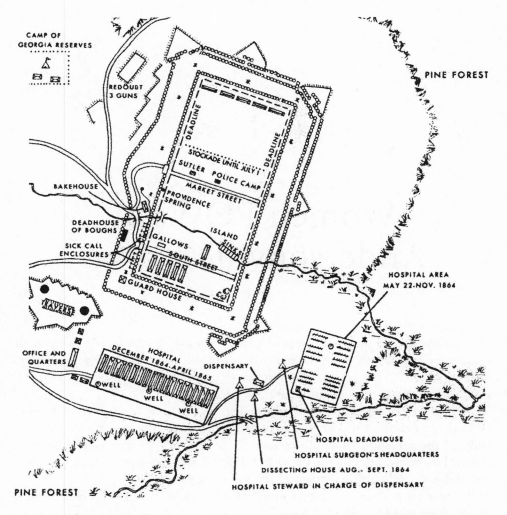

Map of Andersonville. Courtesy of the National Park Service at Andersonville.

were required to live in makeshift tents and dugouts. Official records reveal that Andersonville Prison was the most brutal, unsanitary, and overcrowded prison of the Civil War.

The prison camp was in operation for 13 months and 14 days, from February 25, 1864, to March 10, 1865. During this short period of time, a total of 12,912 prisoners lost their lives. The first Union prisoners arrived on February 25, 1864. By late summer of 1864, the population of the prison had risen to three times its capacity of 6,000. The prison population continued to grow to over 30,000 by the end of the war. During this 13-month period, Andersonville Prison had housed a total of 45,613 prisoners.

Among this huge population of prisoners were two women soldiers who were disguised as men and fought in the Union army. There was also one woman prisoner

Stockade at Andersonville. Courtesy of Hargrett Rare Book and Manuscript Library, University of Georgia.

who chose to stay with her husband when he was captured and sent to the prison. She also had to disguise herself as a man in order to hide her gender from the other prisoners. It is recorded, however, that the Confederate guards knew she was in the prison with her husband. There may have been other women in the prison, but they were not discovered and no record of their involvement exists.

The most interesting fact about these three women prisoners at Andersonville is that they stayed and endured all the suffering and hardships of being confined under such brutal conditions. The two women soldiers only had to reveal themselves to their captors and they would have been returned to their own lines under a flag of truce. Many women, both prisoners and spies, were returned in this manner after being discovered. The third woman could have chosen to leave at any time.

Janie Hunt

The first of these extraordinary women was Janie Hunt, daughter of Thomas L. Scadden of Chicago, Illinois. Janie Scadden was married in June 1863 to Captain Harry Hunt of Buffalo, New York. Captain Hunt operated a coasting vessel out of New York City.

After the wedding, the wedding guests were invited aboard the ship for a plea-
sure cruise. The guests happily accepted and the ship set out from New York Harbor for a short trip. After sailing for only a few hours, they were stopped by a Federal
revenue cutter and ordered to proceed to North Carolina to pick up a load of corn.
It is not known why the wedding guests and the bride were not taken aboard the
revenue cutter and returned safely to New York. Perhaps there was no room for them
on the ship, or perhaps its captain attached no danger to the mission. For whatever
reason, all stayed aboard and the ship sailed to North Carolina.

While the corn was being loaded, the ship was seized by Confederate troops.
The passengers and crew were all taken into custody. Soon thereafter, the wedding
guests were released and allowed to return home. Janie, hoping that her husband
would soon be released, refused to leave and was allowed to remain at his side.

The newlywed couple was held in custody until February 1864 when the Confederate authorities decided to send Captain Hunt to the new prison camp at Andersonville, Georgia. Upon hearing this news, Janie still refused to leave her husband
and after much pleading was allowed to disguise herself as a man and accompany
him to prison.

Upon arrival at Andersonville Prison, they located an isolated spot in the southwest corner of the stockade and set up their makeshift campsite. The isolated campsite would keep them out of the main stream of the prison population and help Janie
in concealing her identity from the other inmates, a task which became more difficult
as time passed because Janie was already four months pregnant when she arrived at
Andersonville Prison in February 1864.

In July 1864, Janie gave birth to a son whom they named Harry Jr. "Little Harry"
was born in their tent at the corner of the stockade. She wrapped the baby in rags,
which she had torn from her own clothes. Four days after the baby was born, a Confederate doctor named Dr. W. J. W. Kerr made a surprise visit to their tent and found
Mrs. Hunt and the baby.

Originally from Corsicana, Texas, Dr. Kerr was sent to Andersonville Prison to
take charge of the dispensary and to superintend the building of a hospital and all
other buildings associated with the prison. Upon his arrival, he set up his office in
the "Star Fort" directly outside the southwest corner of the stockade. While sitting
quietly in his office on the evening of his first day of duty, he thought he heard the
faint cry of a baby. His inquiry resulted in one of the guards informing him that it
was the baby of Captain Hunt and his wife. The next morning, Dr. Kerr went into
the stockade to locate Mrs. Hunt and the baby.

Recognizing that living conditions in the prison would put the lives of the
mother and baby at risk, Dr. Kerr decided to request help for the family. He rallied
the rest of the medical staff to sign a petition, which would allow the mother and
baby to be placed in a nearby home for the remainder of the war. Dr. Kerr presented
this petition to General Winder and, after some persuasion, it was approved. Janie
and the baby were boarded on a farm, less than two miles from the prison. Mr. and
Mrs. Smith, owners of the farm, reluctantly agreed to the arrangement. Janie and

baby remained with Mr. and Mrs. Smith until the end of the war. Dr. Kerr also provided Janie with material to make clothing for herself and the baby.

Dr. Kerr was also successful in getting Captain Hunt paroled to his custody. He placed the captain as a ward master in one of the wings of the hospital where he remained for the rest of the war. Dr. Kerr was responsible for survival of this entire family.

The sacrifices, hardships, and suffering which Janie Hunt endured as well as the loyalty and dedication she displayed during these trying times indicate that she was willing to and did give the greatest measure of devotion for her family and her beliefs.

Florena Budwin

Very little data is available on the second woman at Andersonville Prison. Her name was Florena Budwin from Philadelphia, Pennsylvania. She is reported to have disguised herself as a man and enlisted in the Union army with her husband, Captain Budwin.

The young couple supposedly fought side by side in many battles. According to a statement made by Florena at the prison camp at Florence, South Carolina, her husband was killed and Florena was captured during the same battle by the Confederate forces. Some reports state that Captain Budwin was killed at Andersonville Prison, after being captured along with Florena. However, there is no record that Captain Budwin ever arrived, and there is no one named Budwin buried in the Andersonville National Cemetery. Records indicate that Florena did arrive at the prison still disguised as a man. The exact date of his death and her capture is unknown, but it was in mid-1864.

After her capture, Florena was imprisoned at Andersonville, Georgia. The alias she was using is unknown. She was held at Andersonville until late 1864, when she was transferred with many other prisoners to the new prison being constructed at Florence, South Carolina.

The Confederate government began construction of the stockade at Florence, South Carolina, on September 17, 1864. While construction was underway the Confederate government transferred 6,000 prisoners from Charleston to Florence. These prisoners were all sick or diseased. They suffered from small pox, yellow fever, and exhaustion, among many other illnesses.

In late 1864, Florena Budwin, along with many other prisoners, was transferred to Florence to help relieve some of the extreme overcrowding at Andersonville. During her short time in Florence stockade, Florena helped care for the many sick and diseased soldiers. While serving in this role, she was stricken with pneumonia and required medical attention. The Confederate doctor treating her discovered her gender. Upon making this discovery the doctor moved her to a private room where she could get special treatment. When questioned by the doctor, she stated that her name was Florena Budwin. She revealed that she disguised herself as a man and joined the army to be near her husband, Captain Budwin. She further stated that he was killed in the same battle in which she was captured.

Florena Budwin Tombstone. National Cemetery — Florence, South Carolina. (Photograph by L.G. Eggleston.)

When word spread that there was a woman in the prison, the ladies of Florence donated food and clothing for her. However, despite receiving better treatment, she died on January 25, 1865, at the age of 20. Her death was only one month before all sick prisoners were released to the Union army.

Between September 17, 1864, and the end of February 1865, when the prison closed, 2,322 prisoners had died. Florena is buried with the others in the National Cemetery at Florence, South Carolina. She is buried under her own name in grave number D-2480. She was the first known woman soldier to be buried in a national cemetery. Each year since her death she has been honored on May 30, the National Memorial Day, as flowers are placed on her grave in tribute to her sacrifice.

The reasons prompting this young couple to enlist in the army after being married for such a short time are unknown. The greater mystery is why Florena stayed at Andersonville Prison and why she let the Confederate authorities transfer her to yet another prison. Since, as she reported, her husband was dead, she seemed to have no reason to continue to suffer the hardship of prison life. She could have revealed her gender to her captors and been set free.

Perhaps she stayed to continue doing her duty for her country and to honor the memory of her husband, or maybe she felt a duty toward the sick to help ease the suffering and pain of the war. Whatever her reasons, she stayed true to these beliefs even at the cost of her own life.

Unknown

Even less is known about the third woman discovered at Andersonville Prison. She is buried in the National Cemetery at Andersonville under a tombstone marked "Unknown." Her sex was not discovered until she died in captivity. Possibly her clothing was removed to be given to another needy prisoner. No one knew her real name, so instead of using her alias the grave was marked "Unknown." The only bit of information about this unknown woman comes from the recorded events of another woman soldier named Madame Collier.

Madame Collier was a Federal soldier disguised as a man who was captured and sent to Belle Isle Prison in Richmond, Virginia. Her gender was later discovered and she was taken back to the Union lines under a flag of truce. Once released, she turned to the Confederate soldiers and defiantly stated that there was still a woman at Belle Isle Prison. She refused to give the name of the woman, and only said that she was disguised as a man.

On March 1, 1864, General Judson Kilpatrick, under orders from President Lincoln, led 3,500 mounted raiders on Richmond with the objective of capturing Richmond and releasing the prisoners held at Belle Isle and Libby prisons. The raid on Richmond failed but it made the Confederate government realize that Belle Isle was not a secure place to keep prisoners. The prison was closed and all the prisoners were transferred to the new prison at Andersonville, Georgia.

If Madame Collier's account was accurate, the woman from Belle Isle Prison was among those transferred to Andersonville in early 1864. She very well may be the woman buried in the grave marked "Unknown."

Hopefully, some day, when more information is discovered, a name will be put on her tombstone and she will be given the recognition she rightfully deserves.

❦ 2 ❦

Sarah Rosetta Wakeman: Woman Soldier

Of all the women who became soldiers disguised as men, Sarah Rosetta Wakeman's army career as Pvt. Lyons Wakeman is one of the best documented. It is documented not only in the official records of the Civil War, but in the many letters she sent home which described her life with the 153rd New York Infantry Volunteers.

Sarah Rosetta Wakeman was born on January 16, 1843, on a farm near Afton, New York. She was the eldest of nine children (seven girls and two boys), born to Harvey Anable and Emily Hale Wakeman. The family was poor and despite the hard work they did, the farm could barely support such a large family.

When Sarah was 17 years old, she took a job at a neighboring home as a domestic servant in order to make extra money to help her family. She remained at this job for two years, during which time she concluded that if she wanted to earn better wages and have better jobs available to her, it would be in her best interest to disguise herself as a man and leave home. Later, in a letter to her family, she explained her reasons for leaving.

In August 1862, she changed her name to Lyons Wakeman, cut her hair short, disguised herself as a man, and left home. She traveled to Binghamton, New York, where she took a job for two weeks for $4. She then signed on with a river barge for four trips to carry coal up the Chenango Canal from Binghamton to Utica, New York. However, on the first trip, much to Sarah's surprise, the river barge did not stop in Utica but proceeded eastward down the Mohawk River to Canajoharie, New York. She was angry when she found that she would receive no additional pay for the extra trip.

While at Canajoharie she met several soldiers from the 153rd New York State Volunteers. This new regiment was being formed at Fonda, New York, just 12 miles east of Canajoharie on the river. The idea of joining this regiment sounded good to Sarah because it offered good steady pay and an enlistment bounty of $152.

On August 30, 1862, Sarah, using her assumed name of Lyons Wakeman, upped her age to 21 and enlisted in Company G, later Company H, of the newly formed regiment. Her enlistment was for a period of three years or the duration of the war. Pvt. Wakeman was described as five feet tall, with a fair complexion, blue eyes and brown hair. Sarah adopted the habit of chewing tobacco because it was believed this practice would fight off illness and thus keep her healthy.

The 153rd Regiment remained in Fonda until it had filled its ranks. The regiment was mustered into the United States Service on October 17, 1862, at Fonda, New York, and ordered to depart for Washington the next day. Private Wakeman's official enlistment date into the United States service is recorded as October 17, 1862, even though she enlisted in the regiment on August 30, 1862.

The regiment arrived in Washington on October 22. They were assigned provost martial and guard duty in Alexandria, Virginia. They formed part of the extensive defenses of Washington. The regiment had held this post for nine months when on July 20, 1863, they were transferred from Alexandria to Washington and quartered on Capitol Hill. The new regimental duties were to patrol the city, guard the B & O Railroad depot, convey troops to the front, escort prisoners of war to the prison at Point Lookout, Maryland, guard the "contraband" ex-slave refugee camp, guard Carroll Prison, and guard Old Capitol Prison.

The regiment performed these duties until February 17, 1864, when it was transferred to field duty with Major General Nathaniel P. Banks, to participate in the ill-fated Red River Campaign in Louisiana. The goal of the Red River Campaign was to capture Shreveport, Louisiana, and open a route for a federal assault on Texas.

Up to this point Pvt. Wakeman had not seen nor participated in any action against the enemy. However, the regiment had continually trained for battle while stationed in Washington and spirits were high. It embarked on February 20, 1864, aboard the steamship *Mississippi*. The regiment disembarked upon arrival in Algiers, Louisiana, which is across the river from New Orleans. They then boarded a train to Brasher City where they formed up and marched the final 53 miles to Franklin. The regiment planned to march from Franklin through Alexandria and Natchitochis directly into Shreveport.

The regiment did not reach Shreveport as planned because Confederate troops were waiting for them at Sabine Crossroads, approximately 40 miles south of Shreveport. The 153rd New York Volunteers were assigned to stay back several miles from the battle and guard the wagons and supplies. The regiment was still untested in the field. The battle was a defeat for the Federal troops and caused them to withdraw about 20 miles south to a place called Pleasant Hill where, on April 9, 1864, the 153rd New York Volunteers finally faced the enemy in battle.

Pvt. Wakeman described the battle in a letter home. She had stood firm with

Sarah Rosetta Wakeman. Photograph from *An Uncommon Soldier*. Courtesy of the MINERVA Center, Pasadena, Maryland.

the regiment which repelled six desperate charges by the Confederate troops under Major General Dick Taylor. Pvt. Wakeman wrote that they had "layed" all night on the battlefield among the wounded and dead. The first battle for the 153rd Regiment was successful and they now had a taste of the horrible realities of war.

The battle at Pleasant Hill was a victory for General Banks. Most of the Union weapons and supplies which had been seized by Confederate troops at Sabine Crossroads were recovered during this battle.

Even though this battle was a victory, the Union army did not advance further up the Red River but returned to Grand Encore to rest and re-evaluate its position. While Rosetta's regiment was camped at Grand Encore with the rest of General Banks' forces, they learned that part of General Taylor's Confederate forces had circled around their rear farther down the river.

This alarming news caused General Banks to strike camp late that evening and set out on a 70-mile forced march to Alexandria. They marched from ten o'clock the evening of April 21 until midnight on April 22 and covered only 35 miles, stopping only once for a meal. Those who could not keep up were left behind. One soldier died from exhaustion during the march. They reached Monett's Bluff and the Cane River Crossing on the morning of April 23. They found the Confederate troops strongly entrenched on the opposite bank of the river with battery well located on the high bluff overlooking the crossing.

Rosetta's brigade was ordered to lie down in the woods on the Union side of the river and wait for General Banks' Third Brigade to cross the river three miles north and attack the Confederate troops on their left flank. They lay in the woods all day under constant bombardment from the Confederate cannon. Finally, at four o'clock in the afternoon, while the left flank of the Confederate troops was being attacked, Rosetta's brigade was ordered to cross the river and make a frontal attack. This maneuver was successful and the assault was a victory. This victory allowed the march to Alexandria to continue. Thus, on April 25, the army finally reached Alexandria.

Pvt. Lyons Wakeman headstone. Courtesy of Chalmette National Cemetery, Louisiana.

On May 3, while still encamped at Alexandria, Pvt. Wakeman complained of chronic diarrhea and reported to the regimental hospital. On May 7, she was transferred to the Marine USA General Hospital in New Orleans. This trip usually took only five days but she did not arrive there until May 22. The delay in getting to the hospital was due to the river being under siege by the Confederate troops. When Pvt. Wakeman arrived in New Orleans, her condition was listed as acute. After almost a month in the hospital Pvt. Wakeman died on June 19, 1864. She was 20 years and five months old. There is no record that her gender was ever discovered.

Sarah Rosetta Wakeman was buried south of New Orleans at the Chalmette National Cemetery as Lyons Wakeman, marker number 4066. The 153 New York Volunteers lost 200 soldiers during the Civil War. They reported 1 officer and 38 enlisted men were killed in battle and 1 officer and 160 soldiers died of disease. Among those was Sarah Rosetta Wakeman.

Although she did not survive the war, she displayed exceptional loyalty to her family and her country. Her bravery, loyalty, and dedication rank her among the great American women of the time.

❧ 3 ❧

Jennie Hodgers:
Woman Soldier

Many of the heroic women who disguised themselves and fought as men actually served throughout the entire Civil War without having their gender discovered. Such is the story of a young Irish girl named Jennie Hodgers.

Jennie Hodgers was born in Clogher Head Parish, south of Belfast, Ireland, on December 25, 1843. She was the daughter of Denis and Catherine Hodgers. In her early years, she and her twin brother would herd sheep on their father's farm. She always wore boys' clothing while tending the sheep and doing farm chores because it made the work much easier.

For some reason which is not known, she left Ireland in her late teens, and headed for the United States. She stowed away, dressed as a man, on a ship bound for New York. She made the journey safely and worked her way to Belvidere, Illinois, where she was living when the Civil War began.

On August 3, 1862, at the age of 18, Jennie Hodgers, using the assumed name of Albert D. J. Cashier, enlisted in Company G of the 95th Illinois Volunteer Infantry. Captain Elliot N. Bush, who was the commanding officer of Company G, enlisted her at Belvidere, Illinois. Jennie is described in the company records as having a light complexion, blue eyes, and light (auburn) hair. One of the soldiers in her company described her as the shortest person in the company. She was only 5' 3" tall and weighed 110 pounds.

The 95th Illinois Volunteer Infantry Regiment was formed in Rockford, Illinois, at Camp Fuller on August 3,1862, under the command of Colonel Lawrence S. Church. The regiment was mustered into Federal service on September 4, 1862.

Albert Cashier enlisted for three years or the duration of the war. She served with the 95th Regiment from August 3, 1862, until the regiment was mustered out on August 17, 1865. She holds the record for the longest length of service for a woman soldier in the Civil War.

On November 4, 1862, after two months of intense training, the 95th Regiment was sent to Jackson, Tennessee, to become part of General Grant's Army of Tennessee. The 95th Regiment served in the western theater for the duration of the war and participated in over 40 battles and skirmishes. Among these battles was the Siege of Vicksburg.

Shortly after Christmas 1862, the 95th infantry was ordered to march to Memphis to board steamships bound for Vicksburg, Mississippi, to join General Grant's forces in their assault on Vicksburg. On January 19, 1863, a fleet of 15 steamships left Memphis for Vicksburg. The 95th regiment sailed aboard the steamship *Marie Denning*, along with the 11th Iowa, 17th Wisconsin, and the 2nd Illinois Infantry regiments. Since the ships were vulnerable to being fired on from the riverbanks, they only sailed at night.

The Union forces disembarked 15 miles north of Vicksburg at a place called Milliken's Bend on January 26. They then marched down river to Grand Gulf where they began to meet resistance from the Confederate forces. These skirmishes continued the rest of the way to Vicksburg.

During one of these skirmishes, Pvt. Albert Cashier was captured by Confederate troops. While under guard, she managed to seize the guard's rifle and knock him down with it. She then fled to the safety of the Union lines. On another occasion when the 95th was pinned down behind a group of fallen trees, Pvt. Cashier is reported to have jumped up on the fallen tree and shouted at the Confederate soldiers to show themselves. She also is reported to have scaled a tall tree during a battle to replace the Union flag which the Confederate troops had shot down. Pvt. Cashier was well thought of by the soldiers of the 95th. They considered him to be dependable and resourceful. They knew him as a brave soldier. Pvt. Cashier was often called on for foraging and skirmishing duties.

After the two costly assaults on the Confederate earthworks at Vicksburg, General Grant began a siege. This siege reduced the Confederate forces, by starvation and disease, to the breaking point. On July 4, 1863, they were forced to surrender.

Pvt. Cashier was stricken with chronic diarrhea during the Vicksburg campaign. She reported to the regimental hospital and talked the doctors into treating her as an outpatient, thus avoiding the chance of her gender being discovered. The doctors agreed and somehow she made a miraculous recovery and was able to continue serving with her regiment.

The 95th Illinois Infantry sustained heavy losses at Vicksburg with 25 soldiers killed in battle, 124 soldiers wounded and 10 soldiers missing. A monument has been erected at the Vicksburg Battlefield to honor all the Illinois soldiers who fought there. The Illinois monument lists over 36,000 names including Cashier, Albert D. J. Pvt.

After Vicksburg, the 95th fought many other battles including the Siege of

Jennie Hodgers (right) with an unknown comrade. From the Frank Crawford Collection, U.S. Army Military History Institute, Carlisle, Pennsylvania.

Atlanta, the Red River Campaign, the Battle of Kenesaw Mountain, the Battle of Nashville, the Siege of Mobile and many more.

Pvt. Albert Cashier fought bravely in these battles without ever being wounded. By the end of the war the 95th Illinois had sustained total losses of 289 soldiers, 84 killed in battle and 205 dead from disease.

At the end of the war, the 95th Illinois Infantry returned to Springfield, Illinois, where on August 17, 1865, they were mustered out of Federal service. Pvt. Cashier had served the entire time the regiment was in existence without her gender ever being discovered or even being under suspicion.

Albert Cashier returned to Belvidere, Illinois, and worked as a laborer. She spent two years in Belvidere and two and one half years in Pontiac before finally settling in Saunemin in 1869. Saunemin, Illinois, is a small town south of Chicago.

Albert Cashier found employment with Joshua Chesbro herding cattle and doing chores around Chesbro's farm. He was allowed to live at the farm as part of his wages. Albert later moved into town to take an evening job in addition to his farm work. He worked cleaning Cording's Hardware store after it closed. He was allowed to sleep in the store as part of his wages. This arrangement did not last long because Albert developed a great fear of the store being burglarized while he was sleeping there.

Revealing these fears prompted his daytime employer Joshua Chesbro to build a small 12 X 22 house for Cashier. The house was built next to the Christian Church in Saunemin and was home to Albert the rest of his life.

Albert soon became custodian of the Christian Church next to his house and was responsible for ringing the bell on Sunday and other special occasions. Albert also served the community by lighting the streetlights each night, which required him to carry a ladder around and clean and light the street lamps. He then had to make a second round to turn them off a few hours later. Albert also worked as a handyman and laborer for several of the other families around town. He was often hired by State Senator Ira M. Lish to do household chores and lawn work.

On Memorial Day, Albert would dress in his Civil War uniform and lead the parade through the town. He would always attend patriotic events and was considered an asset to his community.

On February 13, 1890, Albert applied for a pension for his service with the 95th Illinois Infantry. He based his early request for a pension on the fact that he was partially disabled, as a result of the chronic diarrhea he experienced at Vicksburg. The request was denied because Albert refused to submit to a physical examination to verify the claim. However, in early 1907, Albert D. J. Cashier was granted the normal pension of $12 per month. He also became a member of the Grand Army of the Republic (GAR).

In early 1900 Albert became very ill. Concerned for his welfare, Mrs. Lannon, a close friend, sent a nurse to his home to help him. The nurse was the first to discover that Albert D. J. Cashier was a woman. When she reported the discovery to Mrs. Lannon, they both decided to respect Albert's privacy and keep his secret.

Ten years later, while working for Senator Lish, Albert's secret was again discovered. Mr. Lish was backing his automobile out of his garage when he accidentally hit Albert, breaking his leg just below the hip. Mr. Lish called Doctor C. F. Ross, who, while tending the broken leg, discovered that Albert Cashier was a woman. Albert begged them to keep his secret and they both agreed. Later while attending Albert during his convalescence, Nettie Chesbro, the daughter of Joshua Chesbro, somehow also discovered that Albert Cashier was a woman. The Chesbro family also agreed to keep the secret safe.

As time passed it became more obvious that the injury to Albert's leg was disabling and Albert would not be able to continue performing the work he was doing. It was decided that Albert should seek medical care from an institution. With the help of Senator Lish and Dr. Ross, Albert applied and was admitted to the Illinois Soldier's and Sailor's home in Quincy. The commandant of the home and the doctors agreed to keep his gender a secret so he could live at the home as Pvt. Albert D. J. Cashier. The secret was kept safe until 1913 when two male nurses tried to give Albert a bath and discovered that he was a woman. Once her secret was made public she revealed that her name was Jennie Hodgers and that she had come to the United States from Ireland as a stowaway on a ship.

Public disclosure of the story touched off a storm of newspaper articles and stories. She had lived her entire adult life as a man. Because of all the publicity and her secret being revealed, she became erratic and hard to handle. On March 28, 1913, the State of Illinois declared her to be insane. She was transferred to the state asylum

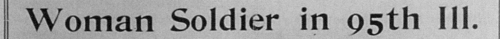

Woman Soldier in 95th Ill.

ALBERT D. J. CASHIER
OF
COMPANY G, 95TH ILLINOIS REGIMENT
Photographed November, 1864

ALBERT D. J. CASHIER
OF
COMPANY G, 95TH ILLINOIS REGIMENT
Photographed July, 1913

Courtesy of the Illinois State Historical Library, Springfield, Illinois.

at Watertown, Illinois. She was forced to wear woman's clothing at the asylum. The dresses she was forced to wear were very awkward for her and it wasn't long before she tripped on a dress and fell down. The fall injured her hip and she never recovered. She died on October 11, 1915, at the age of 72.

While she was in the asylum, the federal government Pension Bureau began an investigation to determine if Jennie Hodgers was in fact Albert D. J. Cashier who had been collecting a pension and if Albert D. J. Cashier really served with the 95th Illinois Regiment. A statement taken from a former comrade is as follows:

Case of Albert D. J. Cashier Cert No. 1001132 on this 24th day of January 1915 at Huron, County of Beadle State of South Dakota before me J. H. Elmes a special examiner of the Bureau of Pensions, personally appeared Robert D. Hannah who, being by me first, duly sworn to answer truly all interrogatories propounded to him during this Special Examination of aforesaid claim for pension, deposes and says: My age is 75 past P.D. and residence Huron, South Dakota,

Above: Jennie Hodgers' (Albert D.J. Cashier's) tombstone at Sunny Slope Cemetery, Saunemin, Illinois. Photograph by L.G. Eggleston. *Right:* Albert D.J. Cashier's original tombstone at Sunny Slope Cemetery, Saunemin, Illinois. Photograph by L.G. Eggleston.

occupation was a farmer. I have lived here eight years. I served as Corporal Company G 95th Illinois Volunteer Infantry. I enlisted about August 1862 and was discharged about June 1865. You showed me a picture without disclosing the name. I was not able to identity same. Further that the picture looked familiar. Since the name is mentioned, I very well recognize that picture as the picture of Albert D. J. Cashier who was a member of my company. I was with the company until after the capture of Vicksburg. I did not know him before the service. After discharge I saw him very often at Belvidere, Illinois where he was working for Samuel Pepper, now dead. About two years ago I learned that Albert D. J. Cashier is a woman. I never suspected anything of that kind. I know that Cashier was the shortest person in the company. I think he did not have to shave. There has never been any doubt in my mind since it came out that Cashier was a woman but that it is so. I have not seen Cashier since a few years after the war. I am not able to identify the right hand figure in the double picture you showed me. It has been to long ago and fifty years make too many changes in a person for me to identify the right hand figure. I have no doubt about the left hand figure being the picture of Albert D. J. Cashier. Albert D. J. Cashier was very quiet in her manner and she was not easy to get acquainted with. I rather think she did not take part in any of the sports and games of the members of the company. When I was examined for enlistment, I was not stripped and a woman would not have any trouble in passing the orientation. I am not related and have no interest in the prosecution of this claim.

The Pension Bureau investigation verified that Jennie Hodgers was Albert D. J. Cashier who did serve with the 95th Illinois Regiment. The depositions taken from other members of the 95th confirmed the truth and the pictures of Albert D. J. Cashier which were shown to the former comrades were readily identified.

The Grand Army of the Republic (GAR) arranged for her burial. She was buried in her Civil War uniform with full military honors, including a flag-draped coffin. She was buried in Sunny Slope Cemetery in Saunemin, Illinois. Her headstone simply read "Albert D. J. Cashier Co. G 95th Ill. INF." In April 1985, an additional headstone was placed on her grave just a few feet behind the original. The new stone reads: "Albert D. J. Cashier Co. G 95th Ill. Inf. Civil War, Born Jennie Hodgers in Clogher Head, Ireland 1843–1915."

Albert D. J. Cashier/Jennie Hodgers achieved many extraordinary goals in her life. She was the first known woman to vote in Illinois, and the only woman soldier to receive a pension as a man for her services as a full time soldier. (Other women received pensions, but their gender was known at the time of payment; Jennie Hodgers' was not.) She holds the record for the longest period of service for a woman soldier in the Civil War, has the only tombstone listing both a man and a woman's name for the same person, and has the only grave marked with two headstones. On each Memorial Day flowers are placed on her grave along with the graves of other soldiers being honored.

Jennie Hodgers served her country faithfully without once wavering. Her loyalty and dedication to duty overshadowed her fear as she endured the horrors of war.

❧ 4 ❧

Sarah Emma Evelyn Edmonds: Woman Soldier, Spy and Nurse

The long periods between battles were times when women were most vulnerable to being discovered. Several of the women soldiers would continually volunteer for other duties they could perform between combat engagements. They would volunteer for nursing duties, for courier duties and for espionage missions. These additional duties kept them up late at night or out of camp much of the time, which lessened the chance of their gender being discovered.

These versatile and courageous women made an enormous contribution to the war effort. Such a woman was Canadian born Sarah Emma Evelyn Edmonds.

Sarah Edmonds was born on a rural farm south of Fredericton, New Brunswick, in December 1841. She was the daughter of Isaac and Elizabeth Edmonds, and was one of five children (four girls and a boy). Since her only brother was frail and sickly, the girls were required to do most of the work on the farm. The girls usually wore boys' clothing while doing their chores.

Sarah became a strong, hard-working farm girl who developed skills in horseback riding, foraging, hunting, shooting, tending live stock, chopping wood, and many other survival skills which would become useful in her later life. In addition, her mother made sure that she did not avoid learning the many tasks and responsibilities of running a home. From her mother she learned how to take care of a home and family, how to prepare home remedies for aches and pains, and the basic nursing practices necessary to care for a sick or injured person. Sarah became very

23

Sarah Emma Edmonds. Courtesy of the State Archives of Michigan.

knowledgeable in these areas and found she had a natural knack for nursing and caring for people.

In 1858, when Sarah was 17 years old, her father decided to arrange a marriage for her to an older neighbor who owned a nearby farm. Sarah obeyed her father and accepted the engagement to the elder farmer. Her mother, seeing that Sarah dreaded the idea of marrying the neighbor, helped her escape. Mrs. Edmonds contacted an old friend, Annie Moffitt, in Salisbury, approximately 90 miles east of Fredericton, to arrange for Sarah to become an apprentice in her millinery shop. Her friend was happy to get the help and accepted Sarah as her student.

Sarah told her best friend, Linus H. Seelye, of her plans for leaving. He provided her with a good set of his clothes to wear on the journey, thinking it would be much safer for her to travel in disguise.

On a dark, moonless night, while wedding plans were still being made, Sarah quietly slipped out of the house and disappeared without a trace. Within a year Sarah had learned the millinery business and, with her new friend, Henriette Perrigo, had opened a shop ten miles east of Salisbury in Moncton, New Brunswick.

Soon after the shop was opened, Sarah received a letter from her mother warning her that her father had discovered where she was. She again feared the loss of her freedom and the horror of being forced into an unwanted marriage. She came to the conclusion that changing her identity and disappearing would solve the problem.

She cut her hair short, changed her name to Franklin Thompson, dressed herself in men's clothing, had an identifying mole surgically removed from her left cheek and moved to Saint John, New Brunswick, 80 miles south of Fredericton. She found employment as a salesman selling Bibles and other religious books in New Brunswick. She was very successful in this new line of work. This success lasted about one year, when, for some unknown reason, she lost all her money along with all her books and supplies. She had one Bible left, which she sold for $5. She decided to head south into the United States to look for work.

It was late 1859 and New Brunswick was covered with snow when Sarah set out walking with only $5 in her pocket. With the exception of a few short rides she received along the way, Sarah walked the entire 450 miles to Hartford, Connecticut. She took a job with Hurlburt and Company selling books in Nova Scotia. This job lasted from February 1860 through November 1860, when Sarah decided to head west. She was living in Flint, Michigan, when the Civil War began.

While living in Flint, Sarah became a friend to William R. Morse, who was a member of the Flint Union Greys, a voluntary military company organized in 1857. On April 17, 1861, only five days after Fort Sumter was fired upon, Sarah enlisted in the Flint Union Greys under her assumed name of Franklin Thompson. At a company meeting on April 18, 1861, the Flint Union Greys voted to become a volunteer company in the Union army. This action was in response to President Lincoln's call for 75,000 troops to put down the rebellion and reunite the nation. On April 25, 1861, the 2nd Michigan Infantry was formed. It included the Flint Union Greys as Company F under the command of Sarah's friend Captain William R. Morse. On May 25, 1861, the 2nd Michigan Infantry was mustered into Federal service at Fort Wayne in Detroit, Michigan.

The 2nd Michigan Infantry was the first three-year regiment mustered in Michigan. The regiment consisted of 1,013 officers and men. By the end of the war, this number had grown to 2,151.

After two months of training, the 2nd Michigan Infantry left on June 6, 1861, for Washington, D.C. They arrived in Washington on June 10 and were reviewed by President Lincoln prior to going into camp.

During the Battle of First Manassas/Bull Run on July 21, the 2nd Michigan Infantry was assigned to guard the escape route back to Washington.

Pvt. Franklin Thompson was on hospital duty in a small stone church between the battlefield and Centerville. Seeing the large amount of wounded soldiers being brought into the makeshift hospital was her first exposure to the horrors of war.

Unaware that the Union army had fled the battlefield, Sarah continued working with the wounded. Once she realized that she was alone and mostly surrounded by enemy soldiers, she had to flee on foot. She worked her way through wooded areas and soon returned safely to the 2nd Michigan Regiment.

Being assigned to General McClellan's Army of the Potomac, Pvt. Thompson with the 2nd Michigan Infantry, participated in most of the major battles of the Civil War, including First Manassas/Bull Run, Fredericksburg, Antietam, Second Manassas/Bull Run, Vicksburg, Wilderness, Spotsylvania, Cold Harbor, and Petersburg.

Over the course of the war, the 2nd Michigan Infantry Volunteers sustained a high casualty rate. Eleven officers and 214 enlisted men were killed in battle, 15 died in

Sarah Emma Edmonds. Courtesy of the State Archives of Michigan.

Confederate prison camps, 4 officers and 143 enlisted men died from disease, and 208 were discharged for wounds sustained. The regiment was mustered out of Federal service on July 28, 1865, at Delaney House, D.C., and discharged at Detroit on August 1, 1865.

Private Franklin Thompson served in many different positions during the war. These positions included serving as a (male) nurse in the regimental hospital, serving as regimental postmaster, serving as a fighting soldier, and working for General McClellan as a spy.

Private Thompson was assigned to be the regimental mail carrier on March 4, 1862. This assignment allowed her to be out of camp much of the time and thus lessened the chance of her gender being discovered. She often would sleep in the woods or alongside the road while on her mail runs. When she was not out on the road, she would work late hours tending the sick and wounded in the regimental hospital. This busy schedule found her going to bed late each night, after everyone else was asleep.

On one occasion Pvt. Thompson was sent out to gather food supplies which were supposedly available at an area farm several miles from the camp. Upon arriving at the farmhouse, Pvt. Thompson inquired about the availability of eggs, meat, and fruit. The woman, who was alone in the house, agreed to supply the requested items. Pvt. Thompson noticed an uneasiness in the woman's manner, as she took her time gathering the supplies.

Pvt. Thompson told her he had to get back to his unit and if she didn't have the supplies readily available he would only take what she had. She nervously apologized, and quickly gathered what she had and gave it to him.

As Pvt. Thompson left and headed toward his horse, he heard the click of a gun. He drew his pistol and turned around to find the woman standing on her porch with a rifle aimed at him. He fired his pistol, hitting her in the hand. She fell down crying in pain. Pvt. Thompson quickly ran up to the woman and pointed his gun at her. She begged not to be killed and explained that her husband, a Confederate soldier, had recently been killed by Union troops and she somehow felt she had to do something to avenge his death.

Pvt. Thompson bandaged the woman's wound, then bound her hands and tied her behind his horse. While riding back to the Union camp it became clear that the woman would not make it back to the camp on her feet. Pvt. Thompson put the woman on the horse and, holding the reins, walked the horse back to the camp.

During the long, slow walk, the woman began to talk about her beliefs, her life, and how glad she was that Pvt. Thompson had stopped her from killing him. The two talked openly and soon Pvt. Thompson began to understand the woman and trust her. The woman asked if instead of turning her in for trying to kill a Union soldier, if she could be put to use as a nurse in the regimental hospital, a job for which she was well qualified.

Pvt. Thompson agreed, and upon entering the camp the woman was introduced as a volunteer nurse who wanted to help the wounded and sick soldiers. The wound to her hand was treated, but never explained. She was grateful to Pvt. Thompson and soon became a well thought of nurse.

Pvt. Thompson's service to General McClellan as a spy came about as a result of two unexpected events. The first event was when she decided to visit an old friend from Canada, James Vesey, who was in a nearby regiment. Upon arriving at his regiment she was informed that he was killed in an earlier skirmish and they were in the process of having his funeral. While in the camp attending the funeral, she was informed of a second event, which would change her life.

One of General McClellan's top agents was captured in Richmond and was to be hanged. This made an opening available in the general's intelligence network. When word came out that the general was looking for another agent, Pvt. Franklin Thompson applied. He was called to Washington to be interviewed by generals George B. McClellan, Samuel P. Heintz, and Thomas S. Meagher. Pvt. Thompson was questioned about his political views, his reasons for wanting to become an agent, and his general knowledge of weapons and fortifications.

The three generals were impressed with Pvt. Thompson's answers and agreed to use him as an agent. Since the Union army was in the process of planning an assault on Richmond, they needed to know the fortifications and troop strength of Yorktown. Pvt. Thompson was assigned to infiltrate the fortifications and report the troop strength, gun placements, armament, and the layout of the defenses.

She began her first spy mission disguised as a black slave named Ned. She covered her face, hands, and neck with walnut stain mixed with silver nitrate to change her skin color to a brownish gray. She dressed in slaves' clothing and used a black wig to cover her cropped hair. Then, late that night, she quietly slipped across the enemy lines into the Confederate camp.

When morning came she joined the other slaves and helped carry breakfast to the Confederate soldiers. If the others slaves realized that she was an imposter, they kept quiet and went along with her. It is hard to imagine that they did not realize that there was an imposter among them. Nevertheless, she worked alongside them in the camp and then accompanied them to Yorktown to work on the Confederate fortifications.

While working at Yorktown, she was able to sketch the layout of the fortifications, including how many guns there were and how they were placed. She also noted the number of "Quaker guns" around the fortifications. (Quaker guns are wooden logs painted to look like guns to give a false impression of the strength of the fortification.)

Later that day while serving food to the Confederate officers, she overheard talk about replacements, plans of attack, and plans to evacuate Yorktown. She recorded the information and concealed it in the insole's of her shoes.

After the officers were fed, she joined them with a pail of water and began filling their canteens. All at once she heard a familiar voice. When she looked up, she saw a peddler who frequently came into the Union camp selling his wares to the soldiers. He was showing the Confederate officers the layout of the defenses around

Washington, including the placement of armament. He was a Confederate spy. She could not wait to return to the Union lines with this important information.

Later that evening she made an attempt to cross back to the Union lines. When she reached the perimeter of the camp, a Confederate officer spotted her, handed her a rifle and assigned her guard duty. In the early morning hours she managed to slip away and return to her own lines, taking the Confederate rifle with her.

The information she had gathered was well received and Pvt. Thompson's daring and courage impressed General McClellan so much that he used her on ten other spy missions during her duty with the battalion.

The other missions helped uncover several Confederate spies, as well as obtain much vital intelligence information needed by the Union army. While working these missions she became a master of disguise. She disguised herself as Ned the slave, a peddler from Kentucky, an Irish woman selling pies (complete with an Irish brogue), and a grieving widow, to name a few. Her greatest disguise, however, was as Pvt. Franklin Thompson for she was never discovered.

Only one man knew her identity. He was her lieutenant and she became very fond of him. When she finally expressed her feelings and revealed her identity to him, he told her he was in love with another woman. However, he kept her secret and was soon transferred out of the regiment.

Shortly thereafter she became ill with malaria. Fearing that a long hospital stay would cause her gender to be discovered, she deserted the regiment on April 19, 1863. She did not consider herself a deserter because she planned to return to the regiment once she recovered. Upon leaving the hospital in Cairo, Illinois, she noticed Pvt. Franklin Thompson was on the desertion list. Therefore, she could not return to her unit for fear of imprisonment. Instead, she joined the United States Christian Commission as a war nurse under her true name, Sarah Edmonds. She served as a nurse for the remainder of the war.

As the war was coming to an end, she was working as a nurse at Harper's Ferry where she met an old acquaintance from New Brunswick. It was Linus H. Seelye, the young man who had given her his suit of clothing when she ran away from home. Linus was now a widower and was working as a carpenter at Harper's Ferry.

The war finally ended in April 1865 and Sarah returned to New Brunswick to visit her family. She found that both her father and mother had died and her brother and sisters were running the family farm. After visiting with her family for several months, she decided to enroll in Oberlin College in Ohio. She moved to Ohio and soon found that college was not very exciting. In the meantime, Linus Seelye had followed her to Ohio where he professed his love for her and asked her to marry him. She happily accepted and on April 27, 1867, they were married in Cleveland, Ohio.

Sarah gave birth to three children. Linus Jr., born on April 14, 1869, lived only three years. Homer, who was born June 21, 1871, lived for only 24 hours. Alice Louise, born on August 12, 1874, lived only six years. The Seelyes then adopted two children. They were George Frederick, born 1872, and Charles Finney, born 1874. They raised these children as their own with loving care.

Sarah Emma Edmonds. Courtesy of the State Archives of Michigan.

Pvt. Thompson's identity was not discovered until 1884 when she attended a reunion of the 2nd Michigan Infantry Volunteers. Though quite stunned, the regiment quickly accepted her and convinced her to apply for a pension for her service.

Following their advice, she applied for a pension and requested that the charge of desertion be dropped. A letter from the Secretary of War helped her get the pension. The letter acknowledges her as "a female soldier who served as a private — rendering faithful service in the ranks."

On March 18, 1884, House Report No. 820 to accompany H.R. 5334 was introduced in the House Military Affairs Committee by Congressman Byron Cutcheon of Michigan. The bill was to remove the charge of desertion from the record of Franklin Thompson, alias S.E.E. Seelye. Two years later the bill was passed by Congress and signed into law by President Grover Cleveland.

Also on March 18, 1884, House Report No. 849 to accompany H.R. 5335 was introduced in the House Invalid Pension Committee by Congressman E. B. Winans of Michigan. This bill was to grant Sarah E. E. Seelye, alias Frank Thompson, a pension for service with the 2nd Michigan Infantry. This bill was passed on July 5, 1884, and signed into law by President Chester Arthur. The pension was approved prior to the bill removing the desertion charge from her record. She was granted a pension of $12 a month, and subsequently received an honorable discharge.

In 1893 the Seelyes lost their home and fell on hard times. They moved to LaPorte, Texas, at the request of their adopted son, George, and lived there comfortably until her death. Sarah Emma Evelyn Edmonds died on September 5, 1898, at the age of 59. She was buried in LaPorte, Texas.

Prior to her death, she was officially mustered into the George B. McClellan Post Number 9 of the Grand Army of the Republic (GAR) in Houston, Texas. She is the only woman soldier to be mustered into the GAR.

In 1901 the GAR exhumed her casket. In a special Memorial Day ceremony and with full military honors, it was re-buried in a GAR plot at Washington Cemetery in Houston, Texas. The headstone reads "Emma E. Seelye, Army Nurse."

Sarah Emma Evelyn Edmonds Seelye not only served faithfully and endured all the hardships of army life, but went far beyond the call of duty in her fearless activities to gather intelligence information for her adopted country. The courage and dedication she displayed make her one of the most extraordinary women of the Civil War.

❧ 5 ❧

Loreta Janeta Velazquez: Woman Soldier and Spy

Not wealth, power, social status, or even family pressure could deter some of the courageous women from serving their country as fighting men. In many cases these brave women enlisted alongside their husbands or loved ones, and served bravely without being detected.

One of the most remarkable women who fought in the Civil War was Loreta Janeta Velazquez, who joined the Confederate army to be near her husband.

Loreta Velazquez was born in Havana, Cuba, in 1842. She was the daughter of a wealthy Cuban aristocrat. Her parents immigrated into the United States shortly after Loreta was born. The family settled in New Orleans, Louisiana, where Loreta was educated.

In April 1856, when she was 14, Loreta's family arranged a marriage for her to a prominent Spanish gentleman. Loreta was not in favor of this arrangement. She had already fallen in love with an army officer named William Rouch. To avoid the unwanted arranged marriage, she and William eloped. After their marriage they moved to Arkansas where they made their home. While living in Arkansas, Loreta and William had three children, all of whom had died by late 1860.

When the Civil War began in early 1861, Loreta's husband decided to enlist in the Confederate army. Not wanting to be separated from her husband, she decided to accompany him disguised as a man. After telling William of her plan, she was very disappointed to find that he was not in favor of the idea. He told her to forget such foolishness and directed her to stay at home while he was away.

In June 1861, William departed with his troops for the Confederate encampment at Pensacola, Florida. Loreta, having no desire to stay at home alone, soon developed a new plan of action. She decided to use her wealth to finance and equip an infantry battalion, which she would take to Pensacola and present to William as his command. She thought this would please him and they would be able to stay together during the war.

Over the next four days she had cut her hair short, purchased a Confederate officer's uniform, purchased a false mustache and goatee, stained her face, neck and hands so she could look tanned, and assumed the name Lt. Harry T. Buford.

Disguised as Lt. Harry T. Buford, she began to recruit her new infantry regiment. In just four days she was able to recruit 236 soldiers, which was enough for the base of a regiment. The newly formed group headed for training at Pensacola, Florida. Lt. Buford called the small regiment "The Arkansas Greys."

When she arrived in Pensacola, Florida, and presented the troops to her husband William, she did not get the reaction she had hoped for. William was quite angry that she had disobeyed his orders. However, his anger and her disappointment were both short lived, because soon after her arrival in Pensacola, William was killed in a gun accident during training.

Devastated first by the loss of her children and then by the loss of her husband, she decided to remain in the Confederate army and do her part for the cause. She applied for a commission as Lt. Harry Buford and for assignment to a permanent regiment. When these requests were not approved she left the Arkansas Greys in the command of someone else and struck out on her own to find a suitable regiment.

Still Lt. Harry T. Buford, she served in several different regiments, both infantry and cavalry. She participated in several major battles, including Blackburn's Ford, First Manassas/Bull Run, Ball's Bluff, Fort Donelson, and Pittsburg Landing/Shiloh.

During the Battle of First Manassas/Bull Run, she was assigned temporary command of a company whose senior officer had been killed. While in this position she bravely led the troops into battle.

The next major battle after First Manassas/Bull Run was the Battle of Ball's Bluff on October 21, 1861. During this battle, the Confederate troops repelled a Union force trying to cross the Potomac River and scale a 70-foot bluff into Virginia. She was appointed temporary commander of the company after all officers had been killed or were missing and presumed to be dead. After the battle ended in a Confederate victory, one of the missing officers showed up and assumed command of the company. He stated that he had been captured by the Yankees but had managed to escape. Loreta noticed the officer had a sheepish look on his face and suspected that he had hidden himself until the battle was over.

Her luck in coming through several major battles without being wounded soon changed. During the Battle of Fort Donelson on February 13–16, 1862, Lt. Harry Buford was wounded in the foot and required medical treatment. Lt. Buford's true gender was not discovered in the hospital. The wound was not serious and was healed in time for Lt. Buford to rejoin the regiment at the Battle of Pittsburg Landing/Shiloh on April 6, 1862.

Loreta Janeta Velazquez in uniform as Lt. Harry T. Buford. Courtesy of Leib Image Archives.

During the Battle of Shiloh, Lt. Harry Buford was assigned temporary command of her original unit, the Arkansas Greys, after the lieutenant in command of the company was killed. Lt. Buford reported to Captain C. De Caulp, who was a friend of her husband in Pensacola, Florida. When Captain De Caulp assigned Lt. Harry Buford to command the Arkansas Greys, he was still unaware that Lt. Buford was Loreta, the wife of his friend, William Rouch.

After William's accidental death in Pensacola, Florida, Captain De Caulp had stayed in touch with Loreta by mail. They had known each other from William's early army days and after William's death had fallen in love and were planning to be married after the war. Captain De Caulp did not know that he had fought alongside her at First Manassas/Bull Run, Balls Bluff and Shiloh. She did not reveal her identity to him, nor did he suspect that Lt. Buford was anything but a good fighting soldier and leader.

Captain De Caulp was later stricken with an illness and sent to the Empire Hospital in Atlanta, Georgia, for treatment. Since Lt. Buford's foot was in need of further treatment he also was sent to the Empire Hospital in Atlanta. While in the hospital, Lt. Buford dropped in, unannounced, to visit with Captain De Caulp.

While the two old friends were visiting, Captain De Caulp showed Lt. Buford a picture of Loreta and expressed his great love for her. Loreta wanted to reveal herself to him but was afraid he would reject her for disguising herself as a man and fighting as a soldier. She finally decided to tell him about herself. She reached into his shirt pocket and removed the picture and quietly asked him if he was sure he hadn't seen someone in the three-year period that looked like his love. The captain seemed confused by the question so she asked if he thought the picture looked like his friend Lt. Harry Buford.

Captain De Caulp was stunned when she revealed her identity. She quickly asked if he despised her for not staying home like other women and for going to war disguised as a man. His reply was the response she was hoping to hear. He said that he did not despise her for what she had done, but loved her more.

They planned for their wedding to be held as soon as possible. They took two doctors into their confidence, Doctor Benton and Doctor Hammond, to act as witnesses. They also took the post chaplain, Reverend Pinkerton, into their confidence and he consented to perform the wedding ceremony. Loreta was provided with a wedding dress and they were married in the parlor of the Thompson House in Atlanta.

After a short honeymoon, Captain De Caulp returned to duty. He had convinced Loreta to stay home since she had already done enough for the cause.

On the way to rejoin his unit, Captain De Caulp had a relapse of his illness and was soon taken prisoner by Union troops. He died in the Federal hospital at Chattanooga, Tennessee.

After the death of her second husband, Loreta returned to the army as Lt. Harry Buford. The long inactive periods between battles soon began to frustrate Loreta and she began to seek ways of becoming more active. She thought about becoming a spy for the Confederacy. This course of action would keep her in the field of activity for longer periods of time and give her a sense of accomplishment.

She was accepted as an agent for the Confederacy. Her first adventure as a spy began by paying a Negro washwoman $20 for a dress, sunbonnet, shawl and shoes to replace her Confederate uniform. She planned to disguise herself as a poor woman and work her way north to Washington, D.C.

As she approached Washington, she began to change her clothes as people along the way took pity on her and offered her better apparel. By the time she reached Washington she was dressed well enough to be able to rent a room at the Brown Hotel.

From this room, she set out daily, gathering intelligence data for the Confederacy. She reported on troop movements, defenses around Washington, and movement of naval vessels.

While gathering information she heard about openings for agents in the Pinkerton Federal Detective Corps. Loreta realized that if she could get accepted as a Union agent she would have access to much more critical information which she could pass on to the Confederate authorities.

She applied and was interviewed by the chief detective of the Washington branch, Mr. Lafayette C. Baker. During this interview she professed her deep loyalty to the Union and her dislike of the Confederacy, whom she claimed had persecuted her for her beliefs. Mr. Baker accepted her and her adventures as a double agent began.

Her first spy mission for the North was to proceed to Johnson's Island Prison in Sandusky Bay to gather information needed by the federal government to put down a Confederate planned insurrection. She was to pass herself off as a Confederate operative and gain the confidence of the prisoners in order to gather the needed information. The Confederate authorities used this opportunity to have Loreta transport funds and messages to their operatives in Canada.

Madame L.J. Velazquez before General Butler. Courtesy of Leib Image Archives.

Because Mr. Baker did not completely trust Loreta, he sent an agent to watch her. She was so well disguised, however, that while on the train the agent could not locate her, even though at one time during the train ride he sat down next to her and began asking questions. He showed her a picture of herself during the questioning. Since she could not identify the woman he was seeking, he moved on to question other passengers.

Upon her arrival in Canada she was able to distribute all funds and messages to the Confederate agents prior to crossing over to Johnson's Island. The prisoners at Johnson's Island honored her disguise and she set out to help the planned insurrection and escape of the Confederate soldiers.

The plan was to release all Confederate prisoners on Johnson's Island and organize them into a force to operate in the area between Canada and the United States. The plan involved capture of the Federal gunboat *Michigan*. One Confederate agent named Charles H. Cole was placed aboard the *Michigan* as a Union sailor. Another Confederate agent, Captain John Yates Beall, was to commandeer two boats to assist in the prison escape, which he successfully accomplished on September 19, 1864. Loreta would work in the prison stockade.

The escape was planned for September 19, 1864. However, a few hours before the plan went into effect, a disgruntled Confederate prisoner named Langhorn informed the Union authorities about the plan. It was quickly put down and the leaders arrested. Confederate agent Charles H. Cole was arrested aboard the gunboat

Michigan. The other Confederate agent escaped. Loreta was not arrested or even suspected.

Returning to Washington, she continued her work as a double agent. She worked as Loreta Velazquez, Lt. Harry T. Buford, and Mrs. Williams. During her career as a spy she gathered information, smuggled much-needed drugs from Cuba to the Confederate soldiers at the front, transported materials, and performed many other needed services for the Confederacy.

During several of these missions between the Union and Confederate lines, she was caught and arrested but somehow always managed to escape back to the safety of the Confederate lines.

Mr. Baker was aware of a double agent in his organization and assigned one of his best agents to find the mole. He assigned Loreta to catch herself. This was her last mission as a spy and a mission she never accomplished.

Loreta Janeta Velazquez. From her memoir, *The Woman in Battle* (1876).

When the Civil War ended, Loreta fled to Europe to escape federal prosecution. She reportedly took $100,000 in cash with her. Once it was safe she returned to the United States and married a third time to a Confederate officer named Major Wasson.

The newlywed couple moved to Caracas, Venezuela, to investigate the 1866 colonization plan for Confederate soldiers. They soon became disenchanted with the plan since it was not what they were promised or expected. They made plans to return to the United States but were delayed when Major Wasson caught black fever. He died in Caracas a few weeks later.

By 1868 Loreta had re-settled in Nevada and married a fourth time to a miner. She bore him a son and shortly thereafter the family settled in California where she wrote a book about her four years of service to the Confederacy. The book was titled *The Woman in Battle* and was published in 1876.

Loreta Janeta Velazquez died in 1897 at the age of 55. She had lived life on her own terms and followed her beliefs. She always served faithfully and without regard for her own safety. She went far beyond the call of duty, and is worthy to be remembered for her courageous spirit.

❧ 6 ❧

Frances Louisa Clayton: Woman Soldier

Some women soldiers who joined the military to be with their husbands also had a deep craving for adventure and excitement. This desire, coupled with their loyalty to their beliefs, made them excellent soldiers. These women fought hard and excelled in all aspects of army life. Never complaining about the hardships they endured, they served with honor.

Such a heroic soldier was a woman from Minnesota named Frances Louisa Clayton, who joined the Union army with her husband.

In April 1861, when the Civil War began, Frances Louisa Clayton and her husband were living in Minnesota. When President Lincoln issued his call for 75,000 volunteers to put down the rebellion and reunite the nation, Frances and her husband decided to enlist and do their part in this historic effort. Frances cropped her hair short (just below the ears), dressed as a man and, with her husband, enlisted in the Minnesota State Militia Cavalry. The photographs in this chapter show Frances Louisa Clayton in the uniform of the State Militia Cavalry.

Frances was tall, masculine looking, and had a bronze complexion. In an effort to maintain her disguise as a man she learned to chew tobacco, spit, smoke, drink, cuss, walk and act like a soldier. She became very good in her deception. She stood guard duty rain or shine with the rest of the soldiers, and she was considered a good fighting soldier by the members of her regiment.

The enlistment in the cavalry must have been up after the initial 90 days, because the further accounts of Frances Clayton and her husband indicate that they were fighting with the infantry or light artillery. They fought side by side in many battles

Frances Clayton. Courtesy of the Trustees of the Boston Public Library.

including the Battle of Stone's River. Since the only unit from Minnesota which fought at Stone's River was the 2nd Minnesota Battery, one can conclude that this was the regiment they joined after the cavalry enlistment expired.

The regiment to which Frances and her husband belonged was assigned to General Rosencrans' army in Tennessee. On December 31, 1862, they met General Bragg's Confederate forces at Murfreesboro, Tennessee. The Battle of Stone's River commenced at dawn on December 31, 1862, with an attack by General Bragg's Confederate troops. The battle lasted through January 3, 1863.

By noon on December 31, the Confederates were on the defensive as the Union forces halted the attack and began advancing. During the four days of fighting there were several attacks and counter attacks. During one of the early offensives against the Confederate forces, Frances was positioned on the rear line of the assault while her husband was on the front line. The regiment was making a bayonet assault on the Confederate forces. During the assault, her husband was killed a few feet in front of her. Filled with grief and rage, she charged over his body with the other soldiers and drove the Confederates back.

As the assault was ending, Frances was struck in the hip with a minié ball and required medical attention. She was taken to the regimental hospital for treatment. The wound was not life threatening and no bones had been broken.

During Frances' treatment, the surgeon discovered that she was a woman. After a short period of recovery, she was discharged from the regiment on January 3, 1863.

The Battle of Stone's River was called a bloody draw with the loss of 12,906 Union soldiers out of the total of 41,400 and 11,379 Confederate soldiers out of the total of 34,737. These two armies would meet again in battle at Chickamauga.

On her way back to Minnesota, while riding between Nashville and Louisville, guerillas attacked and robbed Frances' train. They took all of her money, papers, and valuables. After reaching home and recovering from her wound, she headed back to her regiment under the guise of retrieving her husband's belongings. Her true motive was to plead with the commander to let her return to the regiment.

Frances did not make it back to her regiment. She was stopped in Louisville by the Provost Marshal and ordered to turn around and return home. She was put on a train routed to Chicago and then on to Minnesota. Somehow the reservations became confused and she ended up in Kalamazoo, Michigan, and then went on to Grand Rapids. After getting her reservations corrected in Grand Rapids, she was walking away from the Provost Marshal's office when a group of young half intoxicated soldiers

Frances Clayton in uniform. Courtesy of Buddy Hughes, Pound, Virginia.

began to follow her. When they got too close and too aggressive, she drew her pistols and turned on them. They quickly changed their minds about assaulting her and fled.

Continuing her walk through the town, she was recognized as an old acquaintance by the owner of a local restaurant on Monroe Street. He knew her before she was married and was aware of her disappearance after her husband enlisted in the army.

The restaurant owner provided her with shelter for the night. The next morning she boarded the train for Minnesota and disappeared from the pages of history.

With such resolve to continue to serve her country one wonders if she re-enlisted with some other regiment and re-entered the war. If so, she served undetected.

The desire to continue with the regiment after her husband's death as well as the hardships and suffering she had already confronted shows her deep loyalty and dedication to her country and reflects the hearty spirit of such heroic women of the time.

Frances Clayton. Courtesy of the Trustees of the Boston Public Library.

Among historical accounts of Frances Clayton, there exists some confusion as to the proper spelling of her last name. Different accounts show her name as Clayton, Clalin, Clatin or Claytin. The original photograph of Frances sitting in a chair holding her sword has the signature of Mrs. F. S. Claytin on the front and back. It is not known if she signed her name on the picture or if someone simply labeled it for his or her files. The article "Women Who Wore the Blue and the Gray" in the Time-Life book *The Civil War* shows her name as Clalin. The *Grand Rapids Daily Eagle* article of November 19, 1863, titled "Eventful History of a Soldier Woman," shows her name as Mrs. Frances Louisa Clayton. An article in the *New Orleans Daily Picayune*, November 22, 1863, also shows her name as Mrs. Frances Louisa Clayton. *Patriots in Disguise* by Richard Hall shows her name as Clayton. In researching the records of the Minnesota regiments one can only find the name Clayton. Further research of the regiments who fought at Stone's River, reveals only the name Clayton. It seems most likely that the correct spelling of her name is Clayton.

⤙ 7 ⤚

Frances Hook: Woman Soldier

Incredible as it may seem, one woman soldier's heroism was so impressive that the Confederacy offered her a commission to switch sides. This amazing 14-year-old female was Frances Hook, who disguised herself as a man and joined the Union army.

Frances Hook was born in Illinois in 1847. She is described as having dark hazel eyes, dark brown hair, medium height and rounded features. When she was three, both her parents died, leaving her to be raised by her older brother.

Frances and her brother were living in Chicago, Illinois, when the Civil War began. She was 14 years old when her brother announced that he was going to enlist in the Union army in answer to President Lincoln's call for 75,000 volunteers.

Since her brother was her only living relative, and she did not want to be left alone, she decided to disguise herself as a man and accompany him into the army. She cut her hair short, upped her age to 22, dressed in men's clothing and on April 30, 1861, enlisted with her brother in the 11th Illinois Infantry Regiment as Private Frank Miller.

They served in the 11th Infantry for the full 90-day enlistment without incident and without Pvt. Miller's gender being discovered. Upon discharge from their three-month enlistment on July 30, they re-enlisted in the 11th Illinois Infantry Regiment for three years. The three-year regiment was mustered into Federal service on July 30, 1861.

Some of the major battles fought by the 11th Illinois Infantry were Fort Henry, Fort Donelson, and Shiloh. Frances lost her brother during the Battle of Shiloh. The death of her brother had such a devastating effect on her that she could not continue serving with the 11th Illinois Infantry. It is not known how she managed to get out of her enlistment. She may have revealed her age or gender in order to be released or perhaps she deserted.

Although she was not able to serve with the 11th Infantry, she was still determined to continue her service with the Union army. She assumed a new alias and enlisted in the 33rd Illinois Infantry Regiment, which had been in existence since September 3, 1861. She enlisted under the name Frank Henderson and served only a few months before she was wounded in battle. The two major battles she fought while with the 33rd Illinois Infantry were Big River Bridge on October 15, 1862, and Frederickstown on October 21, 1862. She was wounded at the Battle of Frederickstown. The wound was not life threatening but did require immediate attention. While she was being treated in the regimental hospital the attending doctor discovered her gender.

She was discharged from the 33rd Illinois Infantry and asked to promise to go home. She replied that she had no home or family. Frances was not discouraged and soon began seeking another regiment to continue her service. She soon found the newly formed 90th Illinois Infantry Regiment, which had been mustered into Federal service at Chicago, Illinois, on September 7, 1862.

The 90th Illinois Infantry had served as guards at Camp Douglas until November 27, 1862. They had not yet seen battle. While Frances served with the 90th Illinois Infantry, they fought many battles such as Holly Springs, Coldwater, the Siege of Vicksburg, the Siege of Jackson, and Mission Ridge.

In the late summer of 1863 while passing through Florence, Alabama, Frances obtained permission to enter an empty house to forage for food and medicine as the regiment moved forward. She located several items of food and supplies and began to pack them in her bag. Suddenly two Confederate soldiers came out of hiding and took her prisoner. She was taken to Atlanta, Georgia, to be imprisoned.

Shortly after being imprisoned, Frances made a desperate attempt to escape. An alert guard spotted her and ordered her to halt. When she ignored his orders and continued to run, the guard raised his rifle and fired, wounding her in the leg. Frances was carried into the prison hospital where the doctor dressing her wound discovered that Pvt. Frank Henderson was a woman. She was assigned a separate room and given special treatment. The prison authorities placed her on the list of the next prisoners to be exchanged.

On February 27, 1864, Colonel Burke of the 10th Ohio Infantry went to Graysville, Georgia, under a flag of truce, with authority from General Thomas to exchange 27 Confederate prisoners for 27 Union prisoners. Pvt. Frank Henderson was one of the 27 Union prisoners exchanged. She was placed in a Nashville hospital until she recovered from her wound.

While in the hospital she revealed her story. She had evidently also revealed her story to the Confederate doctors after they discovered her gender. The Confederacy must have been quite impressed with her daring and courage, because while in the prison hospital she received a letter from President Jefferson Davis. He offered her a commission as Lieutenant in the Confederate army if she would switch sides. Her response to President Davis was that she would rather fight as a private soldier for the Union than to be honored with a commission in the Confederate army and that she would let herself be hanged before ever raising a hand against the Union.

Upon hearing this report, Dr. Mary E. Walker, a Union army surgeon, proposed that Frances Hook should be made a Lieutenant in the Union army. She also argued that Congress should assign women to duty in the army, with pay, as well as colored men because patriotism had no sex or color.

Frances Hook served her country well. She stood firm in battle and never wavered in her resolve to do her patriotic duty for her country.

❧ 8 ❧

Charlotte Hatfield:
Woman Soldier

The true last name of Charlotte is unknown; her nickname was "Mountain Charley." She used the name Charley Hatfield when she disguised herself to enlist in the Union army as a fighting soldier.

Charlotte was born in rural Iowa in 1840. Her mother died in 1858 when Charlotte was 18 years old, leaving her in the care of a step-father who treated her as a hired hand and discouraged any young men who seemed interested in her.

At the age of 19 she eloped with a young man who was relatively new to the area. They traveled to Des Moines, Iowa, where they were married. Her new husband was a gambler and his lifestyle kept him away from her for much of the time. One year after their marriage, Charlotte delivered their baby, which was stillborn. Her husband was quite angry with her for losing the baby. He beat her severely and left her alone without a means of support. Charlotte later found out that he had run off with another woman whom he had been seeing throughout their marriage. In her anger, Charlotte vowed that someday she would find them and get revenge for what they had done to her.

She set out looking for work hoping to be able to save enough to fund her quest for revenge. She found employment in St. Joseph, Missouri, and was able, over a period of time, to save enough money to begin her search for her husband. She heard rumors that he was headed west to Colorado. Intent on revenge, she set out for the gold fields around Pikes Peak, Colorado. In order to avoid the many problems of a woman traveling alone, she disguised herself as a man. Much to her surprise she fit the part very well; even her female friends did not recognize her.

While crossing the plains on her mule, she met an old friend named George West. West was a publisher by trade. He and his party were heading for Pikes Peak to search for gold. He did not recognize Charlotte in her disguise and she was allowed to ride with his company the rest of the way to Pikes Peak. She inquired about her husband in each town along the way and with small bits and pieces of information she was able to track him from town to town. Soon after her arrival in Colorado, she was finally successful in locating her husband and the woman he had run off with. She quickly changed into women's clothing so they would recognize her. She faced them while they were together and took her revenge. What the revenge was is unclear. But afterward she was in quite a hurry to get away. As she fled the town a group of intoxicated young men spotted her and gave chase. Once they caught her they were determined to have their way with her. Just as she was about to be assaulted, her old friend George West came upon the scene and ran the young men off. She thanked him and after explaining what she was doing in Colorado, promised to give George her story on the condition that he would not publish it for 25 years. George agreed and Charlotte continued her escape into the night.

The next day George received a note from Charlotte asking him to saddle her mule and bring it with him to an isolated spot in the mountains where she would tell him her story. He complied with her request and met her on the trail. They rode together to a secluded cabin where, after building a fire, she revealed her story. As they parted company, they agreed to keep in touch with each other. George later returned to his home in Golden, Colorado.

In late 1860 George West received a letter from Charlotte stating that she was living in Albuquerque, New Mexico. In 1861, George went to see her in a casino in Denver, Colorado, where she was working as a dealer. She explained to him that she was working her way back to Iowa.

When the Civil War began in 1861, George West enlisted in the Union army and served in Colorado as an officer. During the war he stayed in touch with Charlotte.

In September 1861, at the age of 21, Charlotte enlisted in the 3rd Iowa Cavalry Regiment at Keokuk, Iowa, as Private Charley Hatfield. She was assigned as headquarters clerk for the regiment under General Samuel R. Curtis.

Pvt. Hatfield's service as a spy for General Curtis began shortly after entering the army. He volunteered to infiltrate the Confederate lines dressed as a woman carrying eggs from her home. She would tell the Confederates that she got lost and found herself trapped between the two armies. She would be taken into the Confederate camps where she would be allowed to sell her eggs. She would go about selling the eggs and listening for valuable information.

On the day before the Battle of Westport, Confederate Major Arthur McCoy escorted the crying woman into the Confederate camp where she sold her eggs. He then assigned an escort to help her home. Just then, a courier rushed into the camp with an urgent dispatch. The entire camp reacted with excitement. As General Shelby mounted his horse to depart, a folded piece of paper fell from his jacket pocket.

Charley waited in the shadows until the soldiers had all fled, and then she grabbed the note and made her way back to the Union lines. The note contained vital information about the Confederate forces and their placements for the upcoming Battle of Westport.

On the eve of the Battle of Westport, an orderly reported to George West at his regimental headquarters with a message that he was to report to General Curtis. On the way to the General's office, the orderly whispered to George West that she was his old friend Mountain Charley. George was quite amazed and when he looked closely at her he did indeed recognize his old friend. She told him that she had been in the army for two years without being discovered, and that she often acted as a spy for General Curtis. George West never saw Charley again.

In preparation for the Battle of Westport, on October 22, 1864, the 3rd Iowa Cavalry took positions along the Big Blue River to oppose Confederate General Sterling Price and Confederate General Joseph Shelby. On October 23, 1864, General Shelby attacked the Union forces under General Curtis at Westport, Missouri. General Price checked the Union advance on Shelby's forces with a strong counterattack. The Union cavalry then broke through the Confederate rear defenses and forced them to flee down the border between Missouri and Mississippi. The Battle of Westport was a Union victory.

During the Battle of Westport, Charley carried dispatches throughout the camp and battlefield and was later commended for his bravery. During the second day of battle, however, Charley's horse was shot out from under him and he was seriously wounded. Confederate General Joseph Shelby's men found him lying on the battlefield next to his horse. Charley was weak from loss of blood as a result of a mini ball wound in the leg and a saber cut to the shoulder. He was taken to the Confederate hospital for treatment.

Confederate doctor Jesse Terry treated Charley's wounds and discovered that Private Charley Hatfield was a woman. Charley begged the doctor to keep her secret. The doctor agreed and completed his care of Charley in secret. He also placed her name on the next prisoner exchange list. She was soon exchanged and transported to the army hospital in Ft. Leavenworth, Kansas, to recover from the wounds.

While in the hospital at Fort Leavenworth, she was notified that General Curtis had written the Governor of Iowa recommending that Pvt. Charley Hatfield be promoted to 1st Lieutenant. The request was approved and after returning to the regiment Charley was promoted to a 1st Lieutenant and made aide-de-camp to General Curtis.

Charlotte served as Lt. Charley Hatfield with the regiment for the rest of the war without her sex being discovered. She was mustered out at Des Moines, Iowa, on August 9, 1865.

On January 14, 1885, after keeping his promise to Charley for 25 years, George West published her story. Charley, who was living back home in Iowa, read the article. She wrote to George on February 8, 1885, and let him know that she had been married for eight years and had four children. She sent him a copy of her diary, which was an account of her life since they had last seen each other. Her husband was a man West had known in Colorado. She asked him not to reveal her name or address if he used her diary. George West kept her name and address secret as she requested.

Mountain Charley was one of the most courageous women of the Civil War. Her loyalty, bravery and patriotism make her one of American history's great women.

✤ 9 ✤

Sarah Malinda Pritchard Blalock: Woman Soldier and Guerrilla Raider

As incredible as it seems, there was one woman soldier in the Civil War who fought for both the Union army and the Confederacy. She fought for the Confederacy disguised as a man and later fought for the Union army as a woman guerrilla and raider. Her name was Sarah Malinda Pritchard Blalock.

As guerrillas and raiders for the Union, Malinda and her husband Keith led raids throughout the Blue Ridge and Great Smoky Mountains of western North Carolina and eastern Tennessee. They led their own guerrilla band of raiders under authority of the Union army. They acted as scouts and pilots, guiding recruits out of the South to the Union regiments in Kentucky and Tennessee. They guided Union escaped prisoners of war back to the safety of the Union lines. They acted as scouts and raiders for the 10th Michigan Cavalry Regiment under General George Stoneman's Federal raiders and conducted raids across North Carolina.

Malinda, as she preferred to be called, was born in Alexander County, North Carolina, in 1839, the daughter of John and Elizabeth Pritchard. She was the sixth of nine Pritchard children.

At the age of 17, Malinda married her childhood sweetheart, William McKesson "Keith" Blalock. They were married in early April 1856 at the Presbyterian church in Coffey's Gap in Watauga County, North Carolina. The marriage was unusual for the mountain area since it was between two feuding families, the Pritchards and the Blalocks, who had been enemies for over 100 years.

Keith Blalock was born on November 21, 1837, on Grandfather Mountain five miles from the home of Malinda. Keith and Malinda met in school and were childhood sweethearts.

As the Civil War drew closer and loyalties became stronger, the feelings about secession and an impending war were mixed for the mountain people. Many favored secession and becoming part of the Confederacy while others believed in the Union and keeping the nation united.

In April 1861, when the Civil War began, several of Keith's family went North to join the Union army. Keith stayed in North Carolina and worked his farm with Malinda at his side.

On May 20, 1861, North Carolina adopted an Ordinance of Secession and the Provisional Constitution of the Confederate States of America.

When Confederate recruiters pressured Keith to enlist he refused. He managed to stay out of the war until mid–June 1861, despite harsh criticism from the local people. Finally, two recruiters came to the Blalock home and told Keith that he would either enlist in the Confederate army or face the consequences. The consequences would be conscription, and if he refused he would be treated as a traitor.

Keith reluctantly enlisted for one year in Company F of the 26th North Carolina Infantry Regiment. He was allowed to delay his reporting date until November 15 in order to harvest his crops. Though reluctant, Keith enlisted mainly to keep the mountain people from retaliating against Malinda as the wife of a turncoat.

In November, as Keith was marching down the road to Newton to join his unit, he noticed a short soldier marching beside him. He was quite startled when he discovered that the soldier was Malinda. She had cut her beautiful long hair off with Keith's hunting knife, put on baggy men's clothing to hide her gender, and was carrying Keith's own hunting rifle on her shoulder. She quickly explained to Keith that her place was with her husband and she was going to fight by his side. She had enlisted in the same company as Keith as Sam Blalock, brother of Keith, and gave her age as 20 years. Both Keith and Malinda had received $50 bounty for enlisting.

While with the 26th North Carolina Infantry Regiment, Keith and Malinda participated in three battles. During the third battle Malinda was wounded in the shoulder by a minié ball.

The engagement in which Malinda was wounded was the result of orders to track down a group of partisans who were aiding the Federal scouts for General Ambrose Burnside's advancing army.

While the Confederate patrol was wading across the Neuse River, Keith suddenly had a feeling that something was wrong. He stopped the advance and the group headed back to the riverbank. When they had almost reached the riverbank the Union troops across the river opened fire. The Confederate soldiers threw their rifles upon the bank to keep them from getting wet and submerged themselves in the river to avoid the rifle fire till they reached the shore and could run into the cover of the woods.

Keith came up behind a large pine tree, which had fallen from the bank. He began to look for Malinda, who he found behind another tree. She was clutching her musket with one hand and her shoulder with the other. Seeing that she had taken a minié ball in the shoulder, Keith quickly pulled out his handkerchief and stuffed it into the hole. Keith carried Malinda back to the regimental doctor.

The regimental doctor discovered that Sam Blalock was a woman when he removed her shirt to treat the wound. Keith and Malinda pleaded with him to keep their secret. The doctor agreed to keep quiet for two days only until Malinda would be back on her feet.

Since Keith had planned to desert the Confederate army but found no opportunity to do so, he now decided to act. As he could not escape by slipping away, he decided to try for a medical discharge. He rubbed his entire body down with poison sumac and soon developed a bad rash.

Seeing his body covered with a rash and sores led the Confederate doctor to determine that Keith was unfit for duty. Keith received a medical discharge on April 20, 1862. Malinda immediately revealed her gender to the regiment's colonel, Zebulon Vance.

When she revealed to Colonel Vance that she was Malinda Blalock, the wife of Keith Blalock and not his brother, the colonel demanded that she repay the $50 bounty. She repaid the bounty and was discharged on the same day as Keith. They had served with the Confederate army for six months and had fought in three battles.

Keith and Malinda returned to their home on Grandfather Mountain. Keith was treated for his poison sumac with brine baths and after an extended period of time he made a full recovery.

The State of North Carolina passed the Conscription Act while Keith was recovering from his illness. The area residents began to question Keith about returning to his regiment. Keith refused, stating that he had done his duty and had received a discharge.

When Keith was ordered to re-enlist or be considered a traitor, he realized that under the Conscription Act he could be taken by force. Pickets were set around the Blalock farm to keep Keith from fleeing.

During the night, Keith and Malinda gathered food and provisions and waited for the pre-dawn mist to rise from the valley below to cover their escape. They quietly slipped past the militia who were guarding all routes from their home.

Keith and Malinda gathered a band of Unionist men who, like themselves, had escaped into the mountains. This band of Unionists stayed on top of the mountain until the militia discovered their hideout. When their camp was attacked, Keith was shot in the arm. All Keith's men were captured. Keith and Malinda managed to escape into eastern Tennessee.

During the winter of 1862–1863, Keith and Malinda joined a band of Union guerrilla raiders and raided Confederate camps and depots, burned bridges across the Watauga River and destroyed Confederate railroads. Keith and Malinda were considered Yankee partisans by the Union, but were considered bushwhackers by the Confederacy.

During the winter months Keith and Malinda had helped several men escape from the area around their home to the safety of the Tennessee line where they joined the Union partisans. Also during the winter, two Union officers visited the camp and advised Keith and Malinda that they were seeking someone with knowledge of the mountains to guide potential recruits out of North Carolina. The purpose was to form a regiment of cavalry raiders, which would be designated the 10th Michigan Cavalry under General George Stoneman.

Keith and Malinda volunteered. Keith was appointed recruiting officer and scout captain of the 10th Michigan Cavalry Regiment and Malinda was appointed his aide-de-camp. They were both provided with Federal uniforms.

Keith and another Union officer, George W. Kirk, orga-

Sarah Malinda Pritchard Blalock. Courtesy of the Southern Historical Collection, the Library of the University of North Carolina.

nized a mountain railroad for fleeing Unionists, deserters from the Confederate army, and escaping prisoners who were fleeing the prison at Salisbury, North Carolina.

During one of the raids on the Confederate militia near Keith's home, he was shot in the face. His cheekbone was fractured, destroying his right eye. Even with only one eye, Keith continued his raids until the war was over.

After the war Keith and Malinda lived out their lives in Avery County, North Carolina. Keith received a three-quarters pension of $175 per month for the loss of his eye.

On March 19, 1903, Sarah Malinda Pritchard Blalock died in her sleep at the age of 64. She is buried in Montezuma Community Cemetery.

On the morning of April 11, 1913, William McKesson "Keith" Blalock was killed in a railroad accident. He lost control of his handcar on a curve. The car toppled from the tracks crushing him to death. Keith was buried alongside Malinda on April 14, 1913. The inscription placed on his tombstone would have infuriated him. It read:

Soldier
26th North Carolina Infantry
C.S.A.

The courage and daring of this extraordinary couple helped the Union in its quest to end the bitter fighting and reunite the Union. They have earned a place of honor in American history.

❧ 10 ❧

Fanny Wilson and Nellie Graves: Women Soldiers

One of the most unusual stories of women enlisting in the Union army as men is the story of two close friends who disguised themselves and enlisted in the same regiment. These two young ladies enlisted together to be near their lovers. They adapted well to army life and fought bravely in many battles. The two women were Fanny Wilson and Nellie Graves.

Fanny Wilson was a native of Long Island, New York. In 1860, at the age of 18, she traveled to Lafayette, Indiana, to visit with some of her relatives. Her friend Nellie Graves accompanied her on the trip. Both young girls had left lovers behind whom they missed very much.

Fanny became engaged to her young man prior to her trip west. Both girls spent much of their time composing long love letters to their men during the year they were apart.

In early 1861, with the possibility of a civil war hanging over the nation, the girls decided to return home to their families. To help pass the time on the long trip home, the young girls formulated a bold plan which would allow them to be near their lovers if war broke out. Each of them had already received correspondence indicating that the two men were planning to enlist in the Union army when the time to fight came.

Their plan was to enlist in the same regiment as their lovers but not in the same company. Being in a different company would lessen the risk of suspicion or discovery. They did not plan to tell the two men that they were in the ranks and would be happy just to be near them.

They returned home and in early September 1862, the two young men did enlist in the new regiment being formed at Camp Cadwallader, Beverly, New Jersey. The new unit was the 24th New Jersey Infantry Regiment. It was mustered into Federal service on September 16, 1862.

Fanny Wilson and Nellie Graves set about putting their plan into action. They cut their hair short, put on men's clothing and practiced walking and talking like men. Once confident in their disguise, they presented themselves for enlistment and were accepted in the 24th New Jersey Infantry Regiment.

It was easier for Fanny to conceal her gender since she had a masculine build and a deep voice. Nellie had to work harder to keep her identity hidden. Both, however, adapted to army life quite well. They marched and trained alongside their lovers without once being suspected.

The 24th New Jersey Infantry Regiment was assigned to the defense of Washington until December 1862 when they were sent to Fredericksburg, Virginia, and participated in the Battle of Fredericksburg December 11 through 13. Fanny Wilson and Nellie Graves got their first taste of the horrors of war during this fierce battle. Both women were now veteran fighting soldiers and their romantic view of being in the army changed to a more serious way of thinking. Instead of being frightened enough to reveal themselves and be discharged to get away from the horror they experienced, they became stronger and more determined to continue and do their part for their country. The reality of war had realigned their priorities.

The 24th New Jersey Infantry Regiment proceeded to Chancellorsville in April 1863 where on May 1 through 4, they fought the Battle of Chancellorsville. During the fierce battle Fanny's lover was seriously wounded. After the battle, Fanny sought him out and volunteered to watch over him. She almost revealed herself by her excessive devotion to his care. Despite the special care and all the extra effort on her part, he soon died. Fanny was taken ill by this terrible ordeal and was soon bedridden. Her friend Nellie had also become very ill about the same time.

The two friends were both transferred to the army hospital in Cairo, Illinois. While Fanny and Nellie were recovering in Cairo, the hospital staff discovered that both young soldiers were women. After recovering from their illness, both women were discharged. Nellie Graves was discharged first and the two friends parted company. No further data is available on Nellie Graves. If she re-enlisted in another unit to continue her service, she served undetected.

Fanny Wilson was discharged two weeks later and became a ballet dancer in the Cairo Theater for a while. After only two performances she became restless and began to look for another regiment to join. She felt obligated to continue her service to her country.

Fanny soon rejoined the army in Illinois as a private in the 3rd Illinois Cavalry, which was a well-seasoned group of soldiers. The regiment had been in existence since August 27, 1861, and had seen much action. They were on their way to Vicksburg, Mississippi, when Fanny joined them.

The 3rd Illinois Cavalry participated in the Siege of Vicksburg on May 18 through July 4, 1863, and fought both assaults on Vicksburg May 19 and 22. During the second assault on May 22, Fanny Wilson was wounded in battle. Her wound was not serious enough to cause her gender to be discovered during treatment. She recovered and continued with the regiment.

On August 5, 1863, she was riding through the streets of Memphis, Tennessee, with a fellow soldier when a guard stopped them. Fanny was arrested on suspicion of being a woman in men's clothing and possibly a spy. She was then taken to the police station and questioned where she proved that she was not a rebel spy but a Union soldier.

The authorities procured a proper female wardrobe for her after she promised that she would not disguise herself as a man again. She was discharged from the army and left Memphis dressed as a woman. No further records are available on her life. If she sought out another regiment and re-enlisted, she was not detected.

Fanny Wilson and Nellie Graves were both extraordinary women who put their lives on the line for their country and the cause in which they came to believe.

❧ 11 ❧

Amy Clarke:
Woman Soldier

Going from a quiet, peaceful life as a housewife to a mounted cavalry soldier, then to an infantry soldier and finally to a prisoner of war was the course of Amy Clarke's life during the Civil War.

Amy Clarke and her husband Walter were living in the small town of Iuka, Mississippi, when the Civil War began. Walter, being a patriotic Southerner, soon joined a Confederate regiment and left Amy at home to take care of herself.

Amy, distraught over being somewhat abandoned by her husband, soon met and fell in love with a dashing hussar who was a mounted cavalryman in a Louisiana regiment. She was so taken with her newfound love that she decided to follow him when his regiment moved on.

Amy bought a cavalryman's uniform and a horse and after cutting her hair short and getting used to her new disguise, she enlisted in his company as a mounted trooper. Amy was of medium height, slight build, and had stern, spirited eyes. She has been described as not disagreeable to look at. She adapted quickly to cavalry life. She enlisted under the name Richard Anderson.

For four months she rode with the Confederate cavalry unit during which time she became fatigued by the rigors of the cavalry life. She also experienced several close calls from serious bouts of sickness. She resolved to leave the cavalry and transfer to the infantry, for which she felt she was more suited.

Her request was approved and Pvt. Richard Anderson was transferred to the 11th Tennessee Infantry Regiment. Prior to the transfer, she received word that her husband Walter had been killed at the Battle of Shiloh, Tennessee, on April 6, 1862.

The 11th Tennessee Infantry under General Braxton Bragg fought many battles and on several occasions Amy, "Private Anderson," would stand upon the dead body of a comrade in order to see the enemy while firing her rifle.

On August 29–30, 1862, the 11th Tennessee Infantry met Federal troops in battle at Richmond, Kentucky. During the Battle of Richmond she was wounded and taken prisoner by the Union army. Her wound was treated and she was taken, with the rest of those captured, to the union prison in Cairo, Illinois. It was reported by a correspondent of the *Philadelphia Enquirer* that among these prisoners from Kentucky, there were no less than three women soldiers, one being Amy Clarke.

Amy Clarke, who was 29 years old when she was captured on August 30, 1862, had served with the Confederate army for over 10 months, four in the cavalry and six months in the 11th Infantry without being discovered. However, being a prisoner of war in addition to all the previous hardships she had gone through was too much for her to bear. She longed to be returned to Mississippi and her friends. She promised to assume the proper apparel for her sex and not dress as a man again.

Several ladies and gentlemen from the Cairo area, upon learning of her promise, contributed to the purchase of a dress and other suitable clothing. She was then sent to the provost marshal's office and exchanged with the next batch of prisoners. She was sent to Vicksburg for the exchange.

The Jackson Mississippian of December 30, 1862, stated that she was seen in Jackson, Mississippi, and was on her way back to re-join General Braxton Bragg's command. The determination and courage that she had shown prior to her capture leads one to believe that she did re-join the war effort.

She very well may have re-enlisted in another regiment and continued her service to the Confederacy without being detected. No further record concerning her activities exists.

She served her cause very well and adapted to army life without being suspected of being anything but a good, hard working, brave soldier. She was truly a courageous and dedicated woman.

❧ 12 ❧

Frank Martin:
Woman Soldier

The true identity of the woman who posed as Private Frank Martin is unknown. In all of the accounts of her heroic career as a Civil War soldier she never once revealed her real name.

She was born in 1845 in Bristol, Pennsylvania, and was raised in Allegheny City, by well-to-do, highly respected parents. One could surmise that because of society's low opinion of women who dressed as men and entered the war, she was compelled to keep quiet about her real identity to protect her family from ridicule and embarrassment.

At the age of 12 she was sent to a convent in Wheeling, West Virginia. She remained in the convent until shortly after the Civil War began. In early 1862, she left the convent and returned to Allegheny City to see her parents. After visiting with her family for several months she headed for Louisville, Kentucky, with the intention of enlisting as a private in the 2nd Tennessee Cavalry.

She cut her auburn hair short, dressed as a man and enlisted in the 2nd Tennessee Cavalry as Private Frank Martin. The 2nd Tennessee Cavalry was organized at Murfreesboro, Tennessee, in July 1862 and mustered into Federal service in October 1862. The regiment was part of the Army of the Cumberland. Pvt. Frank Martin served with the 2nd Tennessee Cavalry until the Battle of Stone's River.

The Battle of Stone's River (Murfreesboro) was fought on December 31, 1862, through January 3, 1863, and was a battle between the Union army under General William S. Rosencrans and Confederate troops under General Braxton Bragg. The Union army casualties were 1,730 men killed, 7,802 wounded and 3,717 missing while the Confederate troops had 1,294 killed, 7,945 wounded and 1,027 missing. The battle was a bloody draw. These two armies would meet again at Chickamagua.

Pvt. Martin fought bravely and was in the thickest part of the battle. She fought her way across Stone's River into Murfeesboro on the day Union forces were driven back. During the battle, Pvt. Frank Martin was severely wounded in the shoulder, and taken to the regimental hospital. While she was having her wounded shoulder dressed by the regimental doctor, it was discovered that Pvt. Frank Martin was a woman.

The physician immediately notified General Rosencrans, who ordered her mustered out of the regiment. She begged the general to let her stay and serve with the regiment she loved so well. The general was very impressed with her past record, loyalty and bravery. He, however, did not relent and arranged safe transportation for her back to her parents.

As she left the Army of the Cumberland she vowed to enlist in the first regiment she could find. When she arrived at Bowling Green, Kentucky, she found the 8th Michigan Infantry encamped there. She enlisted as Pvt. Frank Martin again and was accepted. She was described as 18 years old, a seasoned veteran, a good soldier, and a good scout who has endured all the hardships and horrors of war. She was of medium height, with auburn hair which she wore quite short, blue eyes, fair complexion bronzed by the sun, well educated and soft- spoken. She was an excellent horseman and was honored with the position of regimental bugler while with the 8th Michigan.

While escorting Confederate prisoners to Louisville, Kentucky, in 1863, she was noticed as an intelligent, resourceful soldier by the commander of the 25th Michigan Infantry, Colonel Mundy. Being in need of such a soldier, he had Pvt. Martin detailed to the 25th Infantry. Pvt. Martin won the respect of his superior officers very quickly and was considered an asset to the regiment.

Her secret was discovered after a short time with the 25th Michigan Regiment. A soldier who had been raised in her hometown recognized her, remembering not only her but her parents as well. He reported her to the regimental commander. She pleaded to be allowed to remain and serve. Her pleas, along with her past record as a good soldier, convinced the commander of the 25th to allow her to remain in the regiment.

She informed the regimental officers that she had discovered a great number of women soldiers in the army and was even personal friends with a woman lieutenant. She also stated that she had assisted in burying three female soldiers during the battles in which she had fought. The women's gender was unknown to anyone but herself.

She was allowed to continue with the regiment by working in the hospital for the remainder of the war.

❧ 13 ❧

Lizzie Compton:
Woman Soldier

As we have seen, some female soldiers were so determined to fight in the war that they would re-enlist in another regiment each time they were discovered or were in fear of being discovered. The woman soldier who holds the record for re-enlisting in the most regiments is Lizzie Compton.

Lizzie Compton was born in a rural area near Nashville, Tennessee, in 1848. Her parents died when she was an infant and she was left in the care of people whom she described as "unfeeling wretches." She was put into the fields to work at an early age and never received an education or any religious training, and was never tutored in the duties associated with running a household.

As a child she wore a frock and had never fully dressed in women's clothing. When she reached the age of 13 she escaped the drudgery of the life which was forced on her and left home dressed as a boy. She found work as a deck hand on the steamboats of the western rivers.

Lizzie was only 13 years old when the Civil War began. When she reached the age of fourteen, she enlisted in the Union army by falsifying her age and using a male name. The alias she used is not known. She adapted well to army life and became a good fighting soldier.

She became skilled with the use of a musket, and understood the army rules and regulations. She loved camp life and enjoyed being with her comrades.

Lizzie Compton was five feet tall, weighed 155 pounds, had a stout build, light brown hair, and a fair complexion. Though she had no formal education or religious training, she displayed a high moral code of ethics.

Her first battle was the Battle of Mill Springs, Kentucky. She watched the fall of General Felix Kirk Zollicoffer at Logan's Crossroads. General Zollicoffer was killed during his first battle.

Lizzie and her entire company were captured by the guerrilla Morgan and was later paroled. This was the first taste of war for Lizzie. She later stated that she was "skeered" in the first battle but never since. She stated that she had done nothing to make her think that she would go to a bad place in the next life and she was not afraid to die.

Lizzie Compton fought in the Battle of Mill Springs, Kentucky, on January 19, 1862, the Battle of Fort Donelson on February 13–16, 1862, the Battle of Shiloh on April 6–7, 1862, and the Battle of Gettysburg July 1–3, 1863. She is known to have served in seven different regiments in the 18 months she was in the army. She served in the 11th Kentucky Cavalry, 21st Minnesota Infantry, the 8th, 17th, and 28th Michigan Infantry, the 79th New York Infantry and the 3rd New York Cavalry.

While serving in the western theater, she once accepted a dare from her comrades to ride a horse which none of them were brave enough to try. She accepted the challenge and mounted the horse without a saddle. She was thrown to the ground and injured. The doctor who was tending her injury discovered that she was a woman. After her recovery, she was discharged. She usually changed regiments when she was in fear of being discovered but this was the first time a doctor discovered her secret.

After this incident, she moved to the eastern theater and jointed the 79th New York Infantry Regiment. During the Battle of Gettysburg on July 1–3, 1863, she was wounded in battle. A piece of shell fragment hit her in the side and she required medical treatment. While attending her wound, the surgeon discovered her gender. She was discharged again after recovering from her injury.

Lizzie Compton was arrested in Rochester, New York, on February 20, 1864, while trying to enlist in a new regiment. She was thought to be an adventurer by the police. Like many other women who had appeared in disguise, she was regarded as a disorderly person.

The police chief first noticed her talking to a young man in a local saloon and told her the local magistrate wanted to see her. She agreed to report to the magistrate but asked if she could be allowed to leave the saloon alone so that she wouldn't appear to be under arrest. Her request was granted and she soon reported to the local magistrate.

She explained to the magistrate that she was not a camp follower and did not ever want to act like those women who were. She advised the magistrate that she did not want to be a woman and that maybe someday she would be a gentleman, but she could never be a lady.

She revealed her story to the magistrate and showed him a paper she carried. The chief of police of Louisville, Kentucky, Mr. Prest, had signed the paper. The letter explained who she was and commended her to the favor of the railroad superintendents.

When the magistrate advised her that it was against the law for a woman to wear men's clothing and that she must abandon such activities, she replied that she would rather take any punishment, even death, than be forced to act the role of a woman.

Bail was entered for her good behavior and cooperation and she was released. She boarded a train and left town. The last bit of information on her was that she went to Ontario, Canada, where she made her home.

She had served 18 months in at least seven different regiments, had fought bravely in several of the fiercest battles of the Civil War, and was wounded twice. She was an incredibly brave woman who had accomplished all these great feats before she was 16 years old.

❧ 14 ❧

Charles H. Williams: Woman Soldier

The love for a young army lieutenant and a patriotic duty to serve her country are the reasons a young Iowa girl disguised herself as a man and enlisted in the Union army.

The true name of the young lady was never revealed. Only her assumed name of Pvt. Charles H. Williams is known. She was a native of Davenport, Iowa, and living just north of Davenport in Clinton County when the Civil War began.

In May 1861, when her lover left for Keokuk, Iowa, to accept a commission as a lieutenant colonel in the 2nd Iowa Infantry, she devised a plan which would allow her to be near him. She cropped her hair short, disguised herself in men's clothing, upped her age to 20, and changed her name to Charles H. Williams. She and her lover, Lieutenant Colonel Samuel R. Curtis, who later became a brigadier general, enlisted together in Company I of the 2nd Iowa Infantry Regiment.

When she presented herself to Captain Hugh P. Cox and expressed a desire to become a soldier, he looked at her as if he was surprised and said, "You're rather young, ain't you?" She quickly replied, "I'm 20 and anxious to serve my country." She was accepted as Pvt. Charles H. Williams in early June 1861.

At some time during the initial training, Captain Cox discovered that Pvt. Charles H. Williams was a woman. She pleaded with him to keep her secret and let her remain in the army. Captain Cox finally agreed and cautioned her about going out on the streets alone in some of the larger cities such as St. Louis because she might be noticed and arrested.

Pvt. Williams worked extra hard during the training period and became quite proficient as a soldier. The 2nd Iowa Infantry Regiment was mustered into federal service on May 27, 1861. After a few weeks of training, they departed for Missouri on June 13. They were stationed at St. Joseph, Missouri, till July and were responsible for guarding the railroads. Then, in July, they were sent to Bird's Point, Missouri, 125 miles south of St. Louis on the river. They served at Bird's Point till August 14, 1861, when they were sent up river to Pilot Knob (Irontown), 60 miles South of St. Louis. They were at Pilot Knob until August 27, 1861.

On August 27, 1861, the regiment stopped in St. Louis on its way to duty in Jackson, Missouri. Private Williams was not with the regiment since he was assigned duty aboard the steamship *City of Warsaw* from Bird's Point to St. Louis where he was to rejoin his own regiment. The steamship docked in St. Louis the same day the regiment arrived.

Private Williams at once made inquiries about her regiment and found that it was at the St. Louis army barracks waiting for orders to depart for Jackson, Missouri. She decided to stay in the city for the night and join her regiment in the morning. She went to the home of some friends she had known in Iowa who were now living in St. Louis on 7th Street. She made herself known to them and was welcomed into their home.

She rose early the next morning to obtain the latest and most reliable news and locate her regiment. It was Wednesday, August 28, 1861, when some of the police officers at the central station discovered a young soldier passing on the opposite side of the street. The soldier's walk was very different, his complexion was fair, and he had small delicate hands. These characteristics excited the suspicion of the policemen, who followed the young soldier several blocks and then decided to take him into custody.

The young solder gave his name a Pvt. Charles H. Williams and was quite surprised and a little angry that he was being interfered with. Pvt. Williams explained that he was on his way to get a newspaper from the *Republican* office. They still felt that the characteristics displayed by this young solder were not of a masculine nature, and took the young private to the police station where she finally admitted that their suspicions were correct and that she was a woman.

The St. Louis newspaper reporters from *The St. Louis Republican*, along with a Captain Turner, called on her that afternoon and found her reading a copy of the *Republican* that one of the policemen was kind enough to buy for her. She related her story to the visitors.

Captain Turner asked her if she would resume her proper dress if he would release her. She agreed and was released. She was a bit upset that she wasn't allowed to draw any pay for the three months she had served. She stated she had earned $30 and was as much entitled to it as any male soldier.

Captain Hugh P. Cox of Company I resigned from the army on April 1, 1862. Records do not show what her true name was, and it is not known if she re-enlisted in another unit under a different name.

✤ 15 ✤

Marian McKenzie: Woman Soldier

Adventure was the primary motive for several of the women who disguised themselves and enlisted as fighting men during the Civil War. Such was the case of a young Scottish girl named Marian McKenzie.

Marian was born in Glasgow, Scotland, in 1844. A few years after she was born her mother died. She and her father then immigrated to the United States and resided in New York. Her father died shortly after they arrived in New York, leaving her and several brothers and sisters orphaned.

Marian educated herself and studied to become an actress but soon found that the life of an actress was not suitable for her. She began traveling from place to place earning a living the best she could.

Marian McKenzie was in Kentucky when the Civil War began. This gave her a chance for a great adventure in her life. She planned to disguise herself as a man and enlist in one of the Union regiments. At the age of 18, she cropped her hair short, put on men's clothing and enlisted in the 23rd Kentucky Infantry Regiment as Pvt. Harry Fitzallen.

Pvt. Harry Fitzallen is described in the military records as five foot, three inches tall, of Scottish origin, with a dark complexion, light blue eyes, black hair, and coarse-looking and rounded features.

The 23rd Kentucky Infantry Regiment was mustered into Federal service on January 2, 1862. They were assigned garrison and guard duty in southern Kentucky and central Tennessee until August 27, 1862.

After only four months with the 23rd Kentucky Regiment, Pvt. Fitzallen was found out to be a woman. She pleaded with the regimental commander to let her stay in the regiment. The regimental authorities agreed and she was allowed to remain in the army, but not as a fighting soldier. She was assigned to nursing duty in the regimental hospital where she worked for two more months before leaving the regiment.

After leaving the 23rd Kentucky Infantry Regiment, Marian joined the 92nd Ohio Infantry Regiment in August 1862. The 92nd Ohio Infantry was a newly formed regiment, which was organized at Camp Marietta and Gallipolis, Ohio, during August and September 1862.

Marian served with the 92nd Ohio Infantry as Pvt. Harry Fitzallen until her secret was discovered in early 1863. While with the 92nd Ohio Infantry Regiment, she participated in the march to Charleston, West Virginia, on October 14 to November 16, 1862. Then the regiment was assigned duty at Camp Vinton till January 1, 1863.

When her true gender was discovered, she was discharged from the 92nd Ohio Infantry. She promptly sought out another regiment. She enlisted in the 8th Ohio Infantry Regiment, which had been in existence since being formed at Camp Dennison, Ohio, on June 22, 1861. She was discovered after only a few weeks with the 8th Ohio.

Each time she was caught and arrested, she was suspected of being a Confederate spy. She revealed her story to convince the authorities that she was not a rebel spy. She was able to convince the authorities that she was not a spy each time she was arrested. She stated that she had brothers and sisters who were now living in Canada. The provost martial asked for their names and addresses to confirm her story. She refused to supply the names and stated that she would not cause them the embarrassment of being questioned about her.

She explained that her only reason for enlisting in the army was a love of adventure. The only crime she felt that she committed was wearing men's clothing. She was discharged and given women's clothing before being sent on her way.

She went into and out of several more regiments each time her gender was discovered. She was later arrested while serving in a cavalry unit in West Virginia. Once she confessed to being a woman she was provided with suitable women's clothing, with the exception of the dress hoops. She adamantly refused to change into the woman's clothing until the oversight was corrected. The provost martial corrected the mistake and she was discharged. She was mustered out of the army in January 1865, just three months before the war was over, on the basis "proved to be a female."

Marian McKenzie served many different regiments in the three years she was in the army. She only expressed adventure as her motive, but the fact that she served for three years and continually re-enlisted makes one believe that there were other, more patriotic motives involved in her decisions.

❧ 16 ❧

Molly and Mary Bell: Women Soldiers

Out of the mountains of Pulaski County in southwestern Virginia emerged two battling southern belles who fought for two years in the Confederate army without being detected. These two disguised soldiers were Molly and Mary Bell.

Molly and Mary Bell were cousins who were raised by an uncle on a small rural farm in the mountains of Pulaski County, Virginia. In 1862, their uncle left Virginia and went north to join the Union army. The two girls were furious and considered him to be a traitor to the South.

The two young ladies decided to do their part for the South and make up for their uncle being a traitor. They decided to disguise themselves as men and join the Confederate army. They cut their hair short enough to comply with the male style of the times, wore thick woolen work shirts to cover their breasts and curves, and practiced lowering the tone of their voices and walking like men. Being mountain farm girls, they were already used to hard work, riding horses, hunting and foraging.

Once they felt they were well prepared and could maintain the disguise, they presented themselves to the recruiters as volunteers. Molly enlisted under the name of Bob Morgan while Mary enlisted under the name Tom Parker. With their prior riding ability in their favor, they were enlisted in the cavalry.

Within one month of their enlistment, Union forces captured the entire Confederate cavalry unit. Molly and Mary thought that their careers in the military had come to a quick halt. Within a few hours of being captured, however, the attacking forces of General John Hunt Morgan rescued them.

The Bells decided that the cavalry was not their cup of tea and soon switched to the infantry. They were assigned to fight under General Jubal A. Early. They fought at Chancellorsville, Gettysburg, and Spotsylvania Court House, where General Early defeated General Burnside.

Molly was standing guard duty one night when explosions and gunfire broke the quiet of the night as the Union troops attacked their camp. Molly sounded the alarm and stood fast at her post. She was credited with killing three charging Yankees, which was quite a feat with a muzzleloader. She was singled out for heroism and promoted to the rank of sergeant. In the same period of time Mary had been promoted to corporal. The two were considered to be gallant fighting soldiers.

In order to continue concealing their sex, they agreed to take a young captain into their confidence. They felt that they could trust him to keep their secret and protect them against physical checkups and other army duties which might expose them. The captain was amazed by their revelation. His respect for them as soldiers and their accomplishments in battle prompted him to overlook their gender and he agreed to keep their secret.

Later, Molly was wounded in battle by a shell fragment that hit her in the arm. Mary rushed to her side and stated that they had better get a doctor. Fearing detection, Molly jumped to her feet and said, "No doctors for me. It is just a scratch." She and Mary tended the wound, which healed quickly and caused no trouble for Molly. This act made the other soldiers consider Molly a tough fighting solder.

At the Battle of Cedar Creek on October 19, 1864, the young captain who knew the girls' secret was captured. Their protector was gone. They then decided to take a young lieutenant, who now commanded the company, into their confidence. The young lieutenant, however, was an opportunist and reported the two girls to General Early hoping for a pat on the back or promotion.

The girls begged General Early to let them stay with the regiment and reminded him of their excellent fighting record. General Early had the girls arrested and sent to Richmond to be placed in Castle Thunder Prison. They were kept at Castle Thunder Prison for three weeks. No specific charges were ever filed against the girls. The Bells were freed after the three weeks and allowed to return to their home in full uniform.

When the newspapers heard of the discovery of women in the Confederate forces, they quickly labeled the girls as common camp followers who were demoralizing General Early's troops. It seems obvious that the opposite was true. The way society viewed women, at the time, especially those who dressed as men, slanted the objectivity of the reporters.

Mary and Molly Bell fought in some of the fiercest battles of the Civil War and distinguished themselves as brave, loyal, soldiers, serving undetected for over two years. Camp followers and women who disguised themselves for prostitution usually did not last more than a few weeks before being discovered or turned in by one of the soldiers. The achievement and longevity of the Bells speaks for itself.

Molly and Mary Bell should be remembered for their great loyalty, dedication, bravery and the sacrifices they made for the cause they believed in.

❧ *17* ❧

Notable Women Soldiers

As we have seen, there were many women in the armies of both the Confederacy and the Union who were never discovered. Many accomplished heroic deeds before being found out while others were discovered after a short time with the regiment and subsequently discharged.

Those women who were dedicated enough to actually join the army as fighting soldiers should also be counted among the nation's Civil War patriots even though their known service was cut short by being exposed as women. Some of these women are discussed in the following eight accounts.

Henrietta Spencer — Woman Soldier

It was pure revenge that prompted a young Ohio girl to disguise herself as a man and join the Union army. Her name was Henrietta Spencer, and she resided with her family in Oberlin, Ohio, about 20 miles west of Cleveland.

When the Civil War began in 1861 her father and brother enlisted in the Union army. They fought many battles together until December 31, 1862, when they began the three-day Battle of Stone's River (Murfreesboro, Tennessee). During this battle both her father and her brother were killed.

Henrietta was devastated by the loss and felt that she must do something to avenge their deaths. She formulated a plan whereby she would disguise herself as a man and join the Union army. This was the best way she could think of to get revenge for the death of her father and brother.

She cut her hair short, dressed as a man, and practiced talking and walking like a man, all things other women did in order to enlist. When she felt confident in her disguise she presented herself for enlistment in the 10th Ohio Cavalry Regiment. She was accepted and began her training. The name she used with the 10th Ohio Cavalry is not known.

The 10th Ohio Cavalry Regiment was formed at Camp Taylor, Cleveland, Ohio, in October 1862. They were mustered into Federal service and left for Nashville on February 27, 1863, after the Battle of Stone's River. Henrietta's enlistment date was probably in early January 1863 after a very short period of bereavement. The exact date is not known.

Henrietta learned that the 10th Ohio Cavalry was to be assigned duty at Murfreesboro, Tennessee after they trained and were mustered in. She was looking forward to her regiment going to Murfreesboro after training. She worked hard during her training, but forgot to keep up her disguise and her actions gave her away after only three weeks. She was discovered to be a woman during the third week of January 1863. The *New York Times* made the first public report of the discovery on January 24, 1863.

The reason she gave for enlisting was to avenge the deaths of her father and brother. She was discharged from the 10th Ohio Cavalry and sent home. It is not known if she enlisted in another regiment to continue her quest for revenge.

Hatty Robinson — Woman Soldier

The Baltimore provost marshal's office arrested a young female dressed as a Union soldier on Saturday October 15, 1861. Her name was Hatty Robinson, and this is her story as she related it to the provost police.

Hatty Robinson was born in Auburn, New York, in 1842. She reported that she was married to Lieutenant Fuller of the 46th Pennsylvania Infantry Regiment, Company F. Her statement to the provost marshal that her husband was a lieutenant may have been made to impress him. Records do show that a Charles D. Fuller was a private in Company D of the 46th Pennsylvania Infantry but do not show a Lieutenant Fuller.

She had been disguised as a man for several months and joined the 46th Pennsylvania as Pvt. Charles D. Fuller. She stated that all the officers of the regiment were aware of her sex, including the surgeon and assistant. When she enlisted, a doctor at Harrisburg, Pennsylvania, examined her. The examination was held in private. She did not recall the doctor's name, only that he was tall and portly with black hair, whiskers, and dark eyes.

She stated that her guardian was W. H. Pickett of Harrisburg, Pennsylvania. Her only relative was an uncle who was a clerk at the Franklin Hotel in Harrisburg, Pennsylvania. His name was George Whitney.

Hatty was arrested at the hotel near the Northern Central Railroad depot in Baltimore, Maryland. She stated that she was on her way from Washington, D. C., to Harrisburg, Pennsylvania, and stopped over in Baltimore for the night. She gave her disguise away after drinking four glasses of ale in the hotel bar. After four drinks it became hard for her to maintain her disguise and an alert provost marshal spotted her and she was promptly arrested.

She stated that Colonel Joseph Farmer Knipe, the commander of the 46th Pennsylvania, had induced her to accompany him to Washington and that he had bought her train tickets. She further stated that she was traveling under the name Charles D. Knipe on her way to Harrisburg. When she arrived home in Harrisburg, she was planning to change back into female attire and rejoin the regiment as a female nurse.

One wonders if the entire story she relates was a fabrication because the 46th Pennsylvania Infantry was not mustered into Federal service until October 31, 1861, and she was arrested on October 5, 1861, at which time the 46th was still being formed and trained. If her account is true, then she may have been a recruit in training and after discovery was being sent home to Harrisburg where she planned to become a nurse and return to the 46th Regiment.

It is not known if she re-enlisted in another regiment as a soldier under an assumed name or if she served as a nurse during the war.

Louisa Hoffman — Woman Soldier

Being a heroine to both the Union and the Confederate armies was quite a feat. This was the case of a young woman from New York City who enlisted in the Confederate army when the Civil War began. Her name was Louisa Hoffman.

When the Civil War broke out, she left New York and headed south where she enlisted in the 1st Virginia Confederate Cavalry. While serving with the 1st Virginia Cavalry, she fought in both battles of Manassas/Bull Run and many battles in between. After the second Battle of Manassas/Bull Run in August 1862, she had a change of heart and realized that she was on the wrong side — being a northern girl, her loyalties were with the Union.

She switched sides and enlisted in the 1st Ohio Infantry Regiment as a cook. After a period of time she became bored with this assignment and longed for the excitement of the soldier in the field. On August 22, 1864, she enlisted in Battery C of the 1st Tennessee Artillery as Pvt. John Hoffman. Her desire for excitement had been fulfilled, but it was short lived. The next day, August 23, 1864, she made a fatal mistake and her sex was discovered. She was promptly arrested by Lieutenant Fletcher of the 1st Tennessee Artillery Regiment and taken to the provost marshal's office in Nashville.

While being questioned by the provost marshal, Private John Hoffman revealed her real name to be Louisa Hoffman and told her story. She was discharged and sent home.

Elizabeth A. Niles — Woman Soldier

It is rare indeed to find a woman soldier who fought for three full years with the same regiment without her gender being discovered. Elizabeth Niles was such a woman, who, at the side of her husband, Martin, fought most of the major battles of the Civil War without an injury or sickness.

Elizabeth and her husband Martin Niles were on their honeymoon in mid-April 1861 when the Civil War began. After a few months, it was obvious that the war was not going to be over in the short period originally forecast. Martin Niles, being a patriotic American, decided to enlist and do his part in preserving the Union.

When Elizabeth heard of his plans she decided that she wanted to stay with her husband and enlist in the same regiment disguised as a man. Martin agreed to this plan and Elizabeth cut her hair short, donned men's clothing and in August 1861, they both enlisted in the 4th New Jersey Infantry Regiment for a three-year tour of duty.

The 4th New Jersey Infantry Regiment was organized at Camp Olden, Trenton, New Jersey, and mustered into Federal service on August 19, 1861.

During the three years Elizabeth spent with the 4th New Jersey Infantry, she participated in many major battles, including: Siege of Yorktown, April 5 — May 4, 1862; Battle of Gaines's Mill, June 27, 1862; Battle of Second Manassas/Bull Run, August 28–30, 1862; Battle of Crampton's Pass/South Mountain, September 14, 1862; Battle of Antietam, September 16–17, 1862; Battle of Fredericksburg, December 11–13, 1862; Battle of Chancelorsville, May 1–4, 1863; Battle of Gettysburg, July 1–3, 1863; Battle of the Wilderness, May 5–6, 1864; Battle of Spotsylvania Court House, May 4–8, 1864; Battle of Bloody Angle, May 12, 1864; Battle of Cold Harbor, June 1–12, 1864; Battle of Petersburg, June 16–18, 1864.

Elizabeth and her husband were mustered out at Trenton, New Jersey, with the rest of the non-veterans on September 7, 1864, at the end of their three-year enlistment. The remainder of the regiment was then consolidated with the 7th New Jersey Infantry Regiment on November 6, 1864.

During the three years the 4th New Jersey Infantry Battalion was in existence, it lost a total of 223 men; 12 officers and 126 enlisted men were killed and 85 enlisted men died from disease.

Martin Niles died a few years after the war ended. Elizabeth lived the rest of her life in Raritan, New Jersey, where on October 1, 1920, she died at the age of 92.

The Raritan newspaper printed this account of her death:

> Mrs. Elizabeth A. Niles who with close cropped hair and wearing a uniform, concealed her sex and is said to have fought beside her husband during the Civil War is dead here today, aged 92.

To have participated in so many major battles and endured all the horrors of war along with the other soldiers demonstrates the true heroism of Elizabeth Niles. Knowing that she could have walked away from the war at any time, she stood firm and continued to do her duty. This clearly makes her an extraordinary woman and a true American heroine.

Mary Seaberry — Woman Soldier

It was July 1862 and the Civil War had been raging for 16 months when a 17-year-old Columbus, Ohio, girl decided to enlist in the army as a man. Her name was Mary Seaberry. She felt a patriotic duty to serve her country. She also had a strong desire for the adventure and excitement of being in an army during wartime.

Mary began her adventure by cutting her hair short and getting used to wearing men's clothing. She practiced walking and talking like a man and when she felt she was prepared, she enlisted in Company F of the newly formed 52nd Ohio Infantry Regiment as Private Charles Freeman.

The 52nd Ohio Infantry Regiment was organized at Camp Dennison, Ohio, in June 1862. They were mustered into Federal service in August 1862.

During the time she was with the 52nd Ohio Infantry Private Freeman participated in the following battles: Battle of Richmond, Kentucky, August 29–30, 1862; Skirmish at Lexington, Kentucky, September 2, 1862; Pursuit of General Bragg to Crab Orchard, Kentucky, October 3–15, 1862; Battle of Perryville, Kentucky, October 8, 1862.

Mary Seaberry as Private Freeman performed her duties as a soldier and adapted to army life very well. Her disguise and manner never gave anyone in her regiment even the slightest hint that she was not a man.

On November 7, 1862, she was admitted to General Hospital in Lebanon, Kentucky, suffering from a severe fever. She was transferred from the Lebanon hospital to a hospital in Louisville, Kentucky, for treatment. On November 10, 1862, the Louisville hospital personnel discovered that Private Charles Freeman was a woman. Upon regaining her health she was discharged on December 13, 1862, on the basis of sexual incompatibility.

Mary served only five months with the 52nd Ohio Infantry. In that short period of service she distinguished herself as a brave, loyal Union soldier, and a credit to her country.

It is not known if she re-enlisted in another regiment under a different alias. If she did, she did so undetected.

Pvt. Charley — Woman Soldier

Little is known about Pvt. Charley. Only brief accounts of her life in the Civil War and her tragic death have been recorded.

Charley enlisted in Company H of the 14th Iowa Infantry at the age of eighteen, with her friend Leroy A. Crane. She enlisted as Pvt. Charley (last name unknown) to be with Captain Crane who was assigned as Commander of Company H. Captain Crane assigned Charley to be his personal aide.

The 14th Iowa Infantry was formed and mustered into Federal service in Davenport, Iowa, on November 6, 1861. They fought at Ft. Henry on February 2–6, 1862,

Ft. Donelson on February 16, 1862, and at Shiloh on April 6–7, 1862. At Shiloh, the 14th Iowa Infantry held center at the "Hornet's Nest," the Confederate nickname for a position in a wooded area on the left center of the Union line on the first day of battle. During the Battle of Shiloh, most of the 14th Iowa Regiment were captured by Confederate troops. They were exchanged on November 19, 1862.

On April 12, 1863, the 14th Iowa Infantry Regiment arrived in Cairo, Illinois, for some rest and relaxation. Charley, accompanied by several other soldiers, attended the local theater that Saturday night. She was noticed by the local provost marshal and suspected to be a woman in uniform. The provost marshal had her arrested and taken to his office. Captain Leroy A. Crane, commander of Company H, came to her rescue and got her released into his custody on the promise that she would dress in proper woman's clothing and resume her normal life.

The news of this event quickly leaked out and spread through the camp like wildfire. The soldiers in the camp became very curious. A large group of men soon gathered outside of Captain Crane's quarters hoping for a chance to see her.

The regimental commander was informed about the incident and the gathering of men at Captain Crane's quarters. He sent his adjutant to investigate the situation.

Realizing that her secret was out and that she was the talk of the camp was devastating to her. Considering all she had been through in the eighteen months she fought with the regiment, the embarrassment and ensuing discharge were too much for her to bear.

She took Captain Crane's revolver from his room, stepped out of his quarters onto the parade ground in front of the men, placed the muzzle of the pistol to her heart and fired. She fell dead without a groan or exclamation of any kind.

No one could find out her true name or her reasons for following Captain Crane into the war. Captain Crane kept her secret and was mustered out of the regiment at the end of his enlistment on November 16, 1864.

Charley fought bravely and proved to be as good a soldier as her comrades. She stood tall in some of the fiercest fighting of the Civil War. She loved the regiment and army life and could not bear being separated from Captain Crane or the regiment, the two loves of her life.

Mary Owens Jenkins—Woman Soldier

"A more faithful soldier never shouldered a musket" was the comment written on the medical file of a wounded woman soldier during her treatment. This brave woman was Mary Owens Jenkins, who distinguished herself as a fighting soldier during the Civil War.

Mary Owens, a native of Danville, Pennsylvania, was just a schoolgirl when the Civil War began. She fell in love with a young man named William Evans and upon hearing that he was going to enlist in the Union army was determined to go with him. She discussed her plans with William, who agreed for her to go along. They also decided to get married prior to enlisting. They were soon married and, after a short honeymoon, put their plan into action.

Mary cut her hair, dressed as a man and with her new husband enlisted in Company K of the 9th Pennsylvania Cavalry. She enlisted under the name John Evans.

Pvt. John Evans adapted well to army life and became a very reliable soldier. Her secret was safe and no one in the regiment even suspected that Pvt. Evans was anything but an excellent soldier.

Mary and her husband fought side by side in several battles. During one of the battles Mary was wounded. The wound was not life threatening and her gender was not discovered during treatment. She was able to continue with the regiment and fought in the next battle.

During the third battle in which she and her husband fought together, he was killed. Devastated by the loss of her husband, her resolve grew stronger and she wanted more than ever to continue fighting the Rebels. She stayed in the army and continued fighting with the regiment for the next 18 months.

Her career as a fighting soldier came to an end when, during a fierce battle, she was struck in the chest by a minié ball. This wound was serious and required immediate medical attention. The surgeon attending her wound discovered that Pvt. John Evans was a woman. The surgeon noted on the hospital record, "A more faithful soldier never shouldered a musket."

Upon recovering from her wound she was discharged from the 9th Pennsylvania Cavalry. She had served undetected for 18 months and had been wounded twice.

After the war she married a coal miner named Abraham Jenkins. She lived the rest of her life in Ohio. She died in 1881 and was buried in her village cemetery in Ohio. The local veterans decorated her grave to honor her for her courageous service.

Frances Day — Woman Soldier

Many women soldiers were killed in battle without their identity being discovered. Some who died in battle lived long enough after being wounded to reveal their story. Such was the case of Frances Day, a 19-year-old Pennsylvania girl.

Frances Day was born in 1844 and was a native of Mifflin, Pennsylvania, 40 miles northwest of Harrisburg in Juniata County. She fell in love with a young man named William Fitzpatrick. William, in response to President Lincoln's call for 75,000 volunteers to put down the rebellion, decided to enlist in the infantry and do his part. Upon hearing his plans Frances decided to disguise herself as a man and accompany him into the army. Her motive was to be near her lover.

She disguised herself and with William at her side, enlisted as a nine-month recruit in Company F of the 126th Pennsylvania Infantry Regiment. She enlisted at Mifflin, Pennsylvania, on August 5, 1862 and was officially mustered in on August

9, 1862 at Harrisburg. She enlisted under the name Frank Mayne. She was described as having light brown hair, being of average height, and having a light complexion and bright eyes.

The 126th Pennsylvania Infantry Regiment was mustered into Federal service on August 9, 1862, at Harrisburg, Pennsylvania. They left Harrisburg on August 15, 1862, for duty in Washington, D.C., where they served until September 12. The regimental camp was at Cloud Mills, Virginia.

Frances adjusted well. She adapted to army life and displayed sound judgement and leadership qualities and was rapidly promoted to sergeant to fill the needs of the regiment. With only three weeks of training she had come a long way and was quickly becoming an asset to the regiment.

Pvt. William Fitzpatrick became ill after three weeks with the regiment and was placed in an Alexandria, Virginia, hospital for treatment. He died on August 24, 1862. The same day that William died, Sgt. Frank Mayne decided to desert. On August 30, 1862, she deserted the regimental camp at Cloud Mills, Virginia. She deserted because she was grief stricken by the loss of her lover, but did not consider herself a deserter and wanted to continue her service to her country.

Within a short period of time she enlisted in another unit that was fighting in the western theater. Her alias is unknown. She was mortally wounded in a fierce battle and while being treated, her gender was discovered. She survived long enough to make a deathbed confession about who she was and her reasons for being in the army.

The men of the 126th Pennsylvania Infantry Regiment were stunned when they heard the news. Her disguise was so complete that they never suspected that Sgt. Mayne was a woman.

After a taste of the realities of war, her motives changed from following a lover to a feeling of patriotic duty to her country. Frances Day distinguished herself as a brave American woman.

Mary Ellen Wise — Woman Soldier

In many cases, the young female adventurers who disguised themselves as men and enlisted in the army soon changed their motives after a taste of the horror of battle, and became completely dedicated to their cause.

Mary Ellen Wise was one of these women. She was living in rural Indiana near Anderson when the Civil War began. In September 1861, she cut her hair short, disguised herself as a man and enlisted in company I of the 34th Indiana Infantry Regiment as Pvt. James Wise.

The 34th Indiana Infantry Regiment was organized at Anderson, Indiana, on September 16, 1861, and was mustered into Federal service on October 10, 1861.

While Mary Wise was with the 34th Indiana she fought many battles and was wounded three times. The 34th participated in the siege at New Madrid, Missouri, on March 5–14, 1862, the siege and capture of Island #10 on the Mississippi River on

March 15 to April 8, 1862, the capture of Fort Pillow on June 5, 1862, the Battle of Port Gibson on May 1, 1863, the Battle of Champion Hill on May 16, 1863 and the siege of Jackson, Mississippi, on July 10, 1863.

In her last battle, a minié ball wounded her in the shoulder. This was the third time she had been wounded and this time the wound was serious enough to require immediate medical attention. When the surgeon removed Mary's shirt to tend the wound he discovered that Pvt. James Wise was a woman. She was discharged after recovering from her wound.

The discharge on the grounds of "Proved to be a Woman" left her right to receive her pay in doubt. She felt that she had as much right to the pay as any male soldier. When President Lincoln heard of her case, he intervened and ordered the army to give her the pay she had earned.

After her discharge in September 1864, she lived for a while with her friend Mrs. E.B. Gates and her husband, who was a captain in the Union army. Their home was at Lincoln Hospital in Washington, D.C. While living with the Gateses she met and fell in love with an army sergeant named Forehand of the Veteran's Reserve Corps. They were married at Lincoln Hospital and moved to his home in New Hampshire to live.

The eight women here had deep feelings about doing their part for the causes they believed in — such deep feelings that they were willing to put their lives on the line as fighting soldiers.

❧ 18 ❧

Elizabeth Van Lew:
Union Spy

She pledged her life, fortune and her sacred honor for the preservation of the Union. She created a spy ring so complex and widespread that it even reached into Jefferson Davis's home. This great American was Elizabeth Van Lew.

Elizabeth Van Lew was born on October 12, 1818, in Richmond, Virginia. She was the oldest daughter of the three children of John and Elizabeth Van Lew. Her father John was a native of Jamaica, Long Island, New York. He left New York after a business failure and moved to Richmond. He and his partner, Mr. Taylor, opened one of the first hardware businesses in the south. The business was very successful, and the Van Lews became part of the wealthy Richmond society.

John Van Lew was married to Elizabeth Baker of Philadelphia, the daughter of the mayor of Philadelphia, Mr. Hilary Baker. The Van Lew family lived in a three and one half-story mansion, located on Grace Street in Richmond at the top of Church Hill overlooking the James River. Church Hill is the highest of the seven hills of Richmond. Their plush home soon became a gathering place for Richmond society and many high-ranking government officials.

As a young girl Elizabeth Van Lew was sent to Philadelphia for schooling. While there, she lived with her grandfather Hilary Baker, who was still the mayor of Philadelphia. During her time attending school in Philadelphia, Elizabeth developed strong anti-slavery sentiments. When she returned to Richmond these strong beliefs prompted her to beg her father to free the twelve slaves he possessed. Her father was not harsh toward his slaves and he cared for their well-being. When asked to free them, he replied, "They are like children. They could not possibly take care of themselves." Elizabeth did not agree with her father, and after he died she and her mother freed all the slaves and helped reunite them with their spouses and loved ones. Once free, some of the slaves left and were never heard of again, while others chose to stay with the family.

Elizabeth Van Lew was known as an outspoken woman who openly expressed her views on slavery. Her act of freeing the slaves was so uncommon that the people of Richmond began to refer to her as "Crazy Bet." This caused her to lose many of her friends.

When Virginia voted on May 23, 1861, in favor of secession from the Union to join the Confederacy, both Elizabeth and her mother were deeply saddened. She wrote in her diary:

> It broke my heart when Virginia seceded. Mother and I prayed for our country. Secession and war would be the worst thing to happen to the South. It could not possibly survive. Its best hope was for a short war. Tearing a country apart is never good for anyone.

Her deep love of country and her prayer for a short war led her to wonder what she could do to help reunite the country. She soon found a way to help. It came after the first land battle of the war, the Battle of Big Bethel, on June 10, 1861. Prior to the battle two units of Union troops mistakenly fired upon each other causing 21 casualties and alerting the Confederate troops of their presence. With the location of the Union troops known and the element of surprise gone, the battle was an easy Southern victory. The Federal troops numbered 2,500 and sustained losses of 21 accidentally killed, 18 killed in battle, 53 wounded and 5 missing. The Confederate forces had only 1 killed and 7 wounded.

Union prisoners of war began arriving in Richmond soon after this battle. To house these captured Union soldiers, the Confederate government established five prisons in Richmond. They were:

Libby Prison. This prison, located between Cary and Dock Streets at 20th on the James River and just below the Van Lew home, was used for housing captured Union officers. The prison was a converted warehouse owned by Libby and Sons who were manufacturers of ship candles. The prison boasted of its high security.

Belle Isle. This prison was set up to house Union enlisted men. It was an island in the James River.

Castle Godwin. A prison for women suspected, accused, or convicted of disloyalty, spy activities, or harboring deserters.

Castle Thunder. This prison was for men suspected of disloyalty, spying, and being Union sympathizers.

Castle Lightning. This prison was for Confederate soldiers who had committed crimes, deserters, AWOL, drunk and disorderly conduct, and other minor infractions.

Elizabeth openly expressed sympathy for the Federal prisoners and offered to help them by supplying food, clothing and medicine. She also provided them bribe money, books and information about the war. She was allowed to enter the prisons to care for them. While doing this she quickly realized that these men had all been brought through the Confederate lines on their way to Richmond, and thus had knowledge of the Confederate troop movements and their strengths. She realized that such information could be valuable to the Union. She began to gather the information to pass on to the Federal troops.

She also began gathering information from the officers and government officials who visited her plush home, the gathering place for high-ranking officers and Richmond's elite. One of her closest friends was the commandant of Libby Prison, Lieutenant David H. Todd, whose half-sister was Mrs. Abraham Lincoln. When Lieutenant Todd was reassigned, she befriended the new commandant, a Lieutenant Gibbs. She talked him into moving his family into the Van Lew mansion as boarders.

In order to get the information to the Union army, she set up a network of relay stations using former slaves and Union supporters. She also used a farm that she owned on the opposite side of the river, south of Richmond. For security she developed a cipher code which would keep anyone who captured the couriers from reading the message. A copy of the code was found folded up in the back of her watch after her death.

Elizabeth Van Lew used the code name "Babcock" in her spying activities. She worked as a spy for generals George H. Sharp, Chief of the U. S. Bureau of Military Information (Secret Service); Benjamin F. Butler, commander of the Army of the James; George G. Mead, commander of the Army of the Potomic; and Ulysses S. Grant, commander of the Union forces.

Prior to establishing her cipher code, she would tear the message into several pieces and send each piece with a different messenger. Once the code was established, Elizabeth would send former Negro slaves into Richmond with things to sell. These messengers wore brogans with extra thick soles. The soles were hollowed out and contained the coded messages. Each courier had two pairs of shoes and never returned home with the same pair with which he left. The hollow soles were used to not only send coded messages, but maps, plans, and letters which were to be delivered to General Grant at City Point the next morning.

One of the operatives who assisted Elizabeth was Mary Elizabeth Bowser, a former slave in the Van Lew home. When Mary was freed she was sent north by Elizabeth to be educated. After receiving an education she returned to the Van Lew home to work with Elizabeth. In 1863 a friend of Elizabeth's persuaded the personal staff of President Jefferson Davis to hire Mary Bowser as a maid in the Davis home. Acting as an uneducated ex-slave, Mary was able to gather valuable information without being suspected. The information she gathered was not written down but committed to memory.

Her contact was Mr. Thomas McNiven, a Northern spy posing as a baker. When he made his daily deliveries to the Davis home she would verbally relay the information to him. The information she gathered from the Confederate white house was invaluable to the Union.

In addition to her loyalty, dedication, bravery, and love of freedom, Mary Elizabeth Bowser was an exceptional actress; she was never discovered. Acting as an uneducated ex-slave incapable of such activities as spying, she successfully accomplished her mission and was a valuable asset to the Union.

Elizabeth Van Lew was also an exceptional actress. She capitalized on the "Crazy Bet" nickname she was given by the people of Richmond. She pretended to be foolish and eccentric. She would walk around Richmond singing nonsense songs, dressed in strange clothes thus furthering the belief that she

Elizabeth Van Lew. Courtesy of the Valentine Museum, Richmond, Virginia.

was really crazy and incapable of the complex activities in which she was engaged. Although she was never discovered, she always felt that she was in danger of being discovered and arrested. She also felt that she was continually being watched.

Elizabeth Van Lew had a large hidden room in her home, which was only accessible by a secret stairway. She used this room to hide secret documents and messages as well as runaway slaves and escaped prisoners. At one time she had over 100 men hidden in the secret room.

She continued to take food, clothing and medicine to the prisons to help ease the suffering and to continue to gather information. During her visits to Libby Prison she became aware of an upcoming escape plan and began preparing her network to help the escaping officers reach the Union lines.

On February 9, 1864, 109 Union prisoners completed a 60-foot tunnel from the basement of Libby Prison's east end. The tunnel went under the street and up into

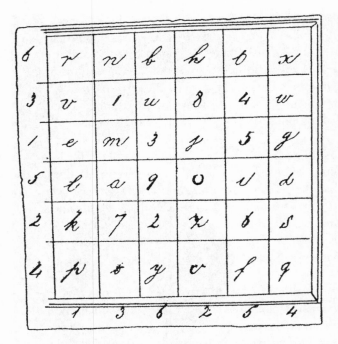

Elizabeth Van Lew's Cipher Code. Reprint from *On Hazardous Service* by William Gilmore Berymer, 1912.

a tobacco storage shed. From there the escaping prisoners crossed a yard and went into the street. It was an easy passage. When some of the escapees emerged from the tunnel, they encountered a security guard. The security guard mistook them for Confederate soldiers. Since the guard had been stealing "Yankee Boxes" stored in the shed, he made no inquiry but let them pass.

The escapees made their way up the hill to the Van Lew home where they were hidden in the secret room and slowly moved out through Elizabeth's network. This was the largest prison break during the Civil War. Of the 109 Union officers who escaped, 48 were recaptured, 2 drowned in the James River, and 59 safely reached the Union lines. Elizabeth Van Lew and her network were responsible for the success of the escape.

Based on information from Elizabeth Van Lew, President Lincoln ordered a raid on Richmond. On March 1, 1864, General Judson Kilpatrick led 3,500 mounted raiders to capture Richmond and set the prisoners free. The raid failed and the Federal troops lost 340 troopers and 500 horses. One of those killed was Colonel Ulric Dahlgreen.

The Confederate soldiers dumped his body in a shallow, unmarked grave. One of the men who witnessed this callous treatment of a Union officer's body reported the incident to Elizabeth Van Lew. Under cover of night she and a few loyal followers stole the body and gave it a proper burial at the gate of the cemetery.

She continued her activities as a spy until the end of the war. On April 3, 1865, when Richmond surrendered, Elizabeth Van Lew immediately raised the Stars and Stripes over her home. It was the first Union flag in four years to fly over Richmond and the first to be displayed in Richmond after the surrender. After she raised the flag the Richmond citizens gathered and threatened her. She faced them down, stating, "General Grant will be here in one hour. I know all of you and if you harm me or my property your homes will be burned to the ground by noon." The crowd then left without taking any action. When General Grant arrived, he assigned a special squad of soldiers to guard the Van Lew home and protect Elizabeth from reprisals.

The people of Richmond treated Elizabeth Van Lew as a traitor for the rest of her life. On December 16, 1866, at her request, the War Department removed all the files containing communications from her acting as a spy, and turned them over to her. She burned them, which was a great loss to history.

When Grant became President, he appointed her postmaster of Richmond for her service to the Union. However, when Rutherford B. Hayes became President, he knuckled under to political pressures and demoted her to a mail clerk, despite the fact that he had a letter from former President Grant recommending that he keep Van Lew as postmaster. Soon thereafter, she was transferred to Washington, D.C. After more demotions she resigned and returned to Richmond penniless. The letter from former President Grant also stated that Elizabeth Van Lew was due $15,000 for her service, however, Congress never got around to approving the funds.

For the rest of her life Elizabeth was financially dependent on others. One of those who helped her was an officer whom she had helped at Libby Prison. This ex-prisoner was from Massachusetts and was a descendant of Paul Revere whom he was named after.

Until her death September 25, 1900, at the age of 82 years and 11 months, she continued to fight for many other causes including women's suffrage. The community remained hostile toward her till her death. She was buried in Shockoe Hill Cemetery in Richmond, Virginia. She was so hated in Richmond that no one attended her funeral except relatives of the Union soldiers she had helped and her devoted servants.

After her death, relatives of Colonel Paul Revere (whom she had helped escape), bought a headstone for her grave. The headstone was made of Massachusetts granite with a bronze plaque that read

> She risked everything that is dear to man—friends, fortune, comfort, health, life itself. All for the one absorbing desire of her heart—that slavery might be abolished and the Union preserved.

The stone has this marking: "This boulder from the Capitol Hill in Boston is a tribute from her Massachusetts friends."

The service rendered by Elizabeth Van Lew was invaluable in the quest to end the war and reunite the Union. Her courage and dedication to her country demonstrate that she was an extraordinary woman who ranks high among those great Americans who helped preserve our nation.

❦ 19 ❦

Rose O'Neal Greenhow: Confederate Spy

She was a Washington socialite, an entertainer of presidents, senators, diplomats, kings and queens. She was also a Confederate spy. Her name was Rose O'Neal Greenhow.

Rose O'Neal Greenhow was born in 1817 in rural Montgomery County, Maryland, where she also spent most of her childhood. She was the daughter of wealthy slaveholders. When she was a young girl her father was murdered by one of his slaves. This tragedy made Rose an anti-abolitionist for the rest of her life.

When she reached her teens, she and her sister Ellen Elizabeth moved to Washington, D.C., to live with their aunt who ran a boarding house in the old Capitol Building, which later became Old Capitol Prison.

Rose had long, black hair, dark eyes, and an olive complexion. She was considered a beautiful young woman. She became a friend to many of her aunt's boarders and learned to love an active social life. Many of the boarders were upcoming statesmen and government officials.

Several years later, at the age of 26, she married 43-year-old Dr. Robert Greenhow of Virginia. Dr. Greenhow was a man of means and well thought of by Washington society. The marriage to Dr. Greenhow assured Rose the kind of social life that she had desired.

Over the next few years she became the mother of four daughters. Her social status continued to grow and her home became a social meeting place for Washington society. Rose had a dynamic personality and made friends easily. She had a keen sense of humor and a quick wit, which earned her the nickname "Wild Rose."

In 1850, the Green-hows left Washington and headed west to San Francisco. Dr. Greenhow saw an opportunity for great wealth in the west, but his vision was short-lived. He suffered an injury to his leg, which eventually led to his death. Devastated and seeing no future for her daughters and herself, Rose moved back to Washington with her girls four years later. She bought a house near the White House at 398 Sixteenth Street. She then set about renewing all her former friendships and re-establishing herself in the Washington social scene. She became a friend to President Buchanan and Secretary of State William H. Seward, both of whom often dined at her home.

Rose O'Neal Greenhow. Courtesy of Leib Image Archives.

She often held dinner parties at her home and also entertained guests from the diplomatic circle as well as from Congress. Invitations to her parties were coveted in Washington society.

As rumors of civil war began, Rose was not hesitant to let it be known that she was not an abolitionist and that her sympathy and loyalty were with the South. After all, she was a southern woman.

In May 1861, one of her close friends, Captain Thomas Jordan, who was a quartermaster in the Union army, stopped at her home to say goodbye. He was resigning his commission and leaving Washington to join General Beauregard's Confederate troops. Rose confided in Captain Jordan that she wanted to help the Confederacy but didn't know what she could do. Jordan and Rose began planning an espionage ring to gather vital information and pass it along to General Beauregard. The ring included army Colonel Michael Thompson, who was based in Washington; William T. Smithson, a Washington banker; Dr. Aaron Van Camp, Rose's personal dentist; an unmarried woman named Bettie Hassler; and 14-year-old Betty Duvall, a close friend to Rose.

Captain Jordan developed a crude code for Rose to use when writing messages. The coded messages were to be carried on tissue paper rolled up in hair curlers or in women's undergarments since searching a lady was considered improper conduct during the 19th century. Rose carried the code in her camisole at all times.

Once the lines of communication to General Beauregard were established, Captain Jordan left Washington to join the Confederate troops. He was later appointed Adjutant General of the Confederate Army at Manassas.

Rose Greenhow first applied her espionage talents on Colonel E.D. Keys, secretary to General Winfield Scott, General-in-Chief of the Union army, and Senator Wilson of Massachusetts. The information she obtained from these two sources gave her the following list of information on the upcoming Battle of First Manassas/Bull Run, which she forwarded to General Pierre Beauregard.

1. The Union forces would leave Washington on July 16 to advance toward Richmond.

2. The Union troops would consist of 50,000 men.

3. They would advance through Arlington, Alexandria, and Centerville to Manassas.

4. The Union would cut the Winchester Railroad line to prevent General Joseph Johnston from coming to the aid of General Beauregard.

Accompanying this information was a copy of General McDowell's actual orders to his troops. This was the first message Rose sent to General Beauregard. The message was sent on July 10, 1861, by courier. The message was coded and carried by Rose's good friend, 14-year-old Betty Duvall, rolled up in her hair. Betty posed as a market girl driving a cart. This message gave General Beauregard the time he needed to ready his troops and General Johnston's army the time to march from the Shenandoah Valley to reach Manassas and reinforce the Confederate troops. General Beauregard was better prepared for the Federal assault, since he now knew where it was to take place. This advantage led to a Southern victory at First Manassas/Bull Run.

On July 21, 1861, Thomas Jordan delivered a message to Rose from General Jackson. The message read "Our president and our general direct me to thank you. We rely upon you for further information. The Confederacy owes you a debt." Later in her life, President Jefferson Davis would thank her in person.

Rose continued gathering and sending information to General Beauregard; she was becoming quite talented in the espionage business. She later wrote of her success, "To this end I employed every capacity with which God endowed me, and the result was more successful than my hopes could have flattered me to believe."

As prisoners of war were being brought into Washington, the federal government took over the old Capitol Building and converted it into a prison. This was previously the boarding house where Rose lived with her aunt. Rose began to visit the Confederate soldiers imprisoned there under the guise of bringing them food and medicine. While visiting the prisoners she was able to gather information from them on troop movements, troop emplacements and their strengths. They passed through Federal lines on their way to prison in Washington and had such knowledge.

Rose was not initially suspected of any other motive for visiting the prisoners than bringing them food and medicine since her sympathy for the southern cause was no secret, but because she had previously been under suspicion due to her outspoken views, her visits to the prison were noted. She was kept under constant surveillance although no espionage activity could be discovered on her part. When her social friends urged her to stop any activity she might be engaged in, she simply replied, "The devil is no match for a clever woman." She continued her espionage activities even though she was under constant surveillance by Pinkerton's Federal Detective Bureau.

On August 23, 1861, upon returning home, she noticed several men at her door. She remarked to one of her operatives as she walked past, "I think I am about to be arrested." Rose was indeed arrested and placed under house arrest. She was charged with communicating with the enemy in the South. Federal troops had found maps, plans, and messages Rose had sent to the Confederate troops. These items were carelessly left behind during a hasty Confederate withdrawal from Fairfax Courthouse. The code used by Rose was quickly broken and considered an amateurish attempt at code.

In her book *My Imprisonment and the First Year of Abolition Rule in Washington*, which was published in London in 1863, she stated that her reply to the charges made against her was

> If it were an established fact, you could not be surprised by it, I am after all a Southern woman, and I thank God that no drop of Yankee blood ever polluted my veins. All of whom I have honored and respected have been driven to seek shelter in the South. It would seem the most natural thing that I should communicate with them.

The initial search of her home after her arrest found nothing. She had, however, written records of her espionage ring concealed in the pages of books on the top shelf of her library. She feared that a second search would uncover the records, as well as a message she had ready for General Beauregard. She quickly began working on the detective who was guarding her. She bribed him with brandy to let her go into her library alone. Once inside, she burned the records in the stove and concealed the message meant for General Beauregard in her stockings. Betty Hassler, while visiting Rose, took the message and the next day delivered it to General Beauregard.

At Rose's house her arrest continued; the home became known as Fort Greenhow. Several other women under house arrest were also placed there. Even with all the security of a prison, Rose continued to send messages out. The Pinkerton Detectives could not figure out how she got the messages past their security. She was under constant surveillance even when she slept; her door was left open and a guard kept an eye on her.

Finally, one of her messages was intercepted and published in the newspaper. This embarrassment to the federal government prompted them to close Fort Green-how and transfer all the women to Old Capitol Prison on January 18, 1862. Rose and her daughter, "Little Rose," were placed in a room on the second floor overlooking the courtyard.

On March 25, 1862, she appeared before the United States commissioners for the trial of state prisoners to answer the charges against her. Judge Peirrepont and General Dix, a close friend of Rose's, headed the inquiry. The outcome of the hearing was that Rose would be exiled to the South.

On May 31, 1862, word came to Rose that she was to be transferred to Fortress Monroe and then to the Southern Confederacy. On the morning of June 4, 1862, she and Little Rose were set ashore at City Point by a boat from the *Monitor*. From there, Confederate officers escorted them to Richmond. That evening, President Jefferson Davis called on her to personally thank her for her service to the Confederacy. He told her, "But for you there would have been no Battle of Bull Run."

Rose was well received in Richmond and was soon enjoying a rich social life. She still wanted to do something to help the Confederate cause and was offered $2,500 to travel to Europe and act as an agent for the Confederacy. She traveled with Little Rose to Charleston where she met with General Beauregard. Several weeks passed and she told her social acquaintances that she planned to go to Europe and enroll Little Rose in the Convent of the Sacred Heart in Paris. Late one night they set sail on a blockade-runner from Charleston to Bermuda and then on to England.

Rose was very successful in Europe in her mission to gain support for the Confederacy. When she arrived in England she was presented to Queen Victoria. Later, upon her visit to France, she was given a private audience with Napoleon III. It was in England that she wrote of her experiences in *My Imprisonment or the First Year of Abolition Rule in Washington*. The book was an instant success and gained much sympathy and support for the Confederacy.

Rose enjoyed her social life in England. She became betrothed to a prominent Englishman and planned to remarry and stay in England. For some reason, though, Rose left England suddenly, and left her daughter in the Convent of the Sacred Heart in Paris. She boarded the *Condor*, which was a new three-funneled steamer on its first trip as a blockade-runner. Delaying her plans to marry and risking her life to return to the Confederacy are strong indications that she carried some very important information or plans for the Southern cause.

The captain of the *Condor* was an English officer named Captain Augustus Charles Hobart-Hampton who was on a one year leave and was blockade running for adventure. The *Condor* slipped through the blockade and approached the North Carolina coast at Cape Fear. When it was almost to the mouth of the river, about 200 yards from shore, the *Condor* spotted a vessel straight ahead. Thinking it was one of the Federal squadron, they swerved the ship sharply and ran aground on New Inlet Bar.

The other ship turned out to be another block-ade-runner, the *Nighthawk*, which had been run down by the Federal blockade the previous night.

It was almost dawn and, fearing discovery by Union gunboats, the captain dived overboard and swam to shore. Rose and two other Confederate agents, Judge Holcombe and Lieutenant Wilson, demanded to be taken ashore. They were placed in a boat and headed for shore, but the rough waters soon capsized the boat and the two men swam to shore after losing sight of Rose. (There is a conflicting report that Admiral Hewitt, who had

Rose O'Neal Greenhow and "Little Rose" at Old Capitol Prison. Courtesy of Leib Image Archives.

been knighted by Queen Victoria as Ambassador to Abyssinia, put Rose into a boat at Cape Fear.) Rose was dragged down by the $2,000 in gold coin she had tied to her waist for safekeeping. She drowned on September 30, 1864.

Early the next morning a Confederate soldier walking near the beach discovered the body of a woman that had washed ashore. He discovered the gold around her waist and took it. He then shoved the body back into the surf. Later that day the body was rediscovered by other Confederate troops who recognized it as that of Rose Greenhow. After finding out who the dead woman was, the soldier who took the gold felt so bad he returned it and joined the mourners.

Her body was placed in the State Capitol at Richmond for public homage. Rose was buried with full military honors on October 1, 1864. Her coffin was draped with the Confederate flag and buried in Oakdale Cemetery in Wilmington, North Carolina. Her grave has a marble cross with the words "Mrs. Rose O'Neal Greenhow, a bearer of dispatches to the Confederate Government."

Every year on the anniversary of her death, the Daughters of the Confederacy place a wreath on her grave. Rose O'Neal Greenhow was an extraordinary woman whose sacrifices and courage made an important impact on the cause in which she believed. Presidents, queens and kings were awed by her character and daring.

❧ 20 ❧

Maria Isabella Boyd: Confederate Spy

She was such a notorious Confederate spy that the Union newspapers labeled her "The Siren of the Shenandoah" and "The Rebel Joan of Arc." Her service to Stonewall Jackson was invaluable in his Shenandoah Valley campaign. She was 17-year-old Maria Isabella "Belle" Boyd.

Belle Boyd was born May 9, 1844, in the town of Martinsburg, Virginia. She was the daughter of a shopkeeper. The family was not wealthy but enjoyed a comfortable life. Belle, as a young Southern girl, developed a deep loyalty for the South. This love of the Southern way of life would manifest itself in her determination to serve the Confederacy during the Civil War.

Martinsburg, Virginia, was a small town located in the northwestern part of Virginia. On April 17, 1861, when Virginia voted on secession, the Loyalist leaders of the western section of the state refused to accept the vote. They then held three conventions from May to August for the purpose of electing a Loyalist state governor and electing their own Senators. They voted to combine the 50 western counties into the state of West Virginia and petition the federal government for statehood. They were finally granted statehood by a proclamation signed by President Lincoln on June 20, 1863. West Virginia was the 35th state in the Union.

Martinsburg was now in West Virginia and part of the Union. However, the 26 months it took to become a state were marked with occupation by Federal troops and treatment of the population as if they were the enemy. Federal troops occupied Martinsburg on July 3, 1861. The area was a mixture of loyalists and southern sympathizers.

Belle was just 17 years old when Federal troops occupied Martinsburg. On the second day of occupation, July 4, 1861, several soldiers became intoxicated and went on a rampage which included shooting out windows, destroying public property, invading homes, destroying personal property, and using loud and offensive language toward the townspeople.

These drunken soldiers had previously heard a rumor that Belle Boyd had decorated her room with Confederate flags. They stormed her home in search of these flags but found nothing. Belle's loyal maid Eliza had quickly gathered the flags and burned them as the soldiers approached the house. The soldiers then decided to raise the Union flag over the Boyd home to indicate submission to the North.

When Mrs. Boyd objected to the Union flag being raised over her home, she was met with a barrage of insults and foul language. Seeing her mother being insulted by the drunken Yankees was more than Belle could bear. She drew out her Derringer and shot the insulting soldier. He was carried out by his comrades and soon died from the wound.

Word quickly spread that a Southern belle had killed a Union soldier. The news almost caused a riot among the occupying Union troops. Several soldiers began preparations to burn the Boyd home, with the occupants still inside. Fearing for their lives, Belle fashioned a handwritten note to the commanding officer of the Federal forces, asking that he intervene and stop the soldiers from burning their home. The message reached the commanding officer in time and the riot was stopped. The commanding officer and his staff then held an inquiry into the incident. They questioned all witnesses and came to the conclusion that Belle had acted properly under the circumstances. He then placed guards around the house to stop any further incidents from occurring.

The commanding officer's decision was the result of many factors. He was well aware of the fact that the area did not support the Virginia vote on secession, and he realized that his men were out of line in their actions. But most important to him was ethics, which dictated that it was not chivalrous to take stern measures against someone of the weaker sex, regardless what offense was committed.

Belle got to know the guards and soon found out how easy it was to extract information from them, which she could forward to the Confederate authorities. Thus began her career as a Confederate spy. She began to send messages to the Confederate leaders by using her friends and her faithful maid Eliza. Both Negro and white couriers were used. She developed several ways of hiding the messages such as sewing them into the soles of shoes, packing them inside loaves of bread, in hollowed-out fruit and in the heads of dolls, and writing them on eggs which could only be read by holding them up to a coal oil lamp.

By the time First Manassas/Bull Run was being fought, Belle had left Martinsburg and was staying with relatives at 101 Chester Street, Front Royal, Virginia. She gained employment in the local hospital but longed for a job as a courier for the Confederacy. By October 1861, she was appointed a courier for General Beauregard. She also provided information to General Thomas (Stonewall) Jackson during the 1862 Shenandoah Valley campaign.

Front Royal being occupied by Federal troops gave Belle an easy source for information. She initially did not use a code in her messages but wrote them out and signed them. This amateur practice got her in trouble again when one of her messages were intercepted. In early 1862, she was arrested on suspicion of spying and taken to Baltimore. She was released after a week of courteous imprisonment. She was told to stop her activities because they were treasonous. Here again, chivalry came to her rescue. She was released and returned to Front Royal where she immediately continued her spying activities.

Union officers frequently used the rooming house in Front Royal. This offered her yet another opportunity to gather information vital to the Confederacy. She would listen at doors, through walls, through knotholes, and hide in closets to gather information to forward to the Confederacy.

On May 23, 1862, Stonewall Jackson planned to recapture the town of Front Royal as part of his drive against General Banks' Union forces. Information from many sources reached Belle concerning the Union plans for withdrawal from Front Royal and the plans to destroy all bridges behind them. She realized that if she could get this information to General Jackson he could hasten his attack and save the bridges.

On May 22, 1862, the day before the Battle of Front Royal, General Richard Stoddard Ewell, under command of General Thomas Jackson, stopped on a hill overlooking Front Royal in order to assess the troop strengths and position of the Union forces. He had no information and was unsure about an attack.

While surveying the situation, the Confederate soldiers spotted a woman dressed in white leaving the town and heading toward their lines. The young woman was Belle Boyd. She had not bothered to take the time to saddle her horse for the journey, but raced on foot over the two-mile gap between the two armies. She delivered her message to General Jackson's staff officer, Henry Kyd Douglas. The message advised General Jackson that the Yankee force was small with only one Maryland regiment, seven pieces of artillery, and several cavalry companies.

Belle stated that she had gone through the Yankee camps and had gathered the information from one of the Yankee officers. General Jackson was concerned about this seemingly good news from her since he had never seen or heard of her before. The information turned out to be accurate and Front Royal was taken easily — Union troops fled and the Confederate troops were able to save the bridges. Belle then became a viable operative for General Jackson in his Shenandoah Valley Campaign.

General Jackson thanked Belle with a written note, which stated, "I thank you, for myself and for the army, for the immense service that you rendered your country today. Hastily, I am your friend, T.J. Jackson C. S. A."

As Union secret service surveillance around Front Royal was tightened, Belle was watched closely until late July 1862 when Secretary of War Edwin Stanton issued an order for her arrest. On July 29, 1862, she was arrested by the Federal Secret Service and taken to Washington, D.C., to be held at Old Capitol Prison.

While in prison she was asked to take an oath of allegiance to the Union. Her reply was that if she ever took such an oath she wished that her tongue would cleave to the roof of her mouth, and if she ever signed such an oath that her arms would fall paralyzed to her side.

She was held without specific charges being made against her. After being in prison for one month, on August 29, 1862, General James W. Wadsworth wrote General Dix at Fortress Monroe and ordered him to place Belle Boyd beyond the Federal lines at the earliest opportunity. As a condition of release, she was forbidden to enter Union territory.

She was returned to Richmond, Virginia, where she enjoyed the southern reception afforded her for her service to the Confederacy. In June 1863, she returned to Martinsburg, now in West Virginia, which was in the process of being accepted into the Union as a state. Her purpose for violating the condition of her release was to visit her ailing mother. The next month, Federal troops again returned to Martinsburg. She was immediately placed under arrest for being within Federal lines in contempt of the orders pertaining to her banishment. She was placed in Carroll Prison, which was an annex to Old Capitol Prison. During this period in prison, she developed a severe case of typhoid fever and in December 1863 was again released from prison and banished to the South for the remainder of the war.

In March 1864, after recovering from the fever, she, at the age of 20, set out on her last mission for the Confederacy. Jefferson Davis gave her $500 expense money to go to England and carry messages to Confederate contacts. She boarded the blockade-runner *Greyhound* at Wilmington, North Carolina, in May and sailed for England. The trip was ill-fated; the Federal ship USS *Connecticut* captured the blockade-runner at sea and sailed it back to Fortress Monroe. Belle Boyd was again arrested and sent to Boston. Fortunately, she had destroyed the messages she was carrying to England. The authorities in Boston banished her to Canada under penalty of death if she returned to Federal soil.

When the *Connecticut* captured the *Greyhound*, a young naval officer took charge of the captured ship to sail it back to Fortress Monroe. His name was Lt. Samuel W. Harding. During the trip back to Fortress Monroe, Belle Boyd and Lt. Samuel W. Harding fell in love and became engaged. Lt. Harding was subsequently dismissed from the Navy for neglect of duty.

Once in Canada, Belle sailed on to England where she completed her mission by relaying the messages to the Confederate contacts. She had committed the messages to memory prior to destroying them when the ship was captured.

Samuel W. Harding, after being dismissed from the U.S. Navy, followed Belle to London. They were married on August 25, 1864. Their wedding was the high point of the social season. Samuel returned to the United States soon after the wedding. When he arrived he was arrested as a Southern spy. It was speculated that he was carrying messages for the Confederacy in place of Belle. In February 1865, he was released and returned to England. The reunion with Belle was short-lived. Samuel was in poor health from his imprisonment and he died within a few months of his return.

Maria Isabella "Belle" Boyd. Courtesy of Leib Image Archives.

Belle began to write about her experiences as a Confederate spy and became an actress while in England. Her book *Belle Boyd in Camp and Prison* was printed in 1865 in New York. She began a theatrical career after the war in England and in America. She performed all over the United States telling of her episodes as a spy and giving talks to many veterans groups. She billed herself as "Cleopatra of the Secession." The press had other names for her such as "The Rebel Joan of Arc" and "The Siren of the Shenandoah."

Belle bore three children over her next two marriages. The first was to a former British officer, John S. Hammond, with whom she lived in California until their divorce in 1884. The third marriage was to the son of a Toledo, Ohio, clergyman named Nathaniel R. High. She lived with him until her death on June 11, 1900, at the age of 66.

Belle Boyd died of a sudden heart attack while in Kilborne, Wisconsin. She was there for a personal appearance at the request of the local GAR post. Belle was buried in the Kilborne Cemetery. Four Union veterans lowered her body into the grave. The inscription on her tombstone read:

Belle Boyd
Confederate Spy
Died in Wisconsin
Erected by a Comrade

In 1929 the United Daughters of the Confederacy had her remains removed from Wisconsin and re-buried in the town of her birth, Martinsburg, West Virginia.

❧ 21 ❧

Antonia Ford: Confederate Spy

Without a shot being fired Colonel Mosby captured General Edwin H. Stoughton, two of his officers, and 30 enlisted men of the 2nd Vermont Brigade. The capture was the result of information supplied by a daring Confederate Spy named Antonia Ford.

Antonia Ford was born in 1838, the daughter of a Virginia shopkeeper. Her father, Edward Rudolph Ford, was a very successful businessman and provided the family with a fine home in Fairfax Courthouse, Virginia. Antonia had dark hair and eyes, and was considered an attractive woman. She was 23 years old in 1861 when the Civil War began.

Her father opened his home to Union officers, after the war began, in an effort to improve his income and gather information which could be passed on to the Confederate army.

Antonia thus began her career as a Confederate spy. Using her quiet, genteel personality, she would entertain the Union officers who were guests in her father's home. She was very careful to talk about everything except the military information she was seeking. This strategy worked in her favor. In their boastfulness, the Union officers revealed information that was useful to Antonia. After gathering information, she would pass it on to General J.E.B. Stuart through other field operatives. She often carried messages for and used couriers from Rose O'Neal Greenhow's spy organization.

In a desperate effort to find out how Union military information was being transmitted to the Confederate army, the Union troops conducted a surprise house-to-house

Antonia Ford. Courtesy of Library of Congress.

search of Fairfax Courthouse. The troops were looking for any notes, messages or information that would reveal the source of the suspected espionage.

Antonia was warned just in time to gather all the documents in her possession and conceal them under her skirts. She was sitting in the parlor reading when the soldiers arrived to search the Ford home. She invited them to search all they wanted to. Upon completion of the search the officer in charge asked her to stand up. She angrily replied that she did not think that even a Yankee would expect a Southern woman to rise for him. The officer then left in haste. The documents hidden under her skirt remained undetected.

During the later part of August 1862, just prior to the Battle of Second Manassas/Bull Run, Antonia acquired some vital information needed by General J.E.B. Stuart. She found no one available to carry the message, so she prepared her carriage and set out on a 20-mile trip to deliver the information herself.

Her trip was slowed down by heavy rains and by having to dodge Union troops along the way. Her ordeal made such an impression on General Stuart that he commissioned her his honorary aide-de-camp. The commission was an honor for Antonia. It read:

> *Honorary aide-de-camp*
>
> Know ye, that reposing special confidence in the patriotism, fidelity and ability of Miss Antonia Ford, I, James E. B. Stuart, by virtue of the power vested in me, as Brigadier General in the Provisional Army of the CSA, do hereby appoint and commission her my honorary aide-de-camp to work as such from this date. She will be obeyed, respected and admired by all the lovers of a noble nature.

Her reputation began to grow and her daring exploits were just beginning to be publicized. Her most unusual accomplishment, however, was yet to happen.

As commands changed and Union troops were replaced by others, the Ford home continued to be used as a headquarters by Union leaders. In December 1862, General Edwin H. Stoughton came to Fairfax Courthouse to command the 2nd Vermont Brigade. He made the Ford home his headquarters while his troops camped five miles out of town. General Stoughton was 24 years old — the youngest general in the Union army.

Antonia learned that General Stoughton was planning a huge party at her home, complete with food, champagne, and caviar. Once she was told the date of the party, she conveyed the information to Colonel John Mosby who was camped 20 miles away.

The party began early in the afternoon and soon Antonia became the belle of the ball. Everyone was having great fun, eating and drinking too much.

While the party proceeded, the Confederate troops quietly surrounded the house, cut all telegraph lines, and waited for the right time to attack. Wearing raincoats over their confederate uniforms, they rode undetected into Fairfax Courthouse at 2 a.m. The few Union pickets did not recognize them as Confederate soldiers.

As guests and sentries left the party or became accessible, they were quietly captured. Soon, all were captured without a shot being fired. The only two not immediately captured were General Stoughton and his personal guard. The General had retired to his room to sleep off the intoxicating party.

General Edwin H. Stoughton. Courtesy of Massachusetts Commandery Military Order of the Loyal Legion and the US Army Military History Institute.

One of Colonel Mosby's men knocked on the bedroom door and called out that he was bearing dispatches for the general. When the door opened the drowsy guard was quickly captured and his mouth covered so he could not call out.

Colonel Mosby then walked over to the bed, pulled back the quilt and slapped the general on the backside. The general awoke and jumped up. "Did you ever hear of Mosby?" asked the Confederate Colonel. General Stoughton replied, "Yes. Have you caught him?" "No," said Mosby. "He's caught you."

Colonel Mosby not only captured General Stoughton, he also took two captains and thirty enlisted men as prisoners, and confiscated eighty horses with all their equipment. This incident ruined General Stoughton's reputation.

Colonel John S. Mosby. Courtesy Library of Congress.

This daring raid on the Ford home also intensified the search for the Confederate spy whom the Union believed lived in Fairfax Courthouse. The information compiled by the Secret Service pointed to the Ford home and Antonia. Mr. Lafayette Baker, head of the Secret Service, reported his suspicions to President Lincoln who placed Antonia on top of the wanted list. He ordered Mr. Baker to get the evidence needed to stop her.

Mr. Baker sent a female detective named Frankie Abel to Fairfax to trap Antonia. The female detective disguised herself as a Confederate lady from New Orleans who had taken refuge in Fairfax. When she arrived at the Ford home she was wearing an old faded calico dress. Her tales of being mistreated by the Yankees outraged the local citizens. She soon won the confidence of the citizens of Fairfax Courthouse as well as Antonia.

Antonia gave her clothing to replace the old dress she was wearing when she arrived. A close, trusting relationship grew over the two months Frankie stayed with Antonia. So trusting was the relationship that the two young women even exchanged confidences about the services they rendered for the Confederacy. Antonia even showed Frankie the commission she received from General J.E.B. Stuart.

Shortly thereafter, Frankie left and Federal agents descended on the Ford home searching for the evidence they needed against Antonia. The needed evidence was found, including the commission Antonia received from General Stuart. Antonia and ten others, including her father, were arrested and taken to Old Capitol Prison in Washington, D.C. Antonia was escorted to prison by Major Joseph C. Willard who had previously escorted her to many parties.

Antonia spent several months in prison and became very ill. She was released in September because of her poor health, and her willingness to sign a loyalty oath.

Throughout her imprisonment, Major Willard, who had had himself transferred to the prison, begged her to sign a loyalty oath to the Union. After much pleading from him and thought from her about her future, she agreed on the condition that Major Willard resign his commission. Major Willard agreed and she was released.

On March 10, 1864, in the Great Parlor of the Metropolitan Hotel in Washington, D.C., Antonia Ford and Joseph Willard were married. They honeymooned in Philadelphia and New York, and made their home in a beautiful house at Fourteenth and G. Streets in Washington.

Over the next few years she bore three children, two of whom died in infancy. Antonia never recovered from the illness she contracted while in prison. She died seven years later in 1871 at the age of 33. Her husband never remarried and mourned her until his death in 1897.

✤ 22 ✤

Charlotte and Virginia Moon: Confederate Spies

A love of adventure and a deep devotion for the Confederacy prompted two young Virginia sisters to become spies during the Civil War. Their adventurous spirits and ability to portray many different roles proved to be invaluable assets in their espionage activities and saved their lives on more than one occasion.

The Moon sisters were daughters of a Virginia planter. They were both quite spirited young women who craved adventure. They often performed on stage in small amateur theatricals.

Lottie often performed as a ventriloquist, and could dislocate her jaw and act as if she was in serious pain. A very convincing loud crack could be heard as she dislocated her jaw.

As a young girl Virginia Moon was expelled from an Ohio school for shooting down a United States flag as it flew over the campus and for using her ring to scratch "God bless Jefferson Davis" on a store window.

Lottie Moon, in one of her wild romantic adventures prior to the beginning of the Civil War, became engaged to a promising young Union officer. As the couple stood at the altar, the minister asked Lottie if she took this man to be her husband. She hesitated for a moment then shouted, "No siree, Bob!" She quickly turned and ran out of the church.

The stunned and jilted young officer would later have an opportunity for revenge. However, when the time came and both sisters stood before him charged with spying for the Confederacy, General Ambrose E. Burnside relented and released them after only trying to frighten them into giving up their spying activities.

After the Civil War began, Lottie had another bizarre romantic adventure. She became engaged to 16 young Southern soldiers at the same time. When questioned about this risky situation, she replied, "If they died in battle, they'd have died happy and if they lived, I didn't give a damn."

The Moon sisters got their initiation into their espionage careers from a Southern agent named Walker Taylor. He convinced them to carry a message from General Sterling Price to General Edmund Kirby Smith in Lexington. Taylor explained that he could not carry the message himself because he was being watched too closely by Federal agents and was afraid that he would be arrested.

The excitement of such an adventure was quite appealing to the sisters. They agreed to the assignment and set out that afternoon. They disguised themselves by wearing shabby old shawls and bonnets posing as two bent-over old women.

By late afternoon they had reached the Ohio River. After crossing the river on the ferry, they changed their disguises and became two grieving Irish widows. The sisters then set out searching for transportation toward Lexington. They requested travel permits from the local authorities but were denied. Finally their grieving Irish widow act drew sympathy from several Irish-born sailors who smuggled them aboard the cargo vessel on which they worked. They sailed undiscovered toward Kentucky.

At the closest point to Lexington they disembarked and proceeded on to their destination. Once they finally reached the city they counted on luck to guide them. As it turned out, the first Confederate officer they met was Colonel Thomas Scott. Lottie thrust the document into his hands and instructed him to give it to no one but General Kirby Smith. Colonel Scott was amazed by the girls and their clever disguises and agreed to deliver the message as they had requested.

Relieved that they had accomplished their objective with no real problems, the girls boarded a train to take them to a point near their home. While they were on the train, a warning was given to watch out for a female spy. The sisters, still posing as grieving widows, befriended a Union officer, General Leslie Coombs, and resorted to their crying act. Their convincing act touched General Coombs, who stayed with them and personally saw them safely off the train at their destination. From this point they worked their way through fields and wooded areas to avoid detection until they reached their home.

Lottie's next major assignment was without her sister. She was to disguise herself as a British subject trying to regain her health. Using forged papers she was to travel to Washington, D.C., and deliver messages to the Southern operatives in and around the Washington area.

Her acting ability made the assignment an exciting role, and she was so convincing that she even fooled Secretary of War Edwin M. Stanton, who was considered a very suspicious man. In her disguise as a British subject, she was even invited to join President Lincoln's party when they reviewed the Army of the Potomac at Fredricksburg. This invitation allowed her to secure a pass for Virginia.

Lottie had delivered all the messages to the Confederate agents and had quietly ridden on to Virginia by the time Secretary Stanton became aware of the deception.

She continued gathering information on the way home, and ran into no problems until she reached Winchester, Virginia, where she was stopped and questioned by Union General F. J. Milroy.

General Milroy listened to her tale about being a British subject trying to recover her health. She told him she was confused and had gone to the wrong Hot Springs. She then begged him for a pass through the lines. He was a bit suspicious of Lottie and had her examined by his surgeon to verify her illness.

On the way to the hospital for the examination, she claimed to have become so ill that she could not go into the hospital unassisted. Two Union soldiers carried her into the hospital in a straight-backed chair. During the examination, Lottie claimed that rheumatism had affected her heart and she cried when the doctor touched her. She moaned with false agony as she dislocated her jaw. The doctor was at a loss and stated that hers was a sad case. She was carried back to her carriage, given a pass, and was soon on her way again. Her acting ability had saved her once more.

While Lottie was busy completing her mission to Washington, Ginnie was delivering messages to Nathan Bedford Forrest about the Union troop movements and strengths around the Memphis, Tennessee, area. She was often captured but arrested only once. Each time she was released as her acting ability, like Lottie's, came to her rescue. The *Memphis Commercial Appeal* described Ginnie: "She needed no pass to get through the Union lines, her eyes and her way won her permission everywhere."

In February 1863, Confederate General Sterling Price had vital information, which needed to be delivered to Confederate agents in Western Ohio. Because Ginnie had relatives in Ohio, she volunteered for the assignment. Her reason for traveling would be to visit relatives. The trip began in an ambulance accompanied by eight Confederate soldiers. When they arrived in Memphis, Tennessee, Ginnie stopped and picked up her mother to further legitimize the purpose for the trip. They then proceeded slowly toward her brother-in-law's home near Oxford, Ohio, 25 miles northeast of Cincinnati.

The trip went as planned and Ginnie was successful in delivering all the messages. After a short visit with their relatives Ginnie and her mother made their way down to the Ohio River to Cincinnati where they had booked passage aboard the cargo ship *Alice Dean*. Ginnie was carrying a secret message for General Sterling Price in her bosom.

Before the ship could set sail, Union officers entered their stateroom and arrested the two ladies for treasonous acts. The Commanding officer, Captain Harrison Rose, demanded that the ladies submit to a physical search. Ginnie was quite upset by such a demand. She reached into her pocket, pulled out a Colt revolver and threatened to kill any man who tried to search her. She then yelled verbal abuses at Captain Rose and told him to get out of their stateroom with the luggage, keys, and his life. As he retreated, Ginnie quickly locked the door, removed the message from her bosom, wetted it with water, and swallowed it.

Soon Captain Rose returned with help and both ladies were escorted to army headquarters where their belongings were thoroughly searched. The search revealed quilted garments, which were filled with opium, a quantity of quinine and forty bottles of morphine, all of which were desperately needed by the Confederacy. Mrs. Moon quietly tried to explain that the drugs were for her sickly children at home. This excuse was not believed and all their traveling attire was confiscated. However, the resourceful Ginnie didn't let that deter her resolve to complete her assignment. By the next morning she had secured and sewn into the hems of her skirt and petticoats a total of forty bottles of morphine, seven pounds of opium, and a small quantity of camphor.

The ladies were free to proceed home, but before passes could be issued they had to appear

General Ambrose E. Burnside. Courtesy Library of Congress.

before General Ambrose Burnside, who severely chastised the ladies for their activities. Ginnie looked the General straight in the eyes and replied, "General, I have a little honor, I could not have let you know what I carried or what I did." The general was sympathetic and decided to handle their case himself in lieu of having the customhouse officers decide their punishment. They were kept under house arrest in a Cincinnati hotel.

While under house arrest a strange thing happened which complicated the situation further. It seems that a young British woman who was requesting a pass through the lines was brought before General Burnside. The general immediately recognized Lottie Moon, the young woman he had once courted and who had jilted him at the altar. She turned on the charm and tried every trick she knew but to no avail. She soon found herself under house arrest with her sister and mother.

General Burnside kept the three ladies in suspense for some time and had rumors of trials and executions passed on to them almost daily—an attempt to scare them into discontinuing their espionage activities. The ladies were held under surveillance for several months even though the charges were never pressed. They were allowed to walk around the city but were always watched. The Moon sisters used this opportunity to collect marriage proposals from Yankee gentlemen as well as to gather valuable information, which they easily passed on to Confederate agents in the Cincinnati area.

The three ladies were finally released and allowed to return home. Hoping to stop their Confederate operations, the Union officers in the area of their home required all three ladies to report at ten o'clock each morning to Union General Hurlbert. This order was short-lived because Lottie and Ginnie used it as an opportunity to gain Union information. After three months of such reporting, the frustrated general ordered the Moon family to leave and not come back.

In late 1864 the sisters received a letter from their brother who was ill from wounds suffered in the war. He, his wife, and their two children had escaped to southern France and invited Ginnie and Lottie to come and live with him. The two sisters and their mother obtained passes and proceeded to Newport, Virginia, where they planned to book passage to France. Union General Benjamin Butler stopped these plans by ordering the three ladies to take an oath of loyalty to the Union if they wanted to continue their trip to France. All three ladies indignantly refused and were kept in custody for several months. Every day of their captivity they were reminded that if they took the oath they could proceed on their way to France. When told that they might as well abandon their Confederate convictions and take the oath because they would be forced to when Butler reached Richmond anyway, Ginnie quickly replied, "If Butler's in Richmond, he'll be nailed to a tree." That was all it took for the Union general to realize they would never take the oath. He then had them escorted back to Confederate territory and they were not allowed to continue on to France.

Even after the war had ended the Moon sisters never accepted defeat. Ginnie ran a male boarding house and was a heroine during the yellow fever epidemic during the 1870s. By the time she was 75 years old she decided to become an actress again but this time she wanted to do so in Hollywood. She contacted producer Jesse Lasky about a job. Mr. Lasky asked her what made her think she could act. Ginnie stamped her foot, folded her arms and firmly replied, "I'm 75 years old and I've acted all of them." Mr. Lasky nodded and said, "You'll do."

Ginnie appeared in many early films with such famous people as Pola Negri, Douglas Fairbanks, and Mary Miles Minter. In September 1926, at the age of 81, she was found dead, stretched out on the floor with her pet cat.

Prior to the end of the war Lottie married Judge Clark who was active in the Copperhead movement in Tennessee. After the war, Lottie and her husband moved to New York where she became a writer and pioneer newspaper correspondent. She covered the European capitals during the Franco-Prussian War. No further records can be found for her remaining years.

23

Olivia Floyd:
Confederate Spy

She was credited with saving the lives of 14 Confederate officers who were being tried for war crimes by the Union. Her name was Miss Olivia Floyd and she was a Confederate spy and smuggler.

Olivia Floyd was born in 1824 in Port Tobacco, Virginia. The Floyd family was living on Rose Hill Estate in Charles County, Maryland, in 1861 when the Civil War began. Olivia was the daughter of David and Sarah Semmes Floyd. The Floyd family considered themselves Southerners and was sympathetic to the Confederate cause. Soon after the war began, Olivia's younger brother Bob went south and joined the Confederate army. Olivia and her mother remained at their home on the Federal side of the Potomac River.

Their large, two-story brick home soon became a popular gathering place for Federal soldiers. As their home became more popular, Olivia had the opportunity to gather important military information which she then could pass on to her Confederate contacts. Olivia became very resourceful at gathering information. She used the hollow brass balls at the top of the fireplace andirons to hide the messages that she prepared for the Confederacy. She also smuggled clothing, money, letters, and other information frequently through the Union lines to the Confederate troops.

Her main contact in the North was a Union officer who was stationed in Alexandria, Virginia. He was a Confederate agent who helped in the escape of many Southern sympathizers to Richmond. His messages were always signed with a "J" to help keep his identity a secret.

As Olivia intensified her methods of gathering and transmitting information, she began to arouse some suspicion. On November 10, 1862, Judge Advocate General L.C. Turner sent a message to Secretary of War Edwin M. Stanton. In it, he indicated that Olivia Floyd was known to be "engaged in all sorts of disloyal practices and is in frequent and intimate communication with an officer in our army who signs himself 'J'." Her name was revealed in a correspondence that the government intercepted, which indicated that one of their Federal officers was a Confederate spy. His code name was "J" and all of his correspondence was signed "J." Judge advocate Turner issued an order that Olivia be arrested and transported to Old Capitol Prison in Washington, D.C., in the hope that she would reveal the identity of the Union officer "J." For some reason Olivia avoided arrest and the order was not carried out. Perhaps Federal authorities discovered the identity of the officer by other means and Olivia no longer seemed to be much of a threat. Whatever the reason, it allowed Olivia to continue her espionage activities until the end of the war.

By the time the war came to a close Olivia had become a vital link in the chain of spies and messengers that operated along the great spy route which ran between Richmond, Virginia, and the Confederate agents in Canada. In early 1865, this ring of agents, working through Olivia, was successful in obtaining the release of 14 Confederate officers who had been arrested on criminal charges and were waiting to be tried.

To save them from being tried and possibly executed, messages and papers needed to exonerate the officers were forwarded to Olivia and were quickly hidden in the andirons. When Union authorities came to search her home, as they often did, she simply invited them in and let them search until they were satisfied. The searchers never found any evidence that Olivia was a spy. She would then boldly invite them to sit by the fire and warm their feet upon the very andirons that contained the hidden messages. As additional messages arrived they were added to the andirons. On February 15, 1865, all of the needed documents were gathered at Olivia's home. The information was then forwarded to the courthouse by special courier. These messages and documents saved the Confederate officers from possible execution.

Near the end of the war Olivia was given $80,000 in bank notes by one of her Confederate contacts. She was to hold the money for him while he was in hiding. She hid the money in the sofa near the fireplace. When she invited the Union officers to sit and warm their feet, they never realized that they were sitting on a fortune. The money was returned to its rightful owner after the war.

Olivia was said to have psychic powers and she was interested in the occult. She also believed in ghosts and spirits, and a huge ghost dog was reported to have guarded her home (supposedly seen by many people). This rumor kept many superstitious Confederates as well as Yankees from crossing her doorstep after dark.

After the war, one of the Confederate officers, Colonel Bennett Young, learned about Olivia's role in his release and the release of the other 13 Confederates and invited her to be his guest at a reunion of Confederate Veterans. She was completely surprised when she turned out to be the guest of honor. The reunion was held in

Louisville, Kentucky, and was the highlight of Olivia's declining years. She spent the remainder of her life at Rose Hill and often talked of this great honor.

She died December 10, 1905, at the age of 81, and was buried in the parish cemetery beside her brother Bob. It is reported that all of Charles County mourned her death because there would never be another person like Miss Olivia of Rose Hill.

The *New York Times* published the news of her death on December 12, 1905, and in the article called her a "famous woman blockade runner of the Confederacy."

❧ 24 ❧

Mrs. E. H. Baker: Union Spy

Although she is credited with only one major mission as a spy, it was of vital importance. She gathered information for the Union about the Confederate secret underwater boat and the building of the ironclad ship C.S.S. *Virginia* (*Merrimac*). Her name was Mrs. E. H. Baker.

Mrs. Baker lived in Richmond, Virginia, prior to the Civil War. Because of her strong loyalty to the Union and the impending possibility of war, she left Richmond and moved to Chicago, Illinois. When the war began in 1861, she was already working as a Pinkerton agent. In early 1862, Pinkerton sent her south on her first major mission. She was an ideal choice for the mission because of the friends and contacts she already had in the Richmond area. Her assigned area was between Richmond and Washington. She was assigned to gather information on the new undersea boats which the Confederates were rumored to be making.

Mrs. Baker accepted the offer and proceeded to Washington where she was trained and briefed on her first assignment. This first assignment began in December 1862, when she was asked to gain the confidence of her old friends, the Atwaters, who lived in Richmond and had a son who was a Confederate captain.

Once she gained the Atwaters' confidence, she was to gain entrance into the Tredegar Iron Works. The security at the Tredegar Iron Works was very tight because this facility was where the Confederacy's underwater boat and ironclads were being built.

Mrs. Baker returned to Richmond and re-acquainted herself with all her old friends, especially the Atwater family. She soon became good friends with Captain

Atwater and his wife, and was warmly welcomed into their home. Captain Atwater and his wife introduced Mrs. Baker into the Richmond social circles where she quickly made many new friends. Her social calendar became so full that it kept her moving all around the Richmond area.

She was always careful not to talk about the war. She accepted invitations from the Richmond society families, went to their parties, attended receptions and went along on many sightseeing trips. These sightseeing trips included viewing the Richmond earthworks and fortifications. She also attended many army drills and demonstrations. This social activity gave her the opportunity to memorize and document the city defenses, troop placements, and strengths.

Finally, in a quiet seductive manner, she mentioned to Captain Atwater that she would like to tour the Tredegar Iron Works. Her manner evidently boosted his ego a bit because he agreed to get her a pass and also to act as her personal tour guide.

However, when the time came, Captain Atwater informed Mrs. Baker that he was required to attend a demonstration and she would have to wait until the next day to visit the Tredegar Iron Works. He then invited her to accompany him and his wife to the demonstration. The demonstration was to test the prototype of the new underwater boat by sinking a ship in the river. Mrs. Baker witnessed this very successful test, after which Captain Atwater informed her that they were building a much larger underwater boat.

The next day Mrs. Baker accompanied Captain Atwater to the iron works. While on this informative guided tour, she noticed many experimental weapons, such as the new submarine battery (commonly called a water mine) and a submarine ram (a rod on the bow of a ship which carried a mine used to ram an enemy vessel). She also saw the construction of the secret underwater boat and the prototype of the Confederate ironclad C.S.S. *Virginia*.

Upon returning to her home, Mrs. Baker drew sketches of all that she had seen and sewed them into the lining of her bonnet.

Several days later she told Captain Atwater that the war had made her so upset that she was afraid to stay in one place too long and she wished to return to her home in Chicago, if he would secure a pass for her. Captain Atwater and his wife both sympathized with her and she was given the pass.

Mrs. Baker left Richmond the next day and met Mr. Pinkerton in Fredericksburg, Virginia. Mr. Pinkerton forwarded the drawings and information that he received from Mrs. Baker to the Navy. Within 24 hours after she left Richmond, the weapon sketches were in the hands of the Union authorities.

Around the time that Captain Atwater had stated to Mrs. Baker that the underwater boats would be in operation, the U.S. Navy began dragging the entrance to the river each night after dark as a precaution. One of the boats caught and pulled up the air hoses from the new Confederate underwater boat as it was preparing to sink a Union warship. The Confederate crew was trapped inside and all drowned. The dragging of the channel entrance by the Union army made the Confederates realize that their element of surprise had failed.

The underwater boat was a submerged craft, which held four men who operated a mechanical propulsion device. Above the craft, at the water line, was a large green raft that supported air hoses down to the underwater boat so the men could breathe. It was to be used only at night to quietly maneuver close to a Union ship and attach an explosive device to its hull. The underwater boat would then quietly back away before setting off the device and sinking the ship.

Although Mrs. Baker continued operating between Richmond and Washington for the remainder of the war, this was her only recorded major mission. When Mr. Pinkerton went back into private business, Mrs. Baker went with him. No further record of her life exists.

Although she only performed one major mission it was of vital importance to the Union army and helped keep the Union strong in its quest to reunite the nation.

❧ 25 ❧

Rebecca Wright:
Union Spy

The one patriotic and heroic act of Miss Rebecca Wright opened the way for General Philip H. Sheridan's conquest of the Shenandoah Valley.

Rebecca Wright was a simple Quaker schoolmistress in Winchester, Virginia, when the Civil War began. Although she was a pacifist living in what became a Confederate state, her deep loyalty was to the Union.

Winchester, Virginia, was in Confederate hands and was the key to conquering the Shenandoah Valley. General Sheridan knew that Confederate General Jubal A. Early was concentrating his troops at Winchester, but he was receiving conflicting reports on the Confederate troop strength and movements around the Winchester area. He sought the aid of General Crook, who was familiar with the area and knew many of the local residents. General Crook was asked to suggest someone he knew to be loyal to the Union who could help get the information needed to plan an attack on Winchester. General Crook suggested Miss Rebecca I. Wright.

While looking for someone to carry General Sheridan's request to Rebecca Wright, the Union troops located an elderly slave named Thomas Laws who lived in Berryville, two miles east of Winchester. Mr. Laws had a pass from General Early that allowed him to travel to and from Winchester to sell vegetables and eggs. He agreed to be the courier for General Sheridan and welcomed the chance to do his part for the Union.

Rebecca was quite shocked and a little scared when, around noon on September 16, 1864, Thomas Laws knocked on her door with a message from General Sheridan. The message was written on a piece of tissue paper rolled tightly in a tin foil

113

Rebecca Wright. Courtesy of the Western Reserve Historical Society. Cleveland, Ohio.

ball. Thomas Laws carried the message in his mouth so if in danger of capture he could swallow it.

To avoid any undue suspicion, Mr. Laws waited until noon when Rebecca's class was dismissed before approaching her house. He told her that he had an urgent message for her. Nervously, she invited him into a small room in the house and closed the door. Thomas took the message out of his mouth and gave it to her. He cautioned her not to destroy the tin foil. He would need it to carry her reply back to General Sheridan. Mr. Laws told Rebecca he would return in three hours for her reply.

General Sheridan had written:

I know from Major General Crook that you are a loyal lady and still love the old flag. Can you inform me of the position of Early's forces, the number of divisions in his army, and the strength of any or all of them and his probable or reported intentions? Have any troops arrived from Richmond, or any more coming or reported to be coming?

I am very respectfully your obedient servant
P. H. Sheridan, Major General Commanding.
You can trust the bearer

Rebecca was afraid that if her neighbors found out she was assisting General Sheridan they might resort to violence against herself and her mother. They already were being shunned by most of the neighbors because of their views about the war. However, she bravely decided to honor the request as best she could.

Rebecca already knew some of the information that General Sheridan needed. The information came from a Confederate officer who was recovering from his battle wounds in a nearby boarding house. He had asked if he could call on Rebecca on

September 14, which was only two days before the request from General Sheridan arrived. She consented and allowed him to call on her after school was out.

During the visit, the wounded officer, while trying to impress Rebecca, talked about the war and in doing so revealed the location of Kershaw's division of infantry and Cutshaw's battalion of artillery.

Rebecca listened quietly like a gracious hostess, absorbing all the information and wondering what use she could make of it. General Sheridan's request gave her the answer. She replied:

> I have no communication whatever with the rebels but I will tell you what I know. The division of General Kershaw and Cutshaw's artillery, twelve guns and men, General Anderson Commanding, have been sent away and no more are expected to arrive as they can not be sparred from Richmond. I do not know how the troops are situated. I will take pleasure here-after learning all I can of the strengths and positions, and the bearer may call again.
>
> Very Respectfully yours

Thomas Laws returned at three o'clock that afternoon for her reply and delivered it to General Sheridan later the same day. The reply was the information General Sheridan needed. Now seemed the time for an attack.

General Sheridan's men slowly positioned themselves and on the morning of September 19, 1864, he threw his entire army at General Early's weakened defenses at Winchester. This was the third Battle of Winchester but the first battle in General Sheridan's ultimately victorious Shenandoah Valley Campaign.

General Sheridan attacked with 33,600 infantry and 6,400 cavalry troops. Union losses in the battle of Winchester were 653 killed, 3,719 wounded and 618 missing.

General Early's forces numbered 8,500 infantry and 2,900 cavalry. Confederate losses were 4,000 killed or wounded and 2,000 taken prisoner.

Rebecca and her mother were awakened by the battle and quickly hid themselves in the cellar of their home to avoid being injured by explosions and flying debris. When the battle was over, General Sheridan rode up to Rebecca's home to personally thank her for the vital information, which led to the Union victory. She pleaded with him to not publicize her assistance because the neighbors might retaliate against her and her mother with violence. General Sheridan assured her that no one would take any action against her or her family, and her part in the Battle of Winchester was kept a secret.

Rebecca continued teaching children in the small school until January 7, 1867, when a letter and gift arrived from General Sheridan. The letter was a thank you for her assistance in the battle and on the back of the letter was an endorsement by General Grant recommending her for a government position in the Treasury Department. Included with the letter was a gold watch and chain. The letter somehow got printed in the valley newspaper and made public her participation in the defeat of Winchester. The residents of Winchester were outraged.

She was a heroine to those still loyal to the Union but the majority of the residents

General Philip H. Sheridan. Courtesy of the Library of Congress.

considered her a traitor. Her life in Winchester became dangerous. She was heckled on the streets, spat upon, and her boarding house was boycotted. She was reduced to poverty and only received the meager income from her schoolhouse.

This went on for two years until General Grant was elected President. She then accepted the promised Treasury Department appointment and moved to Washington, D.C. While working for the Treasury Department, she met and married William C. Bonssall. She continued working for the Treasury Department for the next 47 years.

Her salary with the Treasury Department was $900 per year until 1892 when her salary was increased to $1,000. In 1902 she passed a competitive examination and her salary was increased to $1,200. She retired from the Treasury Department 1914.

She kept as her treasures for the rest of her life the gold watch and chain, the letter with General Grant's endorsement, and the tissue paper note from General Sheridan that began her spying adventure.

❧ 26 ❧

Notable Women Spies

One of the most dangerous forms of service during the Civil War was being a spy. Spying was as dangerous as being a soldier because when caught, spies were usually executed. Women spies during the Civil War were not treated the same as men and usually only served time in prison and or were taken back to their lines and released after receiving a stern warning. Society frowned on taking stern action against a woman, and this social attitude worked in favor of women spies.

The following adventures of two women spies show their willingness to put their lives on the line and their ability to function under dangerous conditions.

Hattie Lawton — Union Spy

Hattie Lawton went to work for the U.S. Secret Service under Allan Pinkerton when the Civil War began. Her husband Hugh became a captain in the Union army under General George Binton McClellan.

Hattie Lawton moved to Richmond, Virginia, at the request of the Federal Secret Service. She posed as a Southern lady who had been driven out of the North. With this cover she was quickly accepted into Richmond social circles and made many new friends. John Scobell, who was the first Negro operative, was assigned to assist her by posing as her servant. His orders were to never leave Hattie alone when she was out of her residence. She was only permitted to work alone as a spy when she was entertaining guests.

Other Federal operatives quickly forwarded the information gathered by these two operatives to General McClellan. As the situation in Richmond became more tense, General McClellan found that it was becoming more difficult to get messages from his operatives. To solve this problem he decided to set up a direct line of communication to Richmond. Hugh Lawton, Hattie's husband, was one of McClellan's officers and appeared to be the perfect choice for her new contact. The General arranged a nightly rendezvous for the couple at an inn in Glandale, Virginia, which was run by a Union sympathizer. The inn was not only used by Federal agents; it was also frequented by Confederate operatives.

Hattie was a familiar sight to the Confederate soldiers as she took her daily ride with her servant to the inn and back home. Hattie, with Scobell posing as her servant, was easily granted passes to go riding in the afternoons. The pair came and went as they pleased and were considered a welcome sight by the war-weary Confederate troops.

When Hattie and Hugh met at the inn, they exchanged riding crops containing messages in the hollowed-out handles. Mr. Scobell served as a lookout during the Lawtons' meetings, thus ensuring their safety.

One evening, a very friendly peddler came into the inn and began to spend money foolishly. Hattie quickly realized that this peddler was actually a Confederate agent. The peddler disappeared after the evening meal, which at first relieved the Lawtons and Mr. Scobell. However, this relief soon turned to great concern because Hattie learned from an informant that the peddler left quickly to alert his men and set a trap to capture her on her way back to her home in Richmond. The Confederate soldiers were not aware of Hugh being there as Hattie's contact.

After Hugh returned to his regiment, Hattie and Scobell decided to try to make a run through the trap and out of Glandale. They saddled two swift horses and Scobell strapped a pistol on his horse so he could have easy access to it if he or Hattie were in peril. The pair then rode out into the night, avoiding the road when possible, but the full moon soon gave them away to the Confederate soldiers who were watching for them.

They were 20 miles from the safety of the Union lines when they began a desperate attempt to outrun the soldiers. Their Confederate pursuers quickly overtook them. As the soldiers closed in, Scobell's horse stepped into a gopher hole and fell. Hattie started back for him but he waved her on. He quickly grabbed his gun and fired six shots at the soldiers. He killed two, wounded one, and scared two others away.

Once safely behind Union lines, Hattie located her husband and with several Union soldiers set out to find Scobell. When they found him, he was not injured, but nursing the wounded Confederate soldier.

Hattie continued her spying career and traveled throughout the Confederacy with either John Scobell or Pinkerton's favorite agent, Timothy Webster.

In early January 1862, Hattie was sent on a mission to Richmond with Timothy Webster. They posed as brother and sister. As they approached Virginia, the weather turned bad and they missed their final connection. They walked the rest of the way through the cold winter rain. By the time they reached Richmond, Timothy Webster was very sick and in pain. They stayed in a hotel for three weeks while Hattie attempted to nurse Mr. Webster back to health.

During this three-week period, no information had been forwarded to General McClellan and concern arose about the safety and whereabouts of the two agents. Mr. Pinkerton decided to send two of his best agents to Richmond to find out what had happened. The two men he sent were Pryce Lewis and John Scully.

When the two reached Richmond they went to the Union contact — the Richmond *Examiner* newspaper office. The editors informed Lewis and Scully that Mr. Webster had been sick and was in bed at his hotel, and had not left the room since his arrival. They did not know why Hattie had not sent word to Pinkerton about the situation.

The two Union agents hurried to the hotel and in their haste made a fatal error. Instead of asking the desk clerk which room Mr. Webster was in, they went directly to his room and knocked on the door. The clerk alerted the authorities of this odd occurrence.

In Webster's room, they found Hattie sitting next to the bed tending to Mr. Webster and a Confederate visitor named Mr. Pierce. While they were upstairs in Webster's room, Captain McCubbin of the Richmond provost martial's office surrounded the hotel and all four were arrested.

Agent Scully was tried and found guilty. Agent Lewis escaped from jail and was recaptured by Confederate soldiers. He was also tried and found guilty. They both were sentenced to hang. The sentence was later changed from death by hanging to imprisonment.

Webster was sentenced to death. The Union did everything possible to save him from being hung. The Confederacy would not listen to the pleas of the Union and on the morning of April 29, 1862, at Camp Lee in Richmond, Virginia, Timothy Webster was hanged twice. The first time, the rope broke or slipped and he fell to the ground. The Confederates marched him back up the scaffold and after properly securing the rope, Webster was hung again. Webster complained that he was being hung twice for the same offense.

Hattie Lawton was tried and sentenced to Castle Godwin Prison in Richmond, a prison for women suspected of being disloyal, spies or committing treacherous acts against the Confederacy. She spent one year in prison and was then freed in a prisoner exchange. She was released in January 1863.

There is no further word on her activities for the rest of the war. She obviously could not return to her previous spying activities in the South.

Mary Elizabeth Bowser — Union Spy

Mary Elizabeth Bowser was a Negro slave in the home of John and Elizabeth Van Lew of Richmond, Virginia. The Van Lews' daughter was also named Elizabeth, and was born on October 12, 1818, in Richmond, Virginia. As a young girl Elizabeth Van Lew (whose story is told in more detail in Chapter 18) was sent to live with her grandfather who was the mayor of Philadelphia. It was while living in Philadelphia that she developed strong anti-slavery sentiments. After her father's death Elizabeth and her mother freed all the 12 slaves owned by the Van Lew family and helped to reunite them with their loved ones. Once free, most of the former slaves stayed with the family, including the maid, Mary Elizabeth Bowser.

Once Mary Bowser was free she was sent north at the expense of Elizabeth Van Lew to be educated. When her education was completed, Mary returned home to work with the Van Lews.

During the Civil War, Elizabeth Van Lew became one of the Union's most productive Union spies. She had organized and set up a complex network of operatives to pass information to General Grant at City Point.

In early 1863, a close friend of Elizabeth Van Lew persuaded the personal staff of President Jefferson Davis to hire Mary Bowser as a dining room servant in the Davis home. Her duties were as a dining room maid and a nanny to the children. Incredible as it may seem, there was another Union Negro spy in the Davis home. He was the personal coachman to Jefferson Davis, and carried the information he gathered to his Union contacts during the night when everyone was asleep. There is no documentation that the two spies in the Davis home were aware of each other's activities. Posing as an uneducated ex-slave, Mary Bowser aroused no suspicion and was able to gather valuable information from overhearing plans being made and discussions between many Confederate generals and President Davis while serving them meals in the dining room.

Mary Bowser wrote nothing down on paper; instead she committed the information to her exceptional memory. She would remember every detail so she could accurately transmit the information to her contact in Richmond.

Her Union contact was Mr. Thomas McNiven, who ran the local bakery, which supplied baked goods to the Jefferson Mansion. When he made his daily deliveries to the Davis home, Mary would verbally pass on the information to him. The information was then sent via the Van Lew spy network to General Grant. The information gathered by Mary Bowser was invaluable to the Union.

27

Harriet Tubman: Abolitionist, Scout, Nurse and Spy

Harriet Tubman led hundreds of slaves to freedom. She set up and operated the Underground Railroad between the North and the South.

Harriet Ross Tubman was born a slave in eastern Maryland in 1821. Her grandparents on both sides were brought over from Africa as slaves. Her parents named her Araminta, but she was displeased with her name and adopted the name Harriet from her mother. In 1844, at the age of 23, she married a free Negro named John Tubman. Some accounts say that she was forced into the marriage as a slave and that John Tubman was also a slave. This point is unclear but moot since it is known that she was still a slave and did not want to be married to John.

In 1849 she made a break for freedom and escaped to Philadelphia, fleeing from slavery and from her husband. John Tubman later married someone else. Harriet was 28 years old, a runaway slave, uneducated, and alone in Philadelphia. She was determined to overcome these obstacles and work to help other slaves escape.

Between 1849 and 1861 when the Civil War began, Harriet had set up and was operating the Underground Railroad, which consisted of safe houses where runaway slaves could hide during the day and a safe route they could travel at night. Her network extended from the Deep South to Canada. Harriet was quite clever and had a knack for organization. She often took elaborate measures to confuse and elude pursuers along the way. With Harriet at the helm, the Underground Railroad never lost a passenger and she was never caught.

Harriet Tubman. Courtesy of the Library of Congress.

Harriet was a religious person with a strong belief in God. She was nicknamed "Moses" for leading her people to freedom. She made 19 trips from the South to Maryland and Delaware to personally lead slaves to freedom. She also was one of the first women to speak out on women's rights.

Harriet's leadership and deeds were becoming well known and admired by the abolitionist movement. She was consulted by John Brown, who admired her greatly. She advised him in planning the raid at Harper's Ferry.

Her notoriety and dedication to her cause prompted Harriet to always carry a loaded pistol with her on her missions. The reasons for the weapon were to ensure her personal safety and to help rouse the timid slaves. They often became fearful and discouraged and wanted to turn back. When this happened she would point the gun at them and say, "Dead Niggers tell no tales, you go or you die." Her stern statement would change their minds and give them assurance that they were in capable hands. She further explained to them that if anyone were allowed to turn back, he could be captured and made to tell all he knew about the route and the safe houses, and thus put the entire enterprise in jeopardy. Slaveholders distressed by Harriet's activities placed a reward of $40,000 for her capture. The reward was never collected, as she was never caught.

When the Civil War began in 1861 Harriet had already had been operating her Underground Railroad for several years. The Union army, realizing that she had extensive knowledge about the geography and many routes in and out of Confederate territory, recruited her to help in their efforts in North Carolina, South Carolina, and Florida. Her involvement included serving as a scout, a nurse, and sometimes as a spy, over a period of three years.

Under the command of Colonel James Montgomery of the 2nd Carolina Volunteers, Harriet led a corps of Negro troops on several missions into Confederate territory to gather information needed by the Union and to bring runaway slaves North to freedom. Harriet and her Negro troops could communicate with the slaves better than the white soldiers and therefore were more successful in gaining their confidence.

Early in the war, Massachusetts Governor John A. Andrew asked Harriet to help as a nurse in some of the camp hospitals since she had an extensive knowledge of the healing properties of herbs and roots. She agreed and traveled from camp to camp, as her time allowed, using her knowledge to help the sick and wounded. While in the camps, she would bake goods and sell them to the soldiers. The extra money she earned she gave to the freed slaves who often sought refuge in the camps.

In March 1862, Major General David Hunter approached Harriet Tubman and asked her to become a Federal agent. General Hunter was the director of the Union's Department of the South, which included South Carolina, Georgia, and Florida. She accepted the task and served as a spy and scout until the spring of 1863. Harriet also recruited a group of former slaves to hunt for Confederate camps and report their position, their strength, and any troop movements to the Union commanders.

Harriet's most famous raid behind Confederate lines was on June 1, 1863. Major General Hunter asked her to go with several gunboats up the Combahee River to take up the torpedoes placed in the river by Confederate troops to destroy railroads and bridges and cut off supplies to the Confederate soldiers in the area.

She agreed to go on the mission on the condition that Colonel James Montgomery was appointed commander of the mission. Colonel Montgomery was one of John Brown's men and was well known to Harriet. The General agreed and Harriet set sail with Colonel Montgomery and 150 black Union soldiers aboard one of the gunboats.

Her scouts surveyed the area ahead of the raiding party; they asked slaves where the explosives were placed in the river. With this information the Union gunboats safely navigated the river, picking off smaller boats of Confederate soldiers as they proceeded up the river. The Confederates were caught by surprise as Union soldiers followed the gunboats on both sides of the river. Realizing they were outnumbered, the Confederate troops fled.

Most plantation owners also fled, and their slaves rushed to the riverbanks hoping to get on the gunboat which had come to set them free. Many slave owners, seeing their slaves run to the river, tried to drive them back to their homes with whips but to no avail. There were over 800 slaves crowding the banks of the river.

When the boats were lowered and taken to shore to transport the slaves to the gunboats, all the slaves tried to get into the boats at once. When the boats were loaded the slaves clung on to them so the boats could not leave. The sailors struggled to get them to let go but they held tight. To solve the problem, Colonel Montgomery shouted to Harriet over the noise of the crowd, "Moses, you will have to give them a song!" Harriet agreed and began singing as loud as she could:

> Of all the whole creation in the East or in the West,
> the glorious Yankee nation is the greatest and the best.
> Come along! Come Along! Don't be alarmed
> Uncle Sam is rich enough to give you all a farm.

At the end of each verse the crowd of slaves threw their hands up and sang "Glory!" The sailors took this opportunity to push off. Eventually all 800 slaves were taken aboard the gunboats.

As the Confederate soldiers and plantation owners fled, the Union soldiers burned their houses, barns, and railroad bridges. The railroad tracks were also torn up and the torpedoes in the river were all destroyed. The mission was a great success.

After the war Harriet Tubman made her home in Auburn, New York, where she spent the rest of her life. She continued her efforts to help freed slaves begin new lives and she continued her work for women's rights. She also lectured on her life as a slave and her experiences running the Underground Railroad, which she had operated for eight years.

She died in 1913 at the age of 92. She was given a military funeral with honors.

❧ 28 ❧

Pauline Cushman:
Union Scout and Spy

It was said that few had suffered more or rendered more service to the Union effort than Pauline Cushman, who served as a scout, courier, and spy during the Civil War. President Lincoln called her "the little major."

Pauline Cushman was born Harriet Wood in 1883 in New Orleans, Louisiana, where she spent most of her young years. When Harriet was a young teenager, her family moved to rural Michigan where she was able to acquire many outdoor skills, which would help her in her future service to the Union. She became well rounded in the outdoor activities normally pursued by boys of her age, such as riding, hunting, shooting, and foraging.

Her adventurous spirit prompted her to begin an acting career in her late teens. She adapted well to acting and was considered a clever actress. During this time she used the stage name of Pauline Cushman. At the age of 20 she fell in love with a man from New Orleans. His name was Charles Dickson. Their wedding was held in 1853 in a New Orleans hotel.

Over the next few years she bore two children, both of whom died in infancy. Devastated by her losses she returned to her acting career. Pauline and her husband were living in Cleveland, Ohio, when the Civil War began. Charles joined the Union army, and in December 1862, he died from an illness while serving with his regiment.

Pauline had again been struck with tragedy. After the death of her husband she started thinking about working with the Union army and doing her part to help shorten the war. Her chance to serve came while she was touring with a theatrical company

Pauline Cushman. Courtesy New York Historical Society.

and performing at Wood's Theater in Louisville, Kentucky. A group of Confederate sympathizers offered her $300 to propose a toast to Jefferson Davis and the Confederacy during one of her performances.

Pauline contacted the local provost marshal with the news. She recognized the dare as an opportunity to work with the Union army to uncover the Confederate operation in the Louisville area. The provost marshal agreed after she explained that she would be perfect — not only was she born in the south, but she had a brother with the Confederate army in Mississippi.

Before Pauline began she was asked to take a loyalty oath to the Union. She gladly complied and the following night during her performance she proposed a toast to Jefferson Davis and the Confederacy. A riot broke out in the theater because Louisville, though under Union control, was a mixture of Union and Confederate sympathizers.

Pauline was immediately fired by the theater company and thus began her espionage career. She carried messages and other items between Louisville and Nashville for the Union while pretending to be a true Southerner. She was successful in uncovering many Confederate spies around Louisville and Nashville when they confided in her as an ally. Pauline gained their confidence when she explained that she was searching for her brother who was a Rebel soldier.

Her manner and acting ability made it easy for her to make the acquaintance of Confederate officers, thus giving her access to vital military information which she promptly forwarded to the Union authorities.

She worked for General William Rosencrans and spent many months with the Army of the Cumberland. She crossed rebel lines many times and soon became quite knowledgeable about all the country roads in Tennessee, northern Georgia, Alabama, and Mississippi.

In May 1863, General Rosencrans was preparing a campaign to drive Confederate General Braxton Bragg across the Tennessee River. Pauline was sent into the Confederate lines to find out the strength and the location of the Army of Tennessee.

During the mission, Confederate Captain Blackman invited her to become his personal aide-de-camp. She very politely refused his offer. He then presented her with a Confederate uniform, which was tailor-made for her. She accepted the gift and went on her way.

On June 23, 1863, the Tullahoma Campaign began. Pauline was leaving Shelbyville, Tennessee, with the information she had gathered. Two Confederate soldiers captured her on the Hardin Pike just 11 miles from Nashville. She was placed on a horse between two mounted guards to be taken to Spring Hill, the headquarters of General Forrest. While on the way to Spring Hill she pretended to be sick and complained that she could not travel any further without falling off her horse. The guards stopped at a deserted roadside house where they found a wounded Confederate soldier hiding. He told them that a Union scouting party had passed by about one hour before and that the house should be safe for them.

Pauline determined by listening to the Confederate guards that they had important papers for General Bragg. She quickly thought of a plan to get these papers and escape her captors. She spotted an elderly Negro man walking nearby. She watched for an opportunity to talk to him. When it came she shoved $10 (Tennessee money) in his hands and told him to go up the road a short way, then, in a few minutes, come running back with news that 400 Federal troops were coming down the road.

The Negro man obeyed and soon returned telling them the story with great excitement. At first the two guards did not believe him and told him that he was lying. The old Negro man then got down on his knees and swore his story was true. The two guards became convinced and, forgetting about Pauline, quickly mounted their horses and fled into the woods. Pauline grabbed a pistol that belonged to the wounded soldier in the house, mounted her horse and raced toward Franklin, Tennessee.

When she reached the first picket line and was challenged, she mistakenly thought she had come upon a Confederate line. When asked who she was, she replied that she was a friend of Jefferson Davis. She was asked to advance and give the counter sign. She promptly presented the guard with a canteen of whiskey and was allowed to pass. Finally, one sentry refused the gift and she was turned back.

She was sad and tired and sought refuge in a farmhouse she had passed which had a light in the window. She requested shelter for the night and was given a room by the old farmer. He agreed to wake her up at the break of dawn so she could continue her journey.

At dawn a knock came at the door, but instead of the farmer, it was the two guards she had eluded the previous day. They took her to General Forrest's headquarters. General Forrest sent her to General Bragg.

General Bragg questioned Pauline and could find nothing against her until a southern woman stole her gaiters and discovered that they were concealing important documents, including some drawings Pauline had stolen from a Confederate army engineer. This evidence and the fact that she carried a Confederate uniform in her bags proved that she was a spy. Captain Blackman, who provided her with the uniform, was also arrested as a spy.

During the trial Pauline was so ill from exposure, she could not rise from her bed. Her jailer, Captain Pedden, kept her advised as the trial proceeded. She was finally convicted and sentenced to death. The sentence was to be carried out at once.

The execution was postponed pending Pauline's recovery. She convalesced for several weeks and when she felt strong enough she pleaded with General Bragg to have mercy. He told her that he would have mercy by waiting until she was well enough to be properly hanged.

While preparing for the execution, the Confederate camp was attacked by Union troops. The Confederate army quickly forgot about Pauline as they evacuated the camp. She was saved from the gallows as General Rosencrans launched his assault on Shelbyville, where she was being held prior to her execution. Once freed she was able to give the information she had gathered to General Rosencrans.

News of her rescue spread quickly and she was now well known to both sides. Her spying activities were over. Had she not been rescued she would have been the only female spy to be hung during the Civil War.

Although her spying activities had ended, Pauline continued to advise the Union army of the geographic terrain of Tennessee, Alabama, and Mississippi, which she knew so well. Her assistance was very useful, as maps were quite scarce at the time.

After her rescue, Secretary Stanton commissioned her a major in the U. S. Army and President Lincoln referred to her as "the little major." She was well received throughout the north. After the war she returned to the stage as Major Pauline Cushman. She never spoke of her life as a spy while on the stage.

As her acting career faded she applied for a pension on the basis that she was the wife of a Union soldier who had died in service. She was awarded a pension of $8 a month.

In 1872 she married August Fitchner of San Francisco. Her pension from the government stopped when she remarried. Her second husband died in 1879, only seven years after their marriage.

Pauline later married Jerry Fryer. This marriage only lasted a few years, ending in separation. She then became a seamstress and housemaid. She also became addicted to morphine and died from an overdose in El Paso, Texas, in early December 1893, at the age of 60.

The Grand Army of the Republic gave her a military funeral on December 6, 1893, with flags, an honor guard, and a rifle salute — a fitting tribute for her loyal, courageous service to the Union. She was buried in the GAR plot of the local cemetery. Her headstone reads:

Pauline Cushman

Federal Spy and Scout

of the Cumberland

Pauline Cushman had a deep sense of loyalty for her country, which she displayed over and over again as she willingly laid her life on the line. Her service to the Union was invaluable. The statement that few had suffered more or given more for their country is a fitting description of her service.

❧ 29 ❧

Kady Brownell: Daughter of the Regiment and Nurse

Unlike most army wives who accompanied their husbands into the war as vivandieres, Daughters of the Regiment, cooks, and laundresses, Kady took up arms and participated in battle as well as nursing the wounded on the battlefield and carrying the regimental flag into battle. Her bravery and dedication while advancing onto one battlefield saved her regiment from being attacked by friendly forces.

Kady Brownell was born Kady Southwell in 1842. She was born in a military barracks in Africa, the daughter of a Scottish soldier and a French mother. Her mother died while Kady was a small child, and she was sent to the United States to live with family friends, the McKenzies, who lived near Providence, Rhode Island.

In March 1861, at the age of 19, she married a millwright named Robert S. Brownell from Providence. When the Civil War began one month later, her husband Robert joined the 1st Rhode Island Infantry Volunteers for three months. Robert was appointed as an orderly sergeant for his company. Because Robert's company was the eleventh company formed and a regiment needed only ten companies, they were trained as sharpshooters for the regiment and became known as the "Mechanics Rifles."

When the newly formed regiment was mustered in and arrived in Washington, Kady revealed her intentions to remain with her husband. The regimental commander, Colonel Ambrose E. Burnside, refused her request and sent her back to Rhode Island. She appealed strongly to Rhode Island Governor William Sprague for his assistance and support. Governor Sprague interceded on her behalf and she was allowed to return to Washington and rejoin her husband.

She was soon accepted by the regiment and named the Daughter of the Regiment. She dressed in a modified uniform — a knee length skirt, dark trousers, and boots. She carried a sword on her belt and a rifle, which she soon learned to use quite well. With dedicated practice she learned to use the sword and rifle as well as or better than any man in the regiment. Her regiment was quite impressed with the way she learned to use the weapons. She trained and marched with the soldiers and expected no special treatment because of her gender.

By the time the Battle of First Manassas/Bull Run commenced on July 21, 1861, the three-month enlistment of the 1st Rhode Island Infantry Regiment had expired. The regiment volunteered to stay in service until the northern Virginia campaign was over.

Kady's first combat experience was at the Battle of First Manassas/Bull Run. When the battle commenced Kady positioned herself to guard the regimental flag and thus provide a rallying point for the troops. She stood firm throughout the battle and in the confusion of the retreat she had to be dragged to safety by a soldier from a Pennsylvania regiment. As Kady and the soldier fled toward the woods, a minié ball struck him in the back of the head, shattering his skull and splashing blood on Kady's uniform. She found a stray horse, mounted it and made her escape toward Centerville.

On July 25, 1861, the 1st Rhode Island Volunteers were disbanded and the regiment and returned to Providence, Rhode Island, where on August 2, 1861, they were mustered out of service. Both Kady and her husband received an army discharge. The 1st Rhode Island Infantry Regiment had sustained 25 losses in the four months of service. The losses were one officer and 16 enlisted men killed or mortally wounded, and 8 enlisted men dead from disease.

Kady and her husband's resolve was unshaken by the confusion at Bull Run and their loyalty to the Union prompted them to re-enlist in the newly organized 5th Rhode Island Infantry in October 1861. The 5th Rhode Island Regiment was mustered into Federal service on December 16, 1861.

With the 5th Rhode Island Regiment, under the command of Ambrose E. Burnside, Kady and her husband participated in the Battle of Roanoke Island on February 9, 1862. The regiment then marched South to capture and occupy New Bern, North Carolina. Kady requested that she be allowed to officially serve as the regimental color bearer during the upcoming battle. Her request was approved with the stipulation that she stop when the order was given to charge the enemy.

On the morning of March 14, 1862, as the Union forces were taking their respective positions in preparation for the battle, the 5th Rhode Island Regiment came out of a wooded area at an unexpected position. The other Union forces thought that these troops were Confederate soldiers preparing to attack and prepared to fire upon them. Kady, who had been returned to the rear of the regiment, immediately realized the danger her regiment was in. She raced forward into the clearing between the two Union regiments. She wildly waved the regimental flag until the attacking Union troops realized that they were not Confederate soldiers. Her heroic act, without

Kady Brownell. Courtesy of Louise Arnold-Friend Collection at U.S. Army Military History Institute.

consideration to her own safety, saved the regiment from being fired upon by friendly troops.

During the battle at New Bern, Kady was reported to have disobeyed Burnside's orders that she stay in the rear. She instead spent the whole time participating in the battle, tending wounded soldiers and displaying the regimental colors. While tending the wounded in the field, she came upon a wounded Confederate soldier. When she attempted to help him he cursed at her. She grabbed her gun and with the bayonet tried to stab him in the chest. A wounded Union soldier grabbed the bayonet and stopped her. He told her that it was wrong to kill a wounded soldier regardless of what he said. After she calmed down she was glad that the soldier had stopped her.

Later during the battle, she was said to have picked up another regiment's flag when its bearer fell. While carrying the flag across the field she was wounded as a shell fragment grazed her leg. The wound was not serious and did not put Kady out of action.

Her husband, Robert, also received a wound during the battle; however, his wound was more serious. He was crippled for life when a minié ball shattered his hip. This crippling wound brought the Brownells' military careers to an end.

Kady stayed for one month at New Bern nursing her husband. During this time, she also took food and coffee to the Confederate hospital for the wounded soldiers. They were transferred to Rhode Island and then to New York where Robert convalesced for several months at the Soldier's Relief Hospital. Kady stayed with her husband and tended him personally during his convalescence. In early 1863, when it became apparent that Robert would not be able to fight again, the Brownells were discharged from the army. General Ambrose E. Burnside personally signed Kady's discharge. Robert received a disability pension of $24 per month.

In 1884, after many years of living on the edge of poverty and Robert working at many different jobs, Kady applied for a pension in her own name and was granted a pension of $8 per month.

In 1905 a reporter on the *New York Times* interviewed Kady and published her story. The reporter published a letter to Kady from General Ambrose E. Burnside, dated 1868, in which he mentioned her heroic deed that saved the regiment from being fired upon by friendly troops. He also praised her devotion to the Union.

On January 5, 1915, just two years after her story was published in the *New York Times*, Kady Brownell died at the age of 72 at a Women's Relief Corps Home in Oxford, New York. Robert petitioned the government for the expenses he had incurred during Kady's illness. He followed her in death nine months later in September 1915.

✆ 30 ✆

Anna Blair Etheridge: Daughter of the Regiment

There are many accounts of the bravery and dedication of Anna Etheridge. Different accounts say she was a vivandiere, nurse, and Daughter of the Regiment. However, Anna Etheridge was much more than that. She marched into battle with her regiment while carrying the flag, nursed the wounded on the battlefields, participated in the capture of enemy prisoners, escorted captured soldiers to the Union authorities, and inspired the men of her regiment by her courage and dedication to duty.

Anna Etheridge was born Lorinda Anna Blair in 1840 in Detroit, Michigan. She married James Etheridge in 1860 at the age of 20. Anna was 21 years old when the Civil War began.

Anna's husband James decided to enlist in the Union army in response to President Lincoln's call for volunteers to put down the revolution and reunite the nation. He decided to enlist in the 2nd Michigan Infantry Regiment, which was being formed at Fort Wayne in Detroit, Michigan.

Anna, not wanting to be left alone and having a desire to do her part, decided to accompany her husband into the 2nd Michigan regiment and serve as a Daughter of the Regiment and nurse. Anna and James were both accepted and enlisted in the regiment as it was being formed.

The 2nd Michigan Infantry Regiment was the first three-year regiment mustered in from Michigan. They were mustered into Federal service on May 25, 1861. The regiment consisted of 1,013 officers and men. After six weeks of training from the date it was formed, the regiment left for Washington, D.C., where it was first reviewed by President Lincoln and then assigned to the defense of Washington.

The 2nd Michigan regiment proceeded to Manassas on July 16, 1861. It occupied Fairfax Courthouse on July 17, 1861, and was at Blackburn's Ford on July 18 when the Union reconnaissance forces came upon two Confederate brigades. The Confederate troops repulsed the Union army and claimed a victory. The Union troops lost 78 men while the Confederate troops lost 68.

This battle was a prelude to the Battle of First Manassas/Bull Run which occurred 30 days later on July 21, 1861. At First Manassas/Bull Run the 2nd Michigan Infantry was assigned to guard the escape route from Manassas back to Washington, D. C.

Shortly thereafter, Anna's husband James deserted from the Union army. For some reason she did not go with him but stayed with the regiment. Anna and her husband were separated after less than two years of marriage.

In the spring of 1862, she left the 2nd Michigan Infantry and worked on hospital ships taking the wounded to the major hospitals in New York, Washington, and Baltimore. She worked on three different hospital ships, the *Knickerbocker*, the *Louisiana*, and the *Daniel Webster*.

She was a hard-working, dedicated nurse while serving on these ships, but she missed the regiment. On August 1, 1862, she returned to regiment life, but instead of re-enlisting with the 2nd Michigan Infantry, she enlisted with the 3rd Michigan Infantry Regiment. While with the 3rd Infantry she experienced some of the bloodiest battles of the Civil War. The 3rd Michigan Infantry Regiment fought at the following battles:

Battle of Groveton, August 29, 1862
Battle of Second Manassas/Bull Run, August 30, 1862
Battle of Chantilly (Ox Hill), September 1, 1862
Battle of Fredericksburg, December 11–13, 1862
Battle of Chancellorsville, May 1–4, 1863
Battle of Gettysburg, July 1–3, 1863
Battle of the Wilderness, May 5–6, 1864
Battle of Spotsylvania, May 8–21, 1864
Battle of Bloody Angle, May 12, 1864
Battle of Cold Harbor, May 31–June 9, 1864

Anna was always on the battlefield during these bloody engagements. She would be tending the wounded, while the battles raged, without any thought for her personal safety. Her reputation for courage, patriotism and kindness earned her the nickname "Gentle Annie." Anna's clothing had many holes caused by bullets and shell fragments which barely missed her while she was helping fallen soldiers on the battlefields. Anna was wounded only once as a piece of shell fragment grazed her hand. The wound was not a serious injury and did not slow her down or hamper her work on the battlefields.

Prior to being killed at the Battle of Chantilly, General Philip Kearny stated that

Anna Etheridge. Courtesy of the State Archives of Michigan.

he would make Anna Etheridge a regimental sergeant so she could get sergeant's pay and rations. He was impressed with her dedication and the fact that she never asked for special treatment. She endured all the hardships along with the rest of the regiment. She slept on the ground wrapped in a blanket with the rest of the troops. She cooked and did other chores for the men in her regiment as well as nursing the sick and wounded.

On September 1, 1862, prior to General Kearny effecting the promotion for Anna, he was killed. Anna never received the promotion.

On June 10, 1864, the non-veterans of the 3rd Michigan Infantry were mustered out of service. The veterans, including Anna Etheridge, were transferred to the 5th Michigan Infantry Regiment. The 3rd Michigan regiment lost 249 men during its three years in service. Four officers and 154 enlisted men were killed or mortally wounded and two officers and 89 enlisted men died from disease.

While with the 5th Michigan Infantry, Anna took part in the Siege of Petersburg from June 16, 1864 to April 21, 1865. However, during the winter months of 1864–1865, Anna served as a nurse at the army hospital at City Point. She had returned to the regiment by the time Petersburg fell on April 2, 1865. Her unit was part of the troops that pursued General Lee to Appomattox Courthouse where on April 9, 1865, he surrendered his army to General Grant.

Prior to the end of the war, General David Bell Birney presented Anna Etheridge with the Kearny Cross for meritorious and distinguished service as Daughter of the Regiment. The Kearny Cross was established in memory of General Philip Kearny. The cross was awarded to non-commissioned officers and privates.

On July 5, 1865, the 5th Michigan Infantry Regiment was mustered out of Federal service. Gentle Annie wept as the regiment bid her farewell. The 5th Michigan regiment sustained losses of 454 men during the war. Sixteen officers and 247 enlisted men were killed or mortally wounded and 3 officers and 188 enlisted men died from disease.

After the war Anna Etheridge took a position as a clerk in the United States Pension Office. In March 1870 she remarried. Her new husband was Charles E. Hooks, a veteran of the 7th Connecticut Infantry.

In 1886, Senator Thomas Palmer introduced a bill into Congress to grant Anna Etheridge a pension of $50 per month for her service during the Civil War. The bill was passed on February 9, 1887, but the amount was reduced to $25 per month.

Anna Etheridge died in 1913 as the age of 74 and was buried with honors in Arlington National Cemetery, Washington, D. C.

General Philip Kearny. Courtesy of the Library of Congress.

❧ 31 ❧

Marie Tepe: Vivandiere and Nurse

Without fear or regard for her personal safety, Marie Tepe was an inspiration to the Union troops as she braved the battlefield of 13 major Civil War battles tending her wounded comrades.

Marie Tepe is reported to have been born Marie Brose in France in 1834. In 1849 she immigrated into the United States and settled in Philadelphia. In 1854, at the age of 20, she married a Philadelphia tailor named Bernardo Tepe.

Prior to the beginning of the Civil War, in January 1861, Marie's husband enlisted in Company I of the 27th Pennsylvania Infantry, which was called the "Washington Brigade." Shortly after Fort Sumter, the 27th Pennsylvania Infantry Regiment returned to Philadelphia and reorganized into a three-year unit. The reorganized unit was mustered into service on May 31, 1861. Marie's husband decided to re-enlist for three years and stay with the 27th Pennsylvania Infantry.

Bernardo wanted Marie to stay at home in Philadelphia and manage their small tailor shop. She refused and followed him into the regiment as a vivandiere and nurse. For her uniform she wore a blue Zouave jacket trimmed with red braid and a short (just below the knees) dress over red trousers. She had a red sash around her waist, wore boots, and covered her head with a sailor hat with the brim turned down.

Marie assumed the task of a female sutler and was a true vivandiere to the regiment. She sold the soldiers goods and supplies (including whiskey), cooked, washed clothes, and mended their uniforms. She also worked in the regimental hospital. Her untiring efforts were an inspiration to the regiment. The soldiers fondly nicknamed her "French Mary."

Marie was on the battlefield at First Manassas/ Bull Run. She always went onto the battlefield during the fighting to tend the wounded and help give courage to the frightened young men. In late 1862 after being with the 27th Pennsylvania Infantry through many major battles, she transferred to the 114th Pennsylvania Infantry Regiment — Clarence H. T. Collis's " Zouaves d'Afrique."

The reason she transferred was that her husband and some of his drunken friends came into her quarters while she was out and stole $1,600 which she had earned being a vivandiere. The men were caught and punished but Marie would have nothing else to do with Bernardo. She did not want to be in the same regiment with him and asked to be transferred. When asked to stay with the 27th Infantry Regiment, she refused. She was then was transferred to the 114th Infantry Regiment and away from her husband and his mischievous friends.

Marie Tepe, known as French Mary, in uniform. Courtesy of the Gettysburg National Military Park.

In December 1862, she participated in her first battle with the 114th Infantry Regiment. She was on the field during the fighting at the Battle of Fredericksburg, which began on December 11th and ended on December 13th. On the last day of the battle she was wounded by a minié ball, which lodged itself in her left ankle. Although the wound healed, the minié ball could not be removed and she suffered the effects of it the rest of her life.

During the Battle of Chancellorsville on May 1 to May 4, 1863, she went onto the battlefield with her canteen to give the soldiers water and to tend the wounded. Her skirt was riddled with holes from bullets and shell fragments during the battle, but she was not harmed.

For her bravery Major General David B. Birney awarded her the Kearny Cross. She refused the medal and told the General to keep it because she did not want it.

By the end of the war she had participated in and been on the battlefield during the fighting in 13 major battles. Some of the more noted battles were:

First Manassas/Bull Run, July 21, 1861
Chancellorsville, May 1–4, 1862
Seven Pines, May 31–June 1, 1862
Fredericksburg, December 11–13, 1862
Spotsylvania, May 8–21, 1863
Gettysburg, July 1–3, 1863

Marie Tepe was mustered out of Federal service with the 114th Pennsylvania Infantry on May 29, 1865. After the war Marie settled in Pittsburgh, Pennsylvania, where she married Richard Leonard. Her first husband had been killed at Gettysburg. Her new husband was a veteran of Company K of the 1st Maryland Cavalry.

In 1893, at the age of 59, she went to Philadelphia for a reunion with her regiment and to celebrate the anniversary of the Battle of Fredericksburg.

In the last few years of her life she became an invalid. She suffered from rheumatism and great pain from the minié ball that was lodged in her left ankle. In the spring of 1901, when the suffering became unbearable, she committed suicide by drinking poison. She died on Rafferty's Hill in Allegheny County, Pennsylvania, and was buried in an unmarked grave.

Researchers have recently located her grave in St. Paul's Cemetery in Allegheny County, Pennsylvania. She was honored on September 25, 1988, when a headstone was placed on her grave.

❧ 32 ❧

Notable Daughters
of the Regiment

Many women who felt a deep loyalty to their husbands and wanted to be at their side during the great conflict accompanied them and served in their regiment. They endured all the same hardships of army life while serving as vivandieres, Daughters of the Regiments, flag bearers, cooks, laundresses, seamstresses, nurses, scouts, soldiers and sometimes as spies.

These brave, dedicated women often distinguished themselves with acts of bravery and loyalty to their regiments. Such is the case of the following two Daughters of the Regiment.

Bridget Divers—Daughter of the Regiment

She had seen more danger and death and endured more hardship than any other woman during the Civil War. Her name was Bridget Divers. She was an Irish immigrant who had entered the United States in 1855 and settled in Michigan. She was in her early twenties when she and her husband decided to enlist in the army.

Her husband enlisted as a private in the 1st Michigan Cavalry. She went into the army with him as Daughter of the Regiment and vivandiere. She was already well skilled in riding, foraging, and hunting and adapted quickly to regimental life.

The 1st Michigan Cavalry was formed at Detroit, Michigan, on August 16, 1861, and was mustered into Federal service on September 13, 1861. The 1st Michigan Cavalry fought in most of the major battles of the Civil War including:

The Battle of Winchester, Virginia, May 25, 1862
The Battle of Cedar Mountain, Virginia, August 9, 1862
The Battle of Second Manassas/Bull Run, August 28–30, 1862
The Battle of Gettysburg, July 1–3, 1863
The Battle of the Wilderness, May 5–6, 1864
The Battle of Cold Harbor, May 31–June 12, 1864
The Third Battle of Winchester, September 19, 1864

After participating in the grand review in Washington, D.C., on May 23, 1865, the 1st Michigan Cavalry was assigned to Ft. Leavenworth, Kansas, and participated in the Powder River Expedition.

This expedition was against the Indians in District of the Plains and Dakota and lasted from July–November 1865. The 1st Michigan Cavalry was then on duty in Utah until March 1866. They were mustered out of service on March 10, 1866. The 1st Michigan Cavalry lost 414 men during its service. Fourteen officers and 150 enlisted men were killed or morally wounded and 6 officers and 244 enlisted men died from disease.

Bridget Divers' courage and dedication to her regiment during the many battles soon earned her the nickname of "Irish Biddy." Some referred to her as "Michigan Bridget."

She went into the battlefields with the regiment either carrying the flag or water and supplies to tend the wounded soldiers. Many times she would take up arms and join in the fighting to replace a fallen soldier. It is reported that she had at least four horses shot out from under her during the fierce battles she participated in. However, as dangerous as it was for her in these many battles, she served through the entire war without once being wounded.

Her deep dedication to her regiment was demonstrated after a battle in which the regiment's colonel was seriously wounded and its captain was killed. She nursed the colonel the best she could but soon realized that he needed professional help. She had him placed on a train and accompanied him to City Point where he could get the help he needed. She rested at City Point and then proceeded back to her regiment.

Upon arriving at her regiment she inquired about the captain and was informed that his body had been left on the battlefield. The battlefield was now behind Confederate lines. This situation was unacceptable to Bridget. She mounted her horse and headed deep into enemy territory to recover the body of her captain.

She located the body and managed to place it on the back of her horse and headed back toward the Union lines. She was stopped several times by Confederate pickets but after explaining that she was only retrieving a body, they let her pass. She had carried her captain's body for 15 miles on horseback, had him placed on the train, procured a coffin for him, and had him sent home. She had worked for 48 hours without sleep, tending the wounded from the battle, which she described as the worst battle they had ever been in.

Bridget Divers' devotion to her regiment became well known among the Union troops. She was many times the last to leave the battlefield and often carried wounded men who would otherwise have been left to die off the field.

There is some confusion among historians about whether Bridget Divers served the entire war with the 1st Michigan Cavalry or if she had also served with the 2nd, 3rd, and 5th Michigan Regiments. This confusion arises from the account of her rallying the Union troops at the Battle of Seven Pines (Fair Oaks), Virginia, on May 31 through June 4, 1862. Historical documentation places her at this battlefield. The 1st Michigan Cavalry was not there, but the 2nd Michigan Volunteer Infantry Regiment was. Perhaps she was temporarily reassigned or volunteered to help at the battle while her regiment was in between engagements. For whatever the reason she was instrumental in giving needed inspiration and confidence to the battle-weary Union troops.

The Union troops were having their lunch when the first volley was let go by the Confederates. This surprise attack caused many Union soldiers to jump to their feet and grab their weapons. However, many others became panic stricken by the surprise and resisted attempts to be rallied into action. When ordered to advance they were hesitant until Bridget Divers stood in front of them, waving her soldiers cap and shouting, "Hurray, go in boys and beat the hell out of them and revenge my husband." With this the troops rallied and gave three cheers for "Irish Biddy." These inspired troops drove the Confederate troops back and held the line. The Union losses during the battle were 5,000 while the Confederate losses were 6,000.

After the Civil War ended Bridget participated in the Grand Review on May 23, 1865, in Washington, D.C., with the 1st Michigan Cavalry. She stayed with the regiment when it was assigned to Ft. Leavenworth to participate in the Powder River Campaign. It is reported that after the 1st Michigan Cavalry was mustered out of service on March 10, 1866, Bridget stayed with the army in a different unit and went west to serve in the Indian Wars during the late 1860s and 1870s. There is no further word about her life or how and where she died. Another great heroine lost to history.

Belle Reynolds:
Daughter of the Regiment

So impressive was her loyalty and dedication to her regiment that the governor of Illinois commissioned her as an honorary major in the army.

Belle Reynolds was born Arabella Macomber in Shelbourne Falls, Massachusetts, in 1843. When she was 14 years old her family moved to rural Iowa. After returning to Massachusetts for an education she came back to Cass County, Iowa, where she was a schoolteacher.

In 1860, at the age of 17, she married John G. Reynolds and moved to Peoria,

Illinois. She was only 18 years old when the Civil War began, and her husband announced that he had decided to enlist in the army. He joined the newly organized 17th Illinois Infantry Regiment as a lieutenant. The 17th Illinois Infantry was formed at Peoria, Illinois, and mustered into Federal service on May 24, 1861. They were sent to Birds Point, Missouri, where Belle joined her husband on August 20, 1861.

With the 17th Illinois Infantry Belle experienced their first taste of war on November 7, 1861, at the Battle of Belmont, Missouri, under the command of a new brigadier general named Ulysses Simpson Grant. The 17th Illinois spent the winter of 1862 at Cape Girardeau, Missouri, as General Grant planned his strategy for opening the way to conquer Tennessee.

Through the winter of 1862 Belle stayed with the regiment. She traveled by army wagon, in an ambulance, by mule, and by marching with the regiment with a musket on her soldier.

The 17th Illinois Infantry participated in the Battle of Fort Henry on February 2–6 and the Battle of Fort Donelson on February 12–16, 1862. After these battles they set up camp at a place called Pittsburg Landing (Shiloh).

On Sunday April 6, 1862, Confederate forces attacked the Union encampment at Shiloh. As the Confederate troops overran the Union camp, Belle and the one other woman in the camp were caught in a crossfire. They fled to the river where the wounded soldiers were being taken aboard the steamer *Emerald*. Belle and her friend took off their bonnets, rolled up their sleeves and went to work on the ship nursing the wounded soldiers. There were 350 wounded soldiers aboard the ship and Belle worked without rest for 36 hours straight. In the early morning hours of April 7, the *Emerald* quietly slipped away from Pittsburg Landing and sailed for Savannah where the wounded were unloaded.

After the Battle of Shiloh, the bravery and dedication of Belle Reynolds became well known. The governor of Illinois signed an order on April 16, 1862, making Belle Reynolds an official Daughter of the Regiment and making her an honorary major in the army, for her distinguished service to the Union.

Her husband, Lt. John G. Reynolds, was made aide-de-camp to General John Alexander McClernand. Belle became a good friend to Mrs. McClernand and Mrs. Grant.

After returning to her regiment she and her husband saw battle two more times. They participated in the Battle of Port Gibson on May 1, 1863, and the siege and surrender of Vicksburg, Mississippi, on May 19 through July 4, 1863.

Except for a short visit home in 1862 Belle stayed with the regiment during its full enlistment period and distinguished herself as a brave, dedicated, nurse and loyal patriot. The 17th Illinois Infantry Regiment was mustered out of service on June 4, 1864. Their losses in the three years were 3 officers and 71 enlisted men killed in battle and 1 officer and 71 enlisted men dead from disease for a total loss of 146 men.

After the Reynoldses were mustered out they returned to their home in Peoria, Illinois. After the war ended they moved to Santa Barbara, California. Belle was honored in 1861 by a visit from the President of the United States, Benjamin Harrison.

❧ 33 ❧

Emma Sansom:
Southern Patriot

Her single act of heroism resulted in one of the most unusual captures of Union troops during the Civil War. This 15-year-old girl's bravery inspired the Southern cause. Her name was Emma Sansom.

Emma Sansom was born in 1847 at Social Circle, Georgia. Her father moved the family to a farm near Gadsden, Alabama, in 1852. Emma had one older sister and one brother. By the time the Civil War had begun, Emma's father had passed away. In August 1861 her brother enlisted in the 19th Alabama Infantry leaving Emma, with her mother and sister, to run the farm.

The events leading up to Emma's heroic deed began when General Rosencrans, who was being harassed by Confederate General Nathan Bedford Forrest, sent a mounted column of 1,500 men under Colonel Abel Streight to hunt down and defeat General Forrest. This would put a stop to General Forrest's raids, which were hampering Union operations in Tennessee.

Colonel Streight set out across Tennessee in pursuit of Forrest. The pursuit did not last long as General Forrest turned and began to chase Colonel Streight. For some reason, Colonel Streight was overly cautious and not knowing Forrest's strength, but well aware of his reputation, began to flee. Forrest pursued the Union troops out of Tennessee and into Alabama.

On the morning of May 2, 1863, Colonel Streight's soldiers rode past Emma's home. They noticed her brother (probably visiting on furlough) and took him prisoner. After searching the house for guns and ammunition, the Union troops took hot coals out of the stove and rode toward the bridge over Black Creek. Black Creek had high bluffs on each side and could only be crossed by the wooden bridge. The Union troops planned to burn the bridge and stop their pursuers.

When General Nathan Bedford Forrest and his Confederate troops rode past the house they noticed the burned-out bridge and saw no way to cross the creek in pursuit of Colonel Streight. Seeking help to solve his problem, General Forrest rode up to the small farmhouse and asked the young girl who was standing on the porch if there was a place his troops could cross the stream either above or below the burned-out bridge. He told Emma not to be afraid, that he was General Forrest and that he would protect her.

When he inquired about the Union troops, Emma's mother told him that the Yankees had burned the bridge and were waiting on the other side for Forrest's troops to come down the hill toward the bridge so they could ambush them. When the rest of Forrest's men arrived and took their positions, both sides began firing across the river at each other.

General Forrest asked Emma if there was another way across the river. She was very excited by this time and began giving him directions to a spot two miles down river where her cows crossed during times of low water. General Forrest could not understand her directions and asked her to show him the way.

Emma, realizing that he did not understand, agreed to show him the way and asked that he saddle a horse for her. General Forrest said that there was no time to saddle a horse and invited her to ride behind him on his horse.

Emma's mother objected to her going off with the soldiers and to her riding behind General Forrest. Emma assured her mother that she was not afraid to trust herself with such a brave man as General Forrest. She then jumped up on the stump of a fallen tree, grabbed General Forrest by the waist and mounted his horse.

As they drew near the ford, General Forrest noticed a Yankee sharpshooter on the ridge above them. Soon a minié ball whistled past his ear. "What was that?" Emma asked. "Bullets," he replied. "Are you afraid?" She told him she wasn't and they proceeded. The undergrowth grew thick as they approached the ford area and they were forced to dismount. Emma went ahead of the general, remarking that they wouldn't shoot her but they would shoot him if he went first. General Forrest appreciated the gesture, but not wanting to shield himself behind the brave young girl, took the lead.

Once the route through the underbrush was found, the general brought up troops with axes and cleared a path for the soldiers to approach the ford. The entire column was able to cross in safety.

Upon saying goodbye and thanking Emma, General Forrest asked if there was anything he might do for her in return for her valuable service. She told him that the Yankees he was pursuing had taken her brother prisoner and if General Forrest would release him she would be more than repaid. The general looked at his pocket watch. It was five to eleven. "Tomorrow at five minutes to eleven your brother will be returned to you."

General Forrest's troops soon were ahead of the Union troops and turned to surround them. Colonel Streight asked for a truce. As the two commanders conferred,

Forrest kept his two cannons and his men circling the Union troops. It was only after Colonel Streight had surrendered his remaining 1,466 men that he found out that General Forrest had only 500 troops with him.

By ten o'clock the next morning General Streight and his whole command had been captured. Emma's brother was located and released. He was given a fast horse and told to return to his heroic sister. General Forrest sent her a thank you note. Emma's courage and patriotism contributed to the success of one of the most remarkable cavalry pursuits and captures of the Civil War.

Two years later, in 1864, she married C. B. Johnson, a Confederate soldier of the 10th Alabama Infantry Regiment. Also in 1864 she was honored by the Alabama legislature which awarded her a medal and promised her a

General Nathan Bedford Forrest. Courtesy of the Library of Congress.

section of land for her heroic contribution to the Confederate war effort. After the war, the promise of land was not honored by the Reconstruction legislature. The promise was eventually made good by the Alabama legislature in 1899.

By 1899, when the promise was honored, Emma was a widow living in Calloway, Texas, with her five sons and two daughters. One year later, in 1900, Emma Sansom died in Calloway at the age of 53.

After her death, John Trotwood Moore composed a ballad to honor her wartime heroism titled "The Ballad of Emma Sansom."

On July 4, 1907, a monument to Emma Sansom was unveiled in Gadsden, Alabama, near the site of her courageous deed, depicting her as a Confederate heroine.

❧ 34 ❧

Anna Ella Carroll: Union Pamphleteer and Spy

Anna Ella Carroll proposed one of the most brilliant plans for shortening or ending the Civil War. The plan worked as she expected, but she never received credit or compensation for her idea.

Anna Ella Carroll was born on August 29, 1815, in Kingston Hall, Maryland. She was the daughter of Thomas King Carroll and Juliana (Stevenson) Carroll. The Carrolls had several children, of which Anna was the eldest. They lived in Kingston Hall until 1829 when her father was elected governor of the state Maryland. Anna accompanied her father to Annapolis, leaving her mother with her younger brothers and sisters at home in Kingston Hall.

Anna, a well-educated and charming young redhead, soon adapted to the Maryland social set. She was referred to as "Princess Anne" by Maryland society.

In 1830, after a year of supporting two households, Anna's father was forced to move the family to a less costly home in Cambridge, Maryland.

Also in 1830, Anna began writing anonymously on political subjects, mostly for the "Know-Nothing Party." She forwarded the majority of her writing income to help her family.

By early 1861 she had become a well-known political writer. Her writing ability caught the attention of President Lincoln and his cabinet. The Assistant Secretary of War, Thomas A. Scott, under orders from President Lincoln, contacted Anna and commissioned her to write and publish 10,000 copies of a document entitled "The Reply" which strongly condemned the secession of the Southern states who had left the Union. In addition to this pamphlet she was commissioned to publish two more documents entitled "The War Powers of the General Government 1861," and "The Relation of the National Government to the Revolted Citizens Defined" (1862). These additional documents pointed out that secession was unconstitutional and the formation of the Confederacy was an act of rebellion.

Anna personally met with President Lincoln to discuss payment for the pamphlets she had published on his behalf. She demanded a payment of $50,000. President Lincoln told her that such an amount was outrageous and offered her $750, which she accepted.

In August 1862, President Lincoln sent Anna on an espionage mission to St. Louis, Missouri. She was assigned to accompany another operative, Lemuel Evans. During the trip, their mission was to scout Confederate fortifications and to deliver messages and information to the Union officers stationed in the area. The trip was a complete success with no problems.

While traveling on the Mississippi River in an attempt to gain the information she needed, she became acquainted with an old ship's captain named Winfred Scott. To occupy her time during the long periods of sailing, Captain Scott allowed her to see his river charts and maps. After reviewing the charts of the Tennessee River and with the help of Captain Scott and Lemuel Evans, a plan to shorten or end the war was formulated. Anna returned to Washington in late November 1861 with her information and the plan the three had made for ending the war.

During her report on the Confederate fortifications she introduced her plan for ending the war. Her plan called for sending the Union army up the Tennessee River to take Fort Donelson and Fort Henry and to open the way for the Union invasion of the Confederacy. The idea was so unusual that the President convened his cabinet to discuss it. The generals did not like this bold plan, especially since a woman thought of it. However, the War Department eventually adopted the plan and credit was given to General Ulysses Grant.

In early February 1862, General Grant began the Tennessee River Campaign by attacking Fort Henry in Kentucky. This was the Tennessee River stronghold. The river was high and Fort Henry was awash with floodwater. Most of the Confederate soldiers had been sent to Fort Donelson, leaving only 100 artillery men at Fort Henry to face General Grant's 15,000 men and four gun boats. They surrendered on February 6, 1862, after a short bombardment from the gunboats.

General Grant then marched to Fort Donelson where, after repelling the gun boats, General John Floyd escaped with 2,000 Confederate troops leaving General Grant's old friend General Simon B. Buckner in charge. General Grant demanded an unconditional surrender. General Buckner agreed and the route to the invasion of the South was established. Anna Ella Carroll's plan had worked as she predicted.

Anna filed her claim with the government for her expenses while on the mission and for the $60,000 President Lincoln promised her for her plan. President Lincoln had also promised her a pension for her service to the Union, but his assassination squashed any hopes she had of ever being paid or receiving a pension.

Anna fought for several years with the government for her pay and her pension

Anna Ella Carroll. From *My Dear Lady*. Whittlesey House, 1940.

but was unsuccessful. She returned to the work of a pamphlet writer and railroad attorney. In 1886 she struck her final blow against the injustice she had suffered when she published a brochure, "North American Review," in which she condemned male injustice.

Her sister, who held a government job in Washington, D.C., was her primary means of support during the last 20 years of Anna's life.

Anna died on February 19, 1893, at the age of 78 in Washington, D.C. She was buried in the churchyard of Old Trinity Church in Cambridge, Maryland.

Her head stone reads:

Anna Ella Carroll
Daughter of Thomas King and Jolianna Stevenson Carroll
Born at Kingston Hall, August 29, 1815
Died at Washington, D.C.
February 19, 1893
A woman gifted — An able and accomplished writer

❧ 35 ❧

Barbara Frietchie: Legendary Union Patriot

Barbara Frietchie was born in Frederick, Maryland, in 1766. The widow of a glove maker, she was still living in Frederick in 1862 when General Lee's army first invaded the North. She died in Frederick, Maryland, in December 1862, just two weeks after her ninety-sixth birthday. Prior to her death she was credited with a brave act of defiance against the Confederacy.

The story goes that at 3 a.m. on September 10, 1862, she was awakened by General T. J. Jackson's troops marching past her home. As the troops entered Frederick, the 95-year-old patriot bravely and defiantly leaned out the upstairs window of her home and waved a Union flag as they passed. Another version of the story states that she thought, at first, that the soldiers who were entering Frederick were Union soldiers and as a patriot she wanted to greet them by waving the flag. When she discovered that the soldiers were Confederates she became angered and defiantly waved it in their faces.

Dr. Lewis H. Steiner of the United States Sanitary Commission wrote of the events of the week that Jackson's troops entered Frederick. He did not mention Barbara Frietchie but claimed that an anonymous old woman in Frederick had shaken her small fists at the Confederate invaders and screamed at them when she saw them dragging the American flag in the dust behind them. She shouted, "My curses upon you and your officers for degrading your country's flag!"

Barbara Frietchie's defiant flag waving merged with Dr. Steiner's anonymous woman and Barbara was credited with both incidents even though another Frederick woman claimed to be the anonymous woman. Some other reports claim that

Barbara was bedridden and could not have stood and leaned out of the window waving the flag. The only supporting evidence of the incident is that General Early demanded a ransom of $200,000 in gold from Frederick for the insult to his troops. The city of Frederick borrowed the money from many other banks and paid the ransom to save their town. It took Frederick, Maryland, so long to pay back the loans that the city ended up paying $600,000 in interest. This retribution does not prove that the incident actually occurred. It only proves that there was a publicized insult to the Confederacy.

Barbara's niece forwarded the story to C. S. Ramsburg of Georgetown, Maryland, who had it published in a Washington newspaper.

Mrs. Southworth, a leading American novelist and a neighbor of Barbara's niece, wrote a narrative of the events and forwarded it to John Greenleaf Whittier.

Whittier, a Quaker poet, was impressed by the story of the brave old woman and composed a 30 verse poem which was published by Mr. Whittier's editor, James R. Field, in the *Atlantic Monthly*.

The poem was an immediate hit, and was reprinted widely. However, Barbara evidently knew nothing about becoming famous because she died two weeks before the poem was published. The poem goes:

> Up from the meadows rich with corn,
> Clear in the cool September morn,
>
> The clustered spires of Frederick stand
> Green-walled by the hills of Maryland.
>
> Round about them orchards sweep,
> Apple and peach tree fruited deep,
>
> Fair as a garden of the Lord
> To the eyes of the famished rebel horde,
>
> On that pleasant morn of the early fall
> When Lee marched over the mountain-wall,
>
> Over the mountains winding down,
> Horse and foot, into Frederick town.
>
> Forty flags with their silver stars,
> Forty flags with their crimson bars,
>
> Flapped in the morning wind: the sun
> Of noon looked down, and saw not one.
>
> Up rose old Barbara Frietchie then,
> Bowed with her fourscore years and ten;
>
> Bravest of all in Frederick town,
> She took up the flag the men hauled down;

In her attic window the staff she set,
To show that one heart was loyal yet.

Up the street came the rebel tread,
Stonewall Jackson riding ahead.

Under his slouched hat left and right
He glanced; the old flag met his sight.

"Halt!"—the dust-brown ranks stood fast,
"Fire!"—out blazed the rifle blast.

It shivered the window, pane and sash;
It rent the banner with seam and gash.

Quick, as it fell, from the broken staff
Dame Barbara snatched the silken scarf;

She leaned far out on the window-sill,
And shook it forth with a royal will.

"Shoot, if you must, this old gray head,
But spare your country's flag," she said.

A shade of sadness, a blush of shame,
Over the face of the leader came;

The nobler nature within him stirred
To life at that woman's deed and word:

"Who touches a hair on yon gray head
Dies like a dog! March on!" he said.

All day long through Frederick Street
Sounded the tread of marching feet;

All day long that free flag tost
Over the heads of the rebel host.

Ever its torn folds rose and fell
On the loyal winds that loved it well;

And through the hill-gaps sunset light
Shone over it with a warm good-night.

Barbara Frietchie's work is o'er,
And the Rebel rides on his raids no more.

Honor to her! and let a tear
Fall, for her sake, on Stonewall's bier.

Over Barbara Frietchie's grave,
Flag of Freedom and Union, wave!

> Peace and order and beauty draw
> Round thy symbol of light and law;
>
> And ever the stars above look down
> On thy stars below in Frederick town!

There is no historical evidence to support this story. The only evidence available shows that it could not have been Barbara since she was bedridden during the Confederate occupation of Frederick and therefore could not have seen General Jackson. It is also known that General Jackson entered the town riding in an ambulance since he had been slightly injured by a horse and therefore she could not have seen him ride in.

What is known, however, is that after the Confederate troops had left Frederick and the Union troops were marching into the town, Barbara was brought out to sit on her porch and watch them pass by. She was given a small flag on a small staff, which she waved as the Union army re-occupied Frederick.

✿ 36 ✿

Civil War Heroines

Many women who were loyal to either the Confederacy or the Union felt the need to do their part. Most who felt this way never had the chance to help. However, when an opportunity did arise, those in a position to help came willingly to the aid of their cause. Such is the case of the following heroic women.

Lola, Panchita, and Eugenia Sanchez—Confederate Patriots

The Sanchez sisters were daughters of a Cuban immigrant who was living in Florida when the Civil War began. These three sisters made their contribution to the Confederate war effort by passing vital military information to the Confederate troops. Their information helped win a Confederate victory.

Several Union officers visiting on the front porch of the Sanchez home turned their discussions to their planned use of a gunboat to attack the Confederate fortifications in the area. Lola, eavesdropping, overheard this conversation and went to tell her sisters.

The girls, realizing the value of this information, immediately formulated a plan to relate the information to the Confederacy. Panchita and Eugenia stayed behind to divert the attention of the Union officers while Lola saddled her horse and rode unnoticed through the woods behind her home to the nearby Confederate lines.

The information Lola gave the Confederates allowed them the time they needed to surprise and capture the Union gunboat. To honor the Sanchez sisters for their service, the Confederacy renamed the gunboat "The Three Sisters." The Sanchez sisters were never caught or arrested.

Antoinette Polk — Confederate Patriot

Antoinette Polk was a young girl from Columbia, Tennessee, who was instrumental in helping a group of Confederate soldiers avoid capture by Union troops. The Confederate officers were visiting her father at the family estate, Ashwood Hall, which was located just outside of Union-occupied Columbia.

Antoinette, like most young girls of the time, was a skilled rider. One day while riding into Columbia with a female cousin, she came upon a division of Union cavalry and soon learned that they were preparing to search the surrounding area for Confederate sympathizers.

Knowing that a group of confederate soldiers were visiting with her father she became determined to save them from being captured and her father from being arrested as a confederate sympathizer. Antoinette and her cousin raced home ahead of the Union soldiers and arrived just in time for the visiting Confederate soldiers to make their safe retreat.

The Union troops never suspected and never knew how close they came to finding their quarry.

Laura Ratcliffe — Confederate Spy

Laura Ratcliffe was living with her mother and two sisters on a small farm at a crossroads west of Washington, D.C., called Frying Pan, Virginia, when the Civil War began.

Laura was described as a beautiful brunette with dark eyes and a fair complexion. She was a loyal southern girl and became involved in the war when she brought attention to herself by nursing the fallen Confederate soldiers in her area.

General J.E.B. Stuart was quite impressed with her after hearing about her devotion to the fallen soldiers and her patriotism to the south. General Stuart was so taken with her that in late December he introduced her to Colonel John Singleton Mosby as a possible source of future information about the area.

On many occasions Colonel Mosby used the Ratcliffe farm as his area headquarters. The farm was also used as a storage area for confiscated Union material and money until it could be safely transferred to the proper Confederate authorities. Confiscated money and documents were safely hidden under a huge rock on the Ratcliffe farm. The Confederates knew this hidden place as "Mosby's Rock." Mosby and other operatives also used the rock as a letter drop and rendezvous spot. Federal agents searched the Ratcliffe Farm many times, but found nothing.

When Laura carried messages and information to and from Colonel Mosby, she concealed the information in a false-bottomed egg basket. She was under suspicion of the Union authorities but never caught or arrested.

On one occasion two Union soldiers under the command of Lieutenant Palmer of the 1st Virginian Regiment stopped at the Ratcliffe home for fresh milk. While there they began to brag to Laura about an ambush they had set up for Colonel Mosby when he rode into Frying Pan. They taunted her that her "pal" Mosby would soon be dead or their prisoner, and there was nothing she could do about it. She had no horse to ride to warn Mosby and the roads were too muddy for her to walk on.

After the two Union soldiers left she was determined to warn Colonel Mosby. She ran through the muddy fields and roads until she spotted a troop of soldiers in blue riding toward the trap. She recognized Colonel Mosby leading his men. She told him of the plan for an ambush as he rode into Frying Pan.

With this information Colonel Mosby quickly changed his plans and turned away from Frying Pan to raid a Federal picket near Dranesville, where he took 15 Union soldiers prisoner and confiscated their horses and equipment.

Colonel Mosby was grateful to Laura for saving his life. He gave her his watch chain with a note as a gift. The note was a short poem to her, which read, "And when this page shall meet your glance / Forget not him you met by chance."

After the war ended Laura lived on the farm with her invalid sister. They were poverty stricken until an elderly Yankee neighbor named Milton Hannah offered to build a house near his own so that he and his mother could care for Laura and her sister. She agreed and a two-story brick house was built on a nearby brook and named Brookside.

After the death of her sister, Laura and Milton were married and resided at Brookside. Upon the death of her husband Laura was left a wealthy woman. She devoted her wealth to helping the poor and destitute. Much of the Brookside property was given to the Presbyterian and Methodist churches.

At the age of 79 Laura fell while feeding her chickens and suffered a broken ankle. The break did not heal properly and she was left partially crippled for the rest of her life. Laura spent the next eight years in solitude and died at the age of 87.

Nancy Hart — Confederate Scout and Spy

Nancy Hart was a Scottish-Irish American girl from the mountains of western Virginia where life was simple and uncomplicated. She was not educated but was knowledgeable about the people of her area and the surrounding mountainous terrain. She knew about the war and her loyalties were to the Confederacy.

She often served as a guide for General Thomas Jonathan "Stonewall" Jackson and his Confederate cavalry to lead them through the rough terrain, which she knew well. She also lead Confederate soldiers to isolated Federal outposts where the element of surprise was on their side.

She became an accomplished spy, entering Union strongholds under the guise of selling eggs and vegetables. While peddling her goods she would learn everything she could about the strength, gun emplacements, and plans of the Union soldiers. She kept the information in her memory, and reported it to the Confederate authorities.

Nancy Hart. Courtesy of the West Virginia Archives.

After many successful missions, the Union authorities realized she was spying for the Confederacy and a bounty was placed on her head. Colonel Starr of the 9th West Virginia Regiment captured her in July 1862 while on a scouting expedition to Somerville, Tennessee.

During her captivity she looked for ways to escape and get even with her captors. Late one night she got her chance when the guard assigned to watch her was not paying close attention to her. She quickly overpowered him, grabbed his gun, which she fired, and fatally wounded him. She then stole Colonel Starr's horse and sped away in the dark of night.

The next morning she led Confederate Major Bailey and 200 men on a raid to Somerville. The Union pickets panicked when they saw the Confederate troops approaching and fled without firing a shot, leaving the Union camp unguarded.

At four o'clock in the morning, the Federal camp was awakened by a single shot fired by one of the raiding party to wake the camp. When the Union soldiers rushed to the assembly area they found themselves completely surrounded by Confederate troops.

Major Bailey confiscated all the Federal supplies, weapons, and ammunition. The Federal troops were all taken prisoner and marched down the same road that they had forced Nancy to walk when she was their prisoner.

Clara Judd — Confederate Spy and Smuggler

Clara Judd was born in Minnesota and was the widow of an Episcopal clergyman from Winchester, Tennessee. During the Civil War she gained a reputation as a Confederate spy and smuggler. Her main expertise was in smuggling and she supplied most of the drugs used by the Confederate troops from Tennessee. She was also a spy for General John Hunt Morgan.

On December 16, 1862, she was sent to Louisville, Kentucky, to gather information for General Morgan about the number of Federal troops stationed there and where they were located. On her way back, while walking between Murfreesboro and Nashville, a man named Delos Thurman Blythe approached her. He was a Yankee agent sent by Allen Pinkerton to trap her. He was posing as a paroled Union prisoner with a pass from General Bragg to enter Nashville.

With his charm and wit he soon won Clara's confidence. As they walked he told her that he was a Confederate agent. He talked about several of his spying exploits in detail and by the time they reached Nashville, Clara was beginning to confide in him about her espionage and smuggling activities. Because of her infatuation with Blythe, she was beginning to let her guard down.

Upon reaching Nashville they found rooms at the Commercial Hotel. Once settled in, Blythe contacted Federal authorities and requested Clara be put under constant surveillance. Blythe continued to romance Clara while they were in Nashville, learning more about her spying activities each day. When she attempted to move on, Blythe faked an illness, which required nursing care. Clara stayed on to nurse her new lover back to health. This gave Blythe time to set the trap.

When Blythe recovered, he joined Clara as she was preparing to leave Nashville. She was busy packing drugs, medicine, and secret documents into the false bottoms of her travelling trunks. She was concerned that her bags would be searched and she would be discovered. Blythe told her not to be concerned because he had taken care of everything and her baggage would not be searched. Clara again let her guard down. She should have suspected something was not right when he told her that he had taken care of everything. But she was too taken with her newfound love to be wary of him.

Federal agents a few miles out of Nashville stopped the train on which she and Blythe were traveling. The train was carefully searched and both Clara and Blythe were arrested as spies when the documents and drugs were discovered in their luggage.

Blythe's plan had worked perfectly. He was roughed up in front of Clara and then supposedly taken to a Federal prison. The Federal agents had Clara lodged in a Nashville hotel under guard. Believing that her lover would soon be executed, she begged to meet with Union authorities to plead for his life. Her request was denied.

She never found out the fate of her lover or that he had so cleverly deceived her.

General William Starke Rosencrans ordered Clara sent to Alton Military Prison, in Alton, Illinois, to await trial. Since the Alton prison had no facilities for women she was kept in a local boarding house. She stayed there until August 4, 1863, when, to her surprise, she was released without trial. She returned home to Minnesota never knowing the fate of her lover, Delos Blythe.

Her capture cost the Confederacy a large amount of drugs and information. It also caused the delay of General Morgan's raid into Kentucky.

37

Sarah E. Thompson: Union Spy and Nurse

It took one courageous woman to bring down the feared Confederate raider General John Hunt Morgan. Her name was Sarah E. Thompson. She accomplished what the Union army failed to do in the three years it chased Morgan.

Sarah E. Thompson was born on February 11, 1838, in Green County, Tennessee. In 1854, at the age of 16, she married Sylvanius H. Thompson. Sarah was 23 years old when the Civil War began. Sylvanius and Sarah were both loyal to the Union even though the area of Tennessee where they resided had mixed loyalties, but leaned toward the Confederacy.

After the war began Sylvanius enlisted in the 1st Tennessee Cavalry and served as a recruiter for the Union army. Sarah worked with her husband and helped organize Union sympathizers for recruitment around the Greenville area.

Sarah would gather all the Union loyalists at a pre-designated spot at night and move them north to join the Union army. She is said to have led over 500 loyal recruits to the Union army this way.

Sarah was captured several times and wounded once by Confederate soldiers while making her way through the woods with recruits or dispatches. She was always able to talk her way out of her arrests and was set free.

In late 1863 Sarah's husband Sylvanius was captured by Confederate forces while carrying a message to General Ambrose Burnside, the commander in Knoxville. Sylvanius was sent to Belle Island Prison in Richmond, Virginia. He escaped and by early January 1864 he was back in the Greenville area where he continued his recruiting efforts for the Union. His return to duty was short-lived because on January 10, 1864, he was ambushed near Greenville and killed by a Confederate soldier.

160

Sarah was grief-stricken by the death of her husband. His death at the hands of the Confederates spurred her to intensify her efforts on behalf of the Union. She delivered dispatches and recruiting information to the Union army and continued her efforts to organize recruits.

Her desire to avenge the death of her husband was finally becoming a reality when in early September 1864 General John Hunt Morgan and his Confederate Raiders rode into Greenville.

General Morgan had been captured by Union forces near New Lisbon, Ohio, in late July 1863 and sent to the Ohio State Penitentiary. In April 1864 he and six of his comrades, using table knives as shovels, tunneled out of the prison and returned to the Confederate army. When

General John Hunt Morgan. Courtesy of the Library of Congress.

he returned to the Confederacy, he was appointed commander of the Department of Southwest Virginia.

On August 23, 1864, Morgan's Raiders headed for Greenville. General Morgan and his 1,600 troops arrived there on September 23. He decided to stay overnight at the Williams mansion, a two-story brick home on Irish Street. He had stayed in the Williams home twice before even though the Fry Hotel was just around the corner.

Dr. Alexander Williams, who died prior to the war, built the mansion. He and his wife Catherine had one daughter, Fanny Williams, and three sons. When the Civil War began, two of Mrs. Williams' sons became Confederate officers. One of the sons was on General Morgan's staff. The third son, Joe, remained loyal to the Union. Joe was married to a loyal Union woman named Lucy.

The night that General Morgan stayed at the Williams mansion, Lucy was visiting a relative at College Farm, four miles from Greenville. Some accounts of General

Morgan's death give the credit to Lucy Williams as the informant who tipped off the Union army. She could not have done so since she was not in Greenville at the time.

As General Morgan rode into town Sarah Thompson noticed that he had posted guards around the town and around the Williams mansion. She quickly grabbed her milk pail and made for the edge of town. When stopped by the Confederate guards she explained that her cows were over the hill and needed milking. The guards let her pass.

Once over the hill she discarded the pail and ran for the woods so she could make her way to the Union lines. She stopped at a neighbor's house and borrowed a horse and rode along the railroad track to Bull's Gap where the Union army was encamped. She reported the whereabouts of General Morgan to Union General Gillem who was somewhat skeptical of her report until Colonel John S. Brownlow of the 3rd Tennessee Calvary and Lieutenant Edward J. Brooks of the 10th Michigan Infantry vouched for her, based on her past performance.

One hundred Union cavalrymen were selected from the 10th Michigan and the 3rd, 9th, 12th and 13th Tennessee Regiments. Sarah was given a fresh horse and accompanied the soldiers toward Greenville.

General Morgan was still asleep when the Union troops swept into Greenville just prior to dawn. When the alarm was sounded by one of the sentries, General Morgan was shaken awake by one of his guards. Quickly donning a pair of pants over his nightclothes he hurried downstairs and asked Mrs. Williams where the Yankees were. She replied, "Everywhere," which made General Morgan realize that he had underestimated the enemy.

General Morgan dashed out the rear door of the mansion and across the huge lawn to Main Street where he hid behind the Fry Hotel. This hiding place did not give him adequate cover so he ran to the Episcopal Church, which was next door to the hotel, and hid himself in its cellar.

Before leaving home Sarah had asked Flora, a servant girl, to keep an eye on the Williams mansion for her. Upon returning home, she asked Flora if she knew where Morgan was hiding. The servant indicated that he was somewhere on the premises. Sarah left the house to search for Morgan. She walked down Depot Street, which bordered the Williams estate on the south.

Meanwhile, General Morgan began to feel insecure in the church cellar. He then ran out the back of the church, through the shrubbery of the Williams lawn and slid under a white fence next to the grapevines.

Sarah spotted him as he slid under the fence. She ran and hailed the first Union trooper she could find. She told him to tear part of the fence down and he would find General Morgan.

The Union cavalryman was Private Andrew Campbell of Company G of the 13th Regiment Tennessee Volunteer Cavalry. When he pulled back a board on the fence he recognized General Morgan and shouted for him to surrender. General Morgan shouted back, "I will never surrender!" Private Campbell noticed Morgan reaching for something and, thinking that it could be a gun, fired his rifle at the

General. The bullet hit General Morgan in the center of his body. "Oh, God," were the last words General John Hunt Morgan ever spoke. He died almost instantly. During the battle, 100 of the Confederate soldiers were killed and 75 were taken prisoner. The rest of Morgan's men managed to escape.

After this, Sarah could not remain in Greenville — especially since the Confederacy had offered a bounty for her capture.

Sarah and Lucy Williams, because of their Union loyalties, had to flee to the safety of the North.

Sarah then served as an army nurse until the end of the war. She served first in Knoxville, Tennessee, and then in Cleveland, Ohio. After the war she supported herself by giving lectures in northern cities on her experience during the war.

On January 1, 1866, she married for the second time, to Orville Bacon of Broome County, New York. Orville died in 1877 and Sarah moved to Washington, D.C., to take a $600 a year clerical job in the Treasury Department.

In the 1880s she married for the third time to James W. Cotton. By 1890 she was widowed for the third time.

Sarah then applied for a pension for her work during the war. A bill (S.1837) was presented before Congress to give her a pension of $12 per month. She was awarded the pension by a special act of the fifty-fifth Congress in 1899.

Sarah then worked for the Post Office until 1903 when she retired at the age of 65 and went to live with her son Orville Bacon, Jr., on Capitol Hill.

One April morning in 1909 Sarah was caught between two trolley cars and received a skull fracture. She died two days later on April 21, 1909. She was buried in Arlington National Cemetery with full military honors.

❧ 38 ❧

Mary Ann Ball Bickerdyke: Union Nurse

Mary Ann Bickerdyke was born in 1817 in Knox County, Ohio. She was the mother of one daughter and two sons. She lost her husband and daughter prior to the beginning of the Civil War. After this tragic loss she decided to become a nurse and devote her life to helping relieve sickness and suffering. She was a trained nurse working in Galesburg, Illinois, when the Civil War began.

One Sunday in June 1861 Mary Ann was attending church when the pastor, Edward Beecher, the brother of Harriet Beecher Stowe, asked the congregation to donate food and supplies to help the military camps in Cairo, Illinois. A full wagonload of food and supplies was soon gathered and Mary Ann Bickerdyke was asked to deliver them to the Union camps. She accepted the task, said goodbye to her sons, and began the trip to Cairo, which marked the beginning of her extraordinary service to the Union army. Other than short visits she would not see her sons until the end of the war.

When she arrived in Cairo she was appalled by the unsanitary conditions in the hospital. She decided to do something about these conditions by offering her services. She rented a room and demanded that the hospital be cleaned up. She explained that the men would have a better chance of recovery if they were bathed and surrounded by sanitary conditions.

Her efforts to clean up the hospital soon spread to five other area hospitals. Although she was not welcomed at first by the surgeons, she was soon receiving praise for her efforts. Doctor J.J. Woodward of the 22nd Illinois Infantry Regiment gave her praise by describing her as "Strong as a man, muscles of iron, nerves of steel; sensitive, but self reliant, kind and tender; seeking all for others, nothing for herself."

Her efforts in getting supplies and food for the soldiers and her untiring nursing of the sick and wounded soon earned her the nickname "Mother Bickerdyke." Her notoriety began to spread and she soon gained the friendship of many high ranking officers including General Ulysses Simpson Grant and General William Tecumseh Sherman.

She would do anything to get proper food and supplies for the sick and wounded. She would even beg food and supplies from any available source. She would on occasion raid government supplies without permission. She always found some way to keep the hospitalized soldiers fed and cared for.

As an agent for the Sanitary Commission, Mary Ann Bickerdyke ran field hospitals for General Grant's Army in Tennessee and Mississippi, then with General Sherman's Army in Chattanooga and Atlanta. She set up army laundries, foraged for food, cooked, and nursed the wounded and sick soldiers through 19 battles. She refused to be tied up with army red tape. She said that there was too much work to do to bother.

On May 30, 1862, while Mother Bickerdyke was serving at a hospital in Corinth, Mississippi, General Harry Wager Halleck was marching his troops past the hospital. Mary Ann had all the hospital's barrels of drinking water set alongside the marching route with drinking ladles. When General Halleck refused to let the men stop, she shouted in a loud rough voice, "Halt!" The troops stopped and while they were trying to figure out what happened the hospital staff gave all the troops water, bread and fresh fruit. As it turned out, this was the only food the men would have for two days. She was reprimanded for her actions but made no apology.

In June of 1863 Mary Ann was put in charge of the Gayoso Hospital in Memphis, Tennessee. The hospital was formerly the Gayoso Hotel and Mary Ann decided to make it the best, neatest, cleanest, and most comfortable hospital in Memphis.

Soon after her arrival she entered one of the wards at eleven o'clock in the morning and found badly wounded soldiers who had not been fed breakfast. After investigating, she found out that the surgeon in charge of the ward had been out on the town the night before and had slept late. He neglected to feed and tend to the men who were under his care.

She was denouncing him quite loudly when he entered the ward and asked what was wrong. She called him a miserable scoundrel and said that these wounded men were worth a thousand of him and were sick and left to starve while he was out getting drunk.

She told him to take off his shoulder straps because he wasn't going to be in the army much longer. Within 30 days he was discharged from the army. The surgeon appealed his discharge to General Sherman who patiently listened to the whole story and then replied, "Well, if it was her, I can do nothing for you. She ranks me. You will have to see Mr. Lincoln."

While she was serving as matron of the army hospital in Cairo, she noticed that

Mary Ann Ball Bickerdyke. Courtesy of the Library of Congress.

food designated for the sick and wounded was disappearing. When she complained to the chief surgeon he threw her out of his office. She decided to set a trap and catch the thief. She laced some peaches with medicine, which would make a person vomit. Soon she heard moans from the kitchen, and upon investigation she found several sick members of the hospital staff who had eaten the peaches. She then warned them that the next time she would use rat poison.

Mary Ann later caught one of the ward masters wearing clothing meant for the wounded soldiers. She made the disgraced ward master stand in front of the patients, strip down to his underwear, and return the clothing.

She had no real authority but her strong manner and determination was such that very few ever questioned her. Once when a surgeon challenged her as to who gave her authority to do what she was doing, she replied, "I have received my authority from the Lord God Almighty. Have you anything that ranks higher than that?"

She later had to challenge a military order when supplies were not getting to the wounded soldiers fast enough. General Sherman issued an order to ban rail travel. She left her duties in the field and went to see him at his headquarters. Bursting into his office unannounced, she demanded that he lift the ban so she could get needed supplies and food to the wounded and sick soldiers. She told him to have a little common sense. He looked at her and asked her if she had ever heard of insubordination. She quickly responded, "You bet I've heard of it ... it's the only way I ever get anything done in this army." General Sherman relented and signed an order allowing trains to carry food and supplies to the troops.

When General Grant headed down the Mississippi River, Mother Bickerdyke went along to set up field hospitals. She soon realized that the troops were not getting enough dairy products and without proper diets their health could be at risk. She headed back up the river to Illinois where she convinced the local farmers to donate 200 milk cows and 1,000 hens to the army. She also organized a convoy to take the animals down river to the troops near Memphis, Tennessee.

She was always searching for ways to help the sick and wounded soldiers. She was usually the last one off the battlefield at night, as she searched to see that all wounded soldiers were taken to the aid stations for treatment.

After one major battle, Major General John Alexander "Black Jack" Logan was resting in his tent when he noticed a light out on the battlefield. He had his orderly check it out and bring whoever it was to him. It was Mary Ann Bickerdyke. She was turning bodies over to make sure that anyone still alive had not been missed. General Logan was very impressed with Mary Ann and often called on her to provide for his men. He also invited her to ride by his side in the gala parade in Washington, D.C., after the war was over.

Mary Ann Bickerdyke was also active in the Underground Railroad. She would use runaway Negro slaves to help her in the hospitals and nursing stations. She would teach them and feed them in return for their help.

In early 1865 while speaking for the Sanitary Commission in a church in Brooklyn, New York, she was explaining how she had on many occasions bound the stumps of soldiers' amputated legs and arms with old rags and how there was a need for bandages. To the surprise of the congregation she then asked all the ladies in the church to stand up and pull up their dresses. She asked that they each drop one of their many petticoats so she could use them for bandages. Once they understood what she was asking, the ladies complied with the request. She filled three trunks with the petticoats and within three weeks she was using them to bandage the terrible sores of the many sick prisoners released from the Confederate prison at Andersonville, Georgia.

At the end of the war she marched at the head of General Sherman's army in a parade past the White House.

She resigned from the Sanitary Commission after the Civil War was over and devoted the rest of her life to charitable causes. She died in 1901.

Mary Ann Bickerdyke served her country with courage and dedication. Her efforts in the hospitals and on the battlefields of 19 major battles saved many soldiers from disease and death.

❧ 39 ❧

Clara Barton: Union Nurse and Humanitarian

She was the first woman to be hired for a government job in Washington, D.C., the first woman to be the head of a government agency and the first woman nurse to arrive on the Civil War battlefields. These are among the great accomplishments of Clara Barton, one of history's most extraordinary women.

Clara Barton was born on Christmas Day, 1821, in North Oxford, Massachusetts, and named Clarissa Harlow Barton. Clara was the youngest of five children in her family.

Clara was quite a gifted young woman with a knack for organization, teaching, and helping others. She began teaching at the age of 15. She taught in North Oxford for ten years and then at the Clinton Liberal Institute in Clinton, New York, for two years. She left teaching to go to Washington, D.C., and accepted a job with the U.S. Patent Office as a clerk. She was the first woman to be hired for a government job in Washington.

Clara was 39 years old and still working at the U.S. Patent Office in April 1861 when the Civil War began. After the Battle of First Manassas/Bull Run on July 21, 1861, the wounded soldiers were brought into Washington for treatment. The Senate Chambers were used as a temporary hospital. Clara began spending time away from the Patent Office helping nurse the fallen soldiers. Her superiors reprimanded her for not staying on the job in the Patent Office, but she ignored the reprimand and continued to aid the wounded soldiers. She was soon terminated for not heeding the warning. This did not bother Clara because she had discovered her true calling in life.

There were over 3,000 sick and wounded soldiers housed in the Senate building. Clara wrote a letter to the Worcester, Massachusetts, *Spy* asking for donations of food, clothing, and bandages for the wounded soldiers. The response was overwhelming and supplies began to pour in. Clara was now sure of her mission. She began writing other newspaper ads for money and supplies for the camps and battlefields around Washington, D.C. These ads were carried in most of the newspapers in the northeast.

Many different types of organizations began to send money and supplies. The responding organizations included churches, civic groups, clubs, sewing circles, and individual donors. She soon had amassed three warehouses full of goods and supplies and with the use of four borrowed army wagons she and her helpers made daily deliveries to the camps and battlefields and army hospitals around Washington, D.C.

Clara continued her nursing of the fallen soldiers and in August 1861 the U.S. Congress finally approved the use of female nurses in the army hospitals. This was five months after the war began and was the result of the large number of soldiers needing help and the desperate shortage of trained male nurses. Statistics reveal that two and one-half Union soldiers died of disease to every one who was killed in battle. The rate for the Confederacy was three soldiers died from disease to every one killed in battle. The nursing requirements during the Civil War were enormous.

In early 1862 Clara Barton decided that she would have a better chance of saving lives if she were on the battlefield. After some convincing by Clara, Surgeon General William A. Hammond approved her request to go onto the battlefields. She was supplied with an army wagon fully loaded with medical supplies and water, the first woman nurse to arrive and serve on the battlefields.

By the end of 1862 Clara Barton had been on the battlefield during some of the fiercest battles of the war including the Battle of Second Manassas/Bull Run, the Battle of Chantilly, the Battle of Antietam, and the Battle of Fredericksburg. Her untiring efforts, bravery, and dedication soon earned her the nickname "The Angel of the Battlefield."

At the Battle of Antietam she set up a nursing station in a nearby farmhouse. In addition to the nursing station she also went on to the battlefield at Antietam to help wounded soldiers. She gave them what aid they needed and helped them to the nursing station.

Clara had many close calls while on the battlefields. Her clothing would be riddled with holes from minié balls and shell fragments. On one occasion she was helping a fallen soldier at Antietam by holding him up so he could get a drink of water when a Confederate minié ball pierced her sleeve and struck the soldier she was holding. He died in her arms.

Clara continued her service to the Union soldiers throughout the war even though she was never officially attached to the U.S. Army.

On March 11, 1865, President Abraham Lincoln issued a press release for information on missing soldiers. This information was for a new government agency, which he set up, called Missing Soldiers Office. It was located on the third floor, room

Clara Barton. Courtesy of Leib Image Archives.

nine, in an office building halfway between the White House and the Capitol Building. President Lincoln appointed Clara Barton to head the office. She was the first woman to head a government agency in Washington, D.C.

The press release from President Lincoln read as follows:

March 11, 1865

To the friends of missing persons; Miss Clara Barton has kindly offered to search for the missing prisoners of war. Please address her at Annapolis, giving her the name, regiment and company of any missing prisoner.

A. Lincoln

Clara headed the office for four years. In that time she helped over 22,000 families discover the fate of their missing loved ones.

The number of missing soldiers located by Clara Barton's agency was only a small portion of those unaccounted for. By the end of the Civil War, only 172,400 Union dead were identified and their graves marked, even though there were 315,515 graves found. There were also 43,973 more deaths recorded during the war than the amount of known graves.

Some of the most valuable assistance she received while trying to locate missing prisoners of war was from a young Union corporal named Dorance Atwater of the 2nd New York Cavalry. Dorance was captured at Hagerstown, Maryland, on July 7, 1863. He was sent to Belle Island Prison in Richmond, Virginia. When the Confederacy closed Belle Island Prison and transferred all the prisoners to Camp Sumter in Andersonville, Georgia, Dorance Atwater was put in charge of the books in which a daily record of deaths were recorded.

Dorance, realizing that this information could be valuable to relatives and loved ones, decided to make a duplicate record for himself. When he was exchanged in March 1865, he took the list with him, hidden in the lining of his coat. He notified

Secretary of War Edwin Stanton and requested 30 days leave to publish the Death Register. He was called to the Secretary of War's office where Major Samuel Breck offered Dorance $300 for the list. Dorance explained that he did not want to sell it, but only wished to have it published for the benefit of the soldiers' families and friends. Major Breck then warned Dorance that he could either take the $300 or if he tried to publish the list it would be confiscated. Dorance Atwater accepted the $300 with a promise of a clerkship in the War Department and the return of his original register when the government was done with it.

While waiting for the government to publish the list, Dorance learned of Clara Barton and her work to locate missing prisoners of war. He met with her and explained the method of burial of the soldiers and showed her the second copy of the list he had made for himself.

Dorance Atwater. Courtesy of the Library of Congress.

Clara called on Commissary General of Prisons, Hoffman, and asked him to send an expedition to Andersonville, Georgia, to identify and mark the graves of the Union soldiers. The request was approved. The expedition was led by Captain James M. Moore and included two clerks, 12 carpenters, 12 letterers, and seven laborers along with Clara Barton and Dorance Atwater.

Captain Moore was not pleased that Clara Barton came along on the expedition. He did not think a woman had any place in his crew. He avoided her and Dorance as much as possible. The crew built a fence around the cemetery, reburied some of the dead whose graves were exposed, and placed wooden markers on each grave showing the name, rank, regiment, and state of the soldier.

Proper identification was made of 12,912 graves. However, on 460 of the grave markers, the statement "Unknown Union Soldier" was written.

When Clara Barton and Dorance Atwater returned to Washington, Clara contacted a friend on the *New York Tribune* staff and supplied him the list of names from Andersonville. The story and the list were then published as a supplement to the paper.

When Major Breck saw the list published he had Dorance arrested and court-martialed because he had previously warned Dorance not to publish the list. Dorance was tried by court martial and received a $300 fine, a dishonorable discharge, and 18 months in prison.

Dorance was placed in Old Capitol Prison, which was the same prison in which Confederate Captain Henry Wirz was being held. Dorance remarked that Captain Wirtz was being tried for the murder of 13,000 Union prisoners while commandant of Andersonville Prison and he was being tried for copying the burial register of those murdered men and publishing it so the families and friends could know where their loved ones are buried.

Clara Barton was quite angry when she learned of the treatment of Dorance Atwater. She began to call on all her contacts on Capitol Hill to intercede for him. She got a copy of the court martial proceedings and tried to get a new trial. Finally, after two months, Dorance Atwater was released from prison by a general presidential pardon for all persons convicted by court martial of crimes other than murder.

Because of this great service to the Union, Dorance Atwater was appointed as United States Consul to the Seychelle Islands on the coast of Africa and later U.S. Consul to Tahiti. He married a Tahitian princess and lived out his remaining life in California where he died in 1910 at the age of 65.

Clara Barton served with the International Red Cross during the Franco-Prussian War in 1870. She followed German troops into Strasbourg after the 30-day siege and remained there for six months while setting up relief programs for the sick and wounded.

In 1876, she had a nervous breakdown and was sent to a sanitarium in Dansville, New York, where she recovered over a two-year period.

She went on to organize and set up the American National Red Cross, which received official recognition of the president in late 1881. She was the president of the American Red Cross until 1904.

In 1898, at the age of 76, she went to Cuba during the Spanish American War to set up Red Cross relief on the battlefields.

Clara Barton died at her Glen Echo home outside of Washington, D.C., in 1912 at the age of 91. She had actively participated in three major wars of the 19th century. She spent her life caring for others. Her compassion, courage, and dedication rank her very high among the great women of American history. The world is indeed a better place because of her.

❧ 40 ❧

Civil War Nurses

The United States Congress approved the use of female nurses in military hospitals in August 1861. This change of policy prompted thousands of women to volunteer their services to help the sick and wounded soldiers.

Louisa May Alcott — Nurse and Author

One of these volunteers was a 30-year-old woman from Concord, Massachusetts, named Louisa May Alcott.

Louisa May Alcott felt a deep patriotic desire to help her country. She volunteered to serve as a nurse in December 1862. When she was accepted she ran home to her family and announced, "I have enlisted!" This excitement and desire for adventure would soon change as she encountered her first glimpse of the horror of war.

She was assigned to work in a Union hospital in Washington, D.C. The hospital was converted from an old musty Georgetown hotel. She arrived in Washington in early December and was assigned to oversee a 40 bed ward which had been the old hotel's ballroom.

She was proud and excited about this opportunity to serve her country. She stated that being a nurse was the next best thing to being a soldier.

Louisa May spent her first morning watching a soldier die and comforting a boy with a bullet wound through his lungs. Within a few hours, wagonloads of wounded soldiers began to arrive from the Battle of Fredericksburg. The battle raged for two days from December 11 through December 12. The hospital became overcrowded with wounded soldiers.

Being brought into such a situation from a relatively sheltered life, she was horrified and wished that she were back home in Concord. She commented, "The first thing I met was a regiment of the vilest odors that ever assailed the human nose." She carried a vial of lavender water with her to help overcome the odor as she worked on the wounded soldiers.

She soon realized that nursing was more than just treating wounds. She spent a large part of her days washing the wounded soldiers, serving them food, administering medicine, reading papers to them, writing letters for them, tending the dressings on their wounds, consoling them, and at times even singing to them. Of these duties the one she disliked the most was scrubbing the wounded and maimed with cakes of brown soap.

After serving for six months in the hospital she became very ill and was diagnosed as having typhoid pneumonia. She was taken home to Concord where she was expected to die. In time, she did recover but never regained her strength. While in the Washington hospital she was nursed by Dorothea Dix. She fondly recalled the experience of Dix, "stealing a moment from her busy life to watch over the stranger of whom she was thoughtfully tender as any mother."

During the six months she served at the hospital she wrote letters home to her family about some of the unusual and humorous incidents she encountered as a nurse. These rather amusing letters were first published in the Boston *Commonwealth* and in 1863 they were put into a book titled *Hospital Sketches*. The book was widely read and won her praise for her style of writing.

Her experiences in Washington and the experiences of so many women whose men went to war prompted her to write *Little Women*, a story about northern sisters during the Civil War. The book was a great success and won her national fame.

Mary Ashton Rice Livermore — Nurse, Teacher, Writer, and Editor

"If this war has developed some of the most brutal, bestial and devilish qualities lurking in the human race, it has also shown us how much of the angel there is in the best men and women." This comment was made by Mary Ashton Rice Livermore to describe the great generosity of the American people in their efforts to help in the Civil War by volunteering their time and their talents and donating their money and goods to the Sanitary Commission.

Mary Ashton Rice Livermore was born in 1820 and was 41 years old when the Civil War began. She was a nurse, teacher, writer, and editor in Chicago, Illinois, and has the distinction of being the only woman reporter to cover the 1860 Republican Convention.

After several ads appeared in the local newspapers requesting donations for the soldiers, people began to respond and food, clothing, and medicine began to pour in. Soon the task of control and distribution became too big to handle. Mary Livermore made an attempt to impose some order to this chaotic situation. She set up and organized the Northwestern Branch of the United States Sanitary Commission in Chicago, Illinois.

The Sanitary Commission derived its name from a British agency, which was established by Florence Nightingale during the Crimean War to improve the living conditions of the soldiers.

Mary Livermore was assigned as director of the Chicago office. Under her leadership, it delivered over 30,000 boxes of supplies to the army camps and hospitals by 1863. However, the shipping costs for this large volume of supplies had seriously depleted the Commission's operating funds. They had to find a way to raise needed funds to continue their aid to the soldiers.

Mary Livermore and her colleagues Jane Hoge and Eliza Porter devised an unusual fund raising scheme, which they called a "Sanitary Fair." When the idea was presented to the officials of the Sanitary Commission, it was laughed at but not completely turned down. The board members tolerated the idea and let the women proceed even though they expected total failure.

The women then went to work. They sent out thousands of circulars to newspapers, churches, and businesses in September 1863 announcing "A Grand North Western Fair" to be held in Chicago in October. The circular solicited donations of any item that could be sold at the fair to raise money for the Sanitary Commission.

The goal of the three women was to raise $25,000 for the Commission. Donations began to pour in and soon so many items had arrived that the Commission had to rent three huge exposition halls for the fair.

The fair opened at ten o'clock the morning of October 27, 1863, with a three-mile long parade through the streets of Chicago. The parade ended at the exposition halls. The Commission charged fairgoers a seventy-five cents entrance fee which allowed them entrance into all three halls and a meal in the dining area.

The fair ran for 14 days with an average daily attendance of over 5,000 people. The original goal was surpassed and the fair raised over $100,000 in revenue for the Commission. The officials who laughed at the plan were no longer laughing.

The idea of a Sanitary Fair spread to other major cities. They raised a combined revenue of $4,000,000 for the Commission. During the entire war it is estimated that the Sanitary Commission collected and distributed more than $25,000,000 in aid to the soldiers. This great outpouring of generosity was the great contribution made by the civilian population to the war effort.

Mary Livermore became the national director of the United States Sanitary Commission. As director she toured army camps, hospitals, and battlefields. She also lectured around the country. She wrote of her experiences in her memoir titled *My Story of the War*.

She indicated in her memoir that she encountered several extraordinary women in her tours of the army camps, battlefield, and hospitals. She mentioned several well-known vivandieres and Daughters of the Regiment such as Bridget Divers, Anna Etheridge, and Kady Brownell, who were in some of the units she visited.

In addition to these women, she encountered some women soldiers. In one account she was visiting the 19th Illinois Infantry Regiment and observing a drill by the troops, when the captain approached her and asked if she saw anything peculiar about one of the soldiers whom he pointed to. She immediately realized the soldier was a woman disguised as a man. She shared her suspicions with the captain who stated that he suspected the same.

The review was halted and the soldier was taken out of the ranks and confronted. She stated that her husband was in the regiment and it would kill her if she could not march by his side. She begged the captain to let her stay. He refused her request and she was discharged from the regiment.

Within three days she attempted suicide by jumping into the Chicago River. An alert Chicago policeman saw her jump and rescued her. She was placed in a charity home. Mary Livermore went to the home to comfort her and convince her to abandon the desire to stay in the army with her husband.

Mary could not dissuade the young woman and left with her mission unaccomplished. However, within a few days the woman had disappeared from the home. It is suspected that she intended to find her way back into the army.

Mary Livermore wrote in her memoir that it was estimated that a little less then 400 women were disguised as men and serving as soldiers. She made an incredible impact on the Civil War by her efforts to get needed supplies, medicine and clothing to the soldiers and hospitals.

Sally Louise Tompkins—Confederate Nurse

There was only one woman commissioned in the Confederate army. Her name was Sally Louise Tompkins.

She was born on November 9, 1833, at Poplar Grove, Virginia, the daughter of Christopher Tompkins, a wealthy businessman and politician. She was 28 years old when the Civil War began and had already established herself as a philanthropist and nurse.

Because her father had died prior to the beginning of the Civil War, Sally and her sister moved to Richmond with their mother. They were living in the Arlington House in Richmond when the war began. Instead of taking her wealth and fleeing to Europe to sit out the war, she felt a patriotic duty to stay in Richmond and do her part for the Confederacy.

After the Battle of First Manassas/Bull Run, a Richmond judge named John Robertson moved out of Richmond into the country. He offered his Richmond home to Sally Tompkins to use as a hospital during the war. The house was a two story home located on the northwest corner of Third and Main streets in Richmond.

Sally equipped the hospital at her own expense and converted the home into a 22-bed infirmary. On the morning of July 31, 1861, she opened the doors of the Robertson Hospital for the care of sick and wounded Confederate soldiers. She charged no fees for her services.

The Confederate government assigned six surgeons to the hospital. Sally ran the hospital with military discipline and demanded the highest standards of sanitation. The government supplied only food, medicine and other supplies for the sick and wounded soldiers, and Sally supplied every thing else at her own expense. She was the first woman in the South to support a hospital.

Being a nurse in the South was not considered to be an acceptable profession for a woman. Females were considered too delicate and weak for such work. However, many dedicated Southern women became nurses on their own, especially when the fighting came close to their homes. These women offered their homes as hospitals and assisted in the treatment of the wounded. Many other Southern women unofficially volunteered and worked in hospitals as helpers.

Since the Confederacy had not established a network of military hospitals such as the Union army had, they relied mainly on the civilian population to care for the wounded. Many private hospitals sprang up across the South and with these hospitals came abuses such as overcharging and poor care. As the problem grew, the Confederate government was forced to take over the hospitals and enact a law that soldiers would be treated in institutions under direct control of the government and managed by a commissioned officer with a rank no lower than captain.

Even though the Confederate government took over the hospitals in late 1861, it wasn't until September 1862 that the employment of women nurses in military hospitals was approved. There were no government standards set for becoming a nurse nor was there a formal training course in place. They relied on natural ability only.

The new law required that all soldiers be removed from private hospitals and moved to the military hospitals. This law put Sally Tompkins' hospital in danger of closing. While several ambulances waited at her hospital to remove the soldiers, Sally went to see President Jefferson Davis.

She asked that her hospital be made exempt from the law. She cited her good reputation and the hospital's record. She had returned more healed soldiers back to their units and had a smaller death rate than any other hospital.

President Davis was already aware of her extraordinary record, but could not overrule a law that was enacted by the Confederate Congress. Realizing that her services were vital to the Confederacy, he found a solution which would not violate the law and would keep Sally working for the Confederacy. He commissioned her a captain in the Confederate army and made her head of the hospital. She accepted the solution on the condition that her name not appear on the military payroll. She would work without pay.

On September 9, 1861, L.P. Walker, the Confederate Secretary of War, signed her commission as a Captain of Cavalry (unassigned).

The Robertson Hospital gained such a good reputation that wounded soldiers were requesting to be sent there for treatment. Many of the worst injured soldiers from the battlefields were sent to Sally Tompkins' hospital. Over the course of the entire war this 22-bed hospital treated 1,333 soldiers and only 73 died of their wounds.

The hospital closed on June 13, 1865, but Sally Tompkins continued working with the southern veterans and often spoke at veteran reunions throughout the South.

She lost her fortune when the Confederacy was defeated. She continued to work as a nurse and when her meager salary became insufficient to support her, she went to live in the Home for Confederate Women in Richmond.

The Sally Tompkins chapter of the Daughters of the Confederacy was formed in her honor. She died in Richmond, Virginia, on July 25, 1916, at the age of 83 and was buried with full military honors.

~ 41 ~

Women Doctors in
the Civil War

By the time the Civil War began, there were only a handful of women doctors in the entire country. Records indicate that as of 1858 there were only 300 women doctors who had actually graduated from a medical school as opposed to 18,000 degreed male doctors. Two of these extraordinary women served the Union army during the Civil War; they were Dr. Mary Edwards Walker and Dr. Elizabeth Blackwell.

Mary Edwards Walker — Doctor

Mary Edwards Walker was born in 1831 in Oswego, New York. Her father was a self-educated local doctor as well as a farmer. Mary was considered a non-conformist and insisted on wearing male attire. She was arrested many times for being in men's clothing but adamantly refused to give up her right to dress as she pleased. She often stated her belief that woman's clothing was too binding, heavy, and uncomfortable to the point of being unhealthy for a person to wear.

Mary Walker followed in her father's footsteps and became a doctor. In 1855, at the age of 24, she graduated from Syracuse Medical College in Syracuse, New York.

She was 29 years old when the Civil War began and her deep loyalty to the Union prompted her to go to Washington, D.C., and volunteer her services as a doctor. She felt that she would be welcomed as a volunteer since she was a degreed doctor and had been practicing medicine for almost six years in Oswego.

When she reached Washington in September 1861 she applied for a commission with the U.S. Army as a surgeon. She was met with strong opposition and was denied a commission. The only position she was offered was as a nurse. She finally went to work without pay as a nurse at the Indiana Hospital in Washington where soldiers from First Manassas/Bull Run were being cared for. She only received meals and lodging during the two months she was at the hospital. After the two months she returned home to Oswego.

In the fall of 1862 she returned to Washington and then on to Warrington, Virginia, to serve with General Ambrose Burnside's army, which was suffering from a typhoid fever epidemic. Still she was denied a commission for her services and was again working without pay.

After the typhoid epidemic was under control, she proceeded to Frederick, Virginia, to help the wounded and sick soldiers. In September 1863, she went to Chattanooga, Tennessee, to assist with the 7,500 wounded survivors of the Battle of Chickamauga.

After two years of service to the Union army she again applied for a commission and was again refused. However, this time she was appointed as a surgeon to the 52nd Ohio Volunteer Infantry Regiment, which was part of the Army of the Cumberland.

While with the 52nd Ohio Regiment she not only fulfilled her duties as a surgeon but also operated as a spy for General Sherman. She would go through the lines into Confederate territory as a doctor to assist the war-torn civilian population of the area. While on these medical missions she gathered information on Confederate troop movements and strengths and reported it to the Union army.

On April 10, 1864, her service as a spy came to an end when she went deep into Confederate territory south of Gordon's Mills, Tennessee, and was captured by a Confederate sentry.

Dr. Walker was taken to Richmond, Virginia, for trial. Upon arrival in Richmond she was greeted with hostility. Confederate Captain B.J. Simmes summed up the feelings toward her when her wrote "We were all amused and disgusted too at sight of a thing that nothing but a debased and depraved Yankee nation could produce — A Female Doctor."

Dr. Walker was kept in Castle Thunder Prison in Richmond until August 12, 1864, when she was exchanged.

After her release from prison, the U.S. Army approved her as a contract surgeon with the 52nd Ohio Regiment and paid her $432.36 for her service to the army from her assignment to the 52nd Ohio until her release from prison. However, they still refused to grant her a commission.

After the war had ended she continued her work as a contract surgeon and again requested a commission in the U.S. Army. Her request for a commission was once again denied, but the government felt that she deserved some recognition for her service to the country. This recognition would be in the form of the nation's highest medal.

On November 11, 1865, President Andrew Johnson signed a bill which awarded the Congressional Medal of Honor to Dr. Mary Edwards Walker for her service to the Union. She cherished this honor for the rest of her life. She was the only woman in the Civil War to earn the Medal of Honor.

In 1917, just two years before her death, the conditions for receiving the Congressional Medal of Honor were revised and resulted in the revocation of 910 previously awarded medals, one of which had been awarded to Dr. Walker. This injustice was later corrected in 1975 when President Jimmy Carter restored the Medal of Honor to her.

Elizabeth Blackwell — Doctor

Although Dr. Mary Walker was one of the earliest women to receive a medical degree in the United States, Dr. Elizabeth Blackwell was the first.

Elizabeth Blackwell was an Englishwoman born in 1821. In her quest to become a doctor, she applied to 25 different medical organizations before the Geneva Medical College in Geneva, New York, finally accepted her. In 1849, at the age of 28, Elizabeth Blackwell graduated from the medical college and became the first woman to receive a medical degree from an American medical school.

Dr. Blackwell helped set up the New York Infirmary for Women and Children in 1857. Her ability to organize and set up organizations was an invaluable asset in her efforts to further the medical profession in the United States. This ability was shown time and time again, especially in the first few months of the Civil War.

Dr. Blackwell was 40 years old when the Civil War began. She immediately recognized that the U.S. Army needed a system for distribution of its supplies, especially medical supplies, to the hospitals. In April 1861, she organized thousands of women from the New York area into a voluntary organization called Women's Central Relief Association. Their purpose was to collect donations from people in the New York area, particularly medical supplies, and get them to the hospitals where they were needed.

Dr. Blackwell also set up training courses for women to become nurses. The Woman's Central Relief Association approved her training program by the end of April 1861, and she began supplying trained nurses to the New York hospitals. It was only three days after Secretary of War Cameron accepted Dorothea Dix's offer of female nursing help that the Women's Central Relief Association began its operations.

The Women's Central Relief Association at this point had no official status or authority. The government also had a need to get an official distribution organization into place to provide medical supplies to its hospitals as well as provide for the staffing and management of those hospitals. The problem was resolved in July 1861 when President Lincoln established the United States Sanitary Commission. The President appointed a clergyman, Reverend Henry Bellows, as head of the Sanitary Commission instead of a medical doctor.

The Women's Central Relief Association was quickly absorbed as a major part of the Sanitary Commission. The training of women nurses for the army continued and a need for an army superintendent of nurses became evident. Both Dr. Blackwell and Dorothea Dix were in consideration for this post. The army selected Dorothea Dix for the job.

Dr. Blackwell continued her work throughout the Civil War. After the war, Elizabeth and her sister Emily founded the New York Medical College for Women. Eventually she became discouraged with the future of medicine in the United States, and in 1869 returned to England.

She became a prominent gynecologist and obstetrician in London. Dr. Blackwell also became a respected author with the publication of several books on health and education.

She died in 1910 at the age of 89. She had helped pave the way for nursing to become a socially accepted and honored profession for women. Her contributions to American medicine were enormous.

❧ 42 ❧

Women Crusaders

Many brave women, both Union and Confederate, volunteered to do their part to ease the pain and suffering of the Civil War. Many of these women distinguished themselves as nurses, humanitarians, authors, social reformers, abolitionists, organizers, and administrators. Several of these extraordinary women are discussed in this chapter, but most of the brave women who volunteered their services remain unsung heroines.

Dorothea Dix — Reformer

In April 1861 after Fort Sumter was fired upon, a reformer from Massachusetts went to Washington to organize and supply women nurses to the Union army. She was told that it was an impossible task and the government would not allow her to do it. Her name was Dorothea Lynde Dix. She was born in 1802 and was 59 years old when the Civil War began. Her grandfather was Elijah Dix, a prominent Boston physician.

Even though Dorothea Dix was not a nurse, she was well known as a social reformer. She crusaded for the better treatment of the insane and had helped establish many state hospitals for their care and treatment. She began her crusade for the insane in 1840 when she wrote a very influential document about the treatment of the insane and presented it to the Massachusetts legislature.

During the 1850s she visited Florence Nightingale and toured hospitals throughout Europe and the Crimea. She returned well qualified for her future service to the army.

Dorothea was told that her reason for going to Washington, D.C., in April 1861 was a waste of time, as the government only used male nurses in military hospitals. To overcome this opposition she hastily organized 75 women nurses and made a protest march in Washington, demanding that the government allow women nurses to help care for the wounded and sick Union soldiers.

The government relented and Secretary of War Simon Cameron accepted Dorothea Dix's offer of help. He appointed her as Army Superintendent of Nurses. Her duties were to assist in organizing army hospitals, recruiting nurses, and supplying nurses to the surgeons as needed. The Surgeon General ordered that at least 30 percent of all hospital jobs would be staffed with women. This was to quell the surgeons' opposition to having women nurses.

Dorothea Dix established very strict rules for hiring nurses. Applicants had to be plain in appearance and at least 30 years old. Applicants with hoop skirts were rejected, jewelry was not acceptable, and no one with romantic ideas about hospital work would be accepted. These harsh rules were short-lived because after the Battle of First Manassas/Bull Run the need became so great that she began to accept anyone who was willing to work.

She also established strict rules for those nurses who were initially hired. Women nurses would not be allowed to reside in the camps or accompany regiments on the march. Those who applied for nursing service and were highly accredited were required to have certificates from two physicians and two clergymen of good standing, and forward the certificates to Dorothea Dix who would then return a certificate accrediting them for service in any military hospital in the United States. These strict rules were also short-lived.

As the war proceeded and the amount of sick and wounded began to rise dramatically, many other women and organizations as well as the army nursing corps helped. These other women's groups included soldiers' wives, vivandieres, local women from the areas of battle, and the U.S. Sanitary Commission.

After the war, on September 1, 1865, Dorothea Dix resigned as Superintendent of Nurses. However, at her own expense she continued to work for another 18 months helping individual soldiers and their families deal with the stress of recovering from the war.

Dorothea Dix spent the next 15 years working for better treatment of the mentally ill. She retired in 1882 at the age of 80. She died in 1887 at the age of 85.

She did not want to be remembered for her Civil War years, but her service to the Union was invaluable and she was duly honored in 1985 when she was featured on a special United State postage stamp.

Harriet Beecher Stowe —
Abolitionist and Author

President Lincoln referred to Harriet Beecher Stowe as the little lady who caused the Civil War.

Harriet Beecher Stowe was born in Connecticut. Her father was a minister and her mother died when Harriet was only four years old. The Beecher family was prosperous and well thought of in the community. They had several Negro servants to take care of the home and the children.

In 1832 the family moved to Cincinnati, Ohio, where Harriet's father accepted a position as head of a new theological seminary. Harriet married the school's professor of biblical literature, Mr. Calvin Stowe, in 1836.

Harriet and her husband raised six children over the next 14 years. In 1849, their infant son died of cholera. After the loss of her own son, she stated she began to understand the suffering of slave mothers forcibly separated from their children.

Harriet and her husband moved to Maine in 1850 where he took a position at Bowdoin College. Because Calvin's health was not good, Harriet began to worry that some time in the future they may find themselves without an income. To compensate for this potential problem, she began writing to earn extra money and hopefully gain financial independence.

Her first effort was a collection of short articles entitled *The Mayflower*, which was not successful. She was not deterred by this initial setback and continued to write.

Harriet became emotionally inspired by the Fugitive Slave Act of 1850. This new law, which was written by Senator James M. Mason of Virginia, allowed slave owners the right to seek runaway human property in any state or territory. No warrant was required to retrieve human property and a third party could be used to capture the runaways.

Harriet began composing a set of four episodes of a story called *Uncle Tom's Cabin, or Life Among the Lowly*. The editors of the anti-slavery magazine *National Era* in Washington began printing the episodes one at a time. The story was such a success that readers demanded more episodes. She ended up writing 45 episodes over the next 10 months.

The complete novel *Uncle Tom's Cabin* was published in Boston, Massachusetts, in 1852 and was an instant success. It sold over one million copies in the first year and was translated into over a dozen different languages. The book had a great influence on the abolitionist movement and rallied millions to the cause. The characters— Uncle Tom, Simon Legree, Little Eva, and Eliza — soon became household names.

As a potential abolitionist weapon the book inspired the nation and huge financial donations began to pour in for the anti-slavery movement. The book was a best seller in the North. The hard line Southerners called it a "filthy Negro novel."

Publication of the book made Harriet Beecher Stowe an international celebrity, an honor she used to raise large sums of money for the anti-slavery movement. *Uncle Tom's Cabin* was published at a time when the nation was already divided over the issue of slavery. The dispute was more than a question of whether slavery was right or wrong; it was also over the control of the destiny of the nation as it continued to grow and new states were being added. Both sides of the issue argued when new states such as Missouri, Texas, Kansas, and Nebraska were being accepted into the union whether they would be free or slave states.

Those arguing in favor of slavery were the minority of Southerners yet were very influential. By 1850 only 25 percent of Southern whites had slaves. These slave-holders were mostly wealthy farmers who considered slavery a means of gaining wealth as well as a status symbol. They supported slavery with the excuse that abolition would destroy the Southern way of life.

Harriet Beecher Stowe had a great influence on the way society thought about slavery. When President Lincoln called her into the White House after the Civil War began, he commented as he was introduced to her, "So you are the little woman who wrote a book that started this big war."

She was later invited to Washington when President Lincoln signed the Emancipation Proclamation. Once it was signed those attending the celebration began to chant "Harriet Beecher Stowe." She stood up and accepted her applause.

Julia Ward Howe — Author and Social Reformer

Her desire to help in the war effort and the fact that she thought she had nothing to offer troubled Julia Ward Howe. However, she used her talent for writing prose and poetry to arouse patriotism and instill confidence and hope into the many battle-weary soldiers and Union prisoners of war. Her song "The Battle Hymn of the Republic" was a great contribution to the war effort.

Julia Ward Howe was born in New York City in 1819 and was the daughter of a prominent New York banker. She was a writer, lecturer, reformer, abolitionist and an advocate of women's suffrage. She married Dr. Samuel Gridley Howe, who was 17 years her senior. He was born 1802 and was a prominent Boston philanthropist and abolitionist.

Julia and her husband edited the abolitionist newspaper *Commonwealth*. She was the first woman to be elected to the American Academy of Arts and Letters.

Early in the war she was visiting Washington, D.C., and arranged for a trip across the Potomac to visit one of the Union army camps. While she was visiting a battle began. As the Confederates advanced toward the camp, she and her party were forced to go back to Washington. During her visit to the camp she had noticed soldiers singing the song "John Brown's Body." On the way back to Washington she began to sing some of the lyrics when one of her companions asked her, "Why don't you write more suitable words to that song?"

While staying at the Willard Hotel in Washington that night she again heard a column of Union soldiers singing "John Brown's Body" as they passed by the hotel. She awoke early the next morning and while still half-asleep, she lay in bed and began to change the words to the song. She forced herself out of bed to jot down the lyrics lest she fall asleep again and forget them.

She went back to sleep and when she woke she found that she had written a very nice poem which required very few changes. That day she showed the poem to Massachusetts's governor John A. Andrew, who was with her on her tour of some of the army camps in and around Washington. The governor encouraged her to publish the poem. She found only one publisher who was interested and she sold the poem for $4 to *The Atlantic Monthly* magazine.

The poem appeared in print in 1862 at the time when the Western Campaign was getting underway and General Grant was preparing his assault on forts Henry and Donelson. The poem was published and sheet music was also printed and made available. It was an instant success and became very popular with the troops as they marched.

The song instilled patriotism, confidence, and spirit into the battle-weary soldiers. It also was sung by the prisoners of war at Andersonville and Libby Prisons, and gave the mistreated and weak prisoners a ray of hope and determination to survive.

Julia Ward Howe, with her gift for writing poetry, made an incredible contribution to the war effort. "The Battle Hymn of the Republic" became the Union's theme song and aroused patriotism and confidence among the soldiers.

Julia Ward Howe died in 1910 at the age of 91.

Bibliography

Women POWs at Andersonville Prison

Bowman, John S. *Encyclopedia of the Civil War*. pp. 9, 25, 106. Greenwich, Connecticut: Brompton Books Corp., 1992.

Catton, Bruce, and the editors of American Heritage. *The American Heritage Picture History of the Civil War*. pp. 500–505. New York: American Heritage Publishing Co., 1960.

Denney, Robert F. *Civil War Prisons and Escapes*. p. 187. New York: Sterling Publishing Co., 1993.

Hesseltine, William B. *Civil War Prisons*. pp. 9–32. Kent, Ohio: Kent State University Press, 1997.

Kerr, Dr. W. J. "Sad Ending of a Wedding Trip." *Confederate Veteran*. Vol. XXIII. No. 7. p. 318. Nashville, Tennessee: The Confederate Veteran Co., July 1915.

Leonard, Elizabeth D. *All the Daring of the Soldier*. p. 216. New York: W. W. Norton and Co., 1999.

National Park Service Staff. Andersonville National Historic Site. Andersonville, Georgia, 1999.

Robertson, James I., Jr. and the editors of Time-Life Books. "The Prisoners Plight." pp. 117–119, 122, 129–135. *The Civil War: Tenting Tonight: The Soldier's Life*, Alexandria, Virginia: Time-Life Books, 1984.

Sheppard, Peggy. *Andersonville, Georgia. U. S. A.* p. 4. Andersonville, Georgia: Sheppard Publications, 1998.

Times staff. "A Woman Soldier of the North." *The New York Times*. New York: The New York Times Corp., May 27, 1934.

Sarah Rosetta Wakeman

Burgess, Lauren Cook. *An Uncommon Soldier*. New York: Oxford University Press, 1994.

Dyer, Frederick H. *A Compendium of the War of the Rebellion*. Part 3. p. 1462. Regimental Histories, New York Volunteers 153rd Infantry Regiment. The Civil War CD-ROM. Carmel, Indiana: Guild Press of Indiana, Inc., 1997.

Leonard, Elizabeth D. *All the Daring of the Soldier*. pp. 191–197. New York: W.W. Norton and Co., 1999.

Morning Herald staff. "History of the 153rd Regiment, New York State Volunteers." *Fonda New York Morning Herald*. Fonda, New York, September 17, 1914.

National Archives. RG No. 94. *Records of the Adjutant General's Office. 1780–1917: Compiled Military Service Records*. Pvt. Lyons Wakeman. Company G, Co. H. 153rd New York Infantry. Washington, D.C.

_____. RG No. 94. *Carded Medical Records: Volunteers Mexican and Civil Wars 1846–1865*. Card #3, Medical Record of Pvt. Lyons Wakeman, Company H, 153rd New York Infantry. National Archives. Washington, D. C.

Jennie Hodgers

Bailey, H. Woody. "Woman Hid Her Gender for Years." Pontiac, Illinois: *The Daily Leader*, April 29, 1985.

Burgess, Lauren Cook. *An Uncommon Solider*. p. 70. New York: Oxford University Press, 1994.

Chang, Ina. *A Separate Battle*. p. 49. New York: Lodestar Books, 1991.

Chicago Tribune staff. "2 Women Fought as Soldiers: One in '76, One in '61." Chicago, Illinois: *Chicago Daily Tribune*, April 6, 1923.

Clausius, Gerhard P. "The Little Soldier of the 95th: Albert D. J. Cashier." pp. 380–387. Springfield, Illinois: *Journal of The Illinois State Historical Society*. Vol. LI. Number 4, Winter 1958.

Conklin, Mike. "Jennie." Section 5. pp. 1, 5. *Chicago Tribune*. Chicago, Illinois. Chicago Tribune Corp., September 5, 2001.

Daily Leader staff. "Historical Society Hears Civil War Soldier Story." *The Daily Leader*, Pontiac, Illinois, March 15, 1996.

Davis, Rodney O. "Private Albert Cashier: As Regarded by His/Her Comrades." pp. 109–112. Springfield, Illinois: *Journal of The Illinois State Historical Society*. Vol. 87. No.7, Summer, 1989.

Dyer, Frederick H. *A Compendium of the War of the Rebellion*. Part 3. p. 1087. Regimental Histories, Illinois Volunteers 95th Infantry Regiment. The Civil War CD-ROM. Carmel, Indiana: Guild Press of Indiana, Inc., 1997.

Flick, Mary Ann. "Civil War Veteran's Sex a 48-year Secret." *The Pantagraph*. Bloomington, Illinois, August 17, 1981.

Hall, Richard D. *Patriots in Disguise: Women Warriors of the Civil War*. pp. 20–26. New York: Paragon House, 1993.

Leonard, Elizabeth D. *All the Daring of the Soldier*. pp. 185–191. New York: W.W. Norton and Co., 1999.

Lowry, Thomas P., MD. *The Story the Soldiers Wouldn't Tell*. p. 121. Mechanicsburg, Pennsylvania: Stackpole Books, 1994.

National Archives. RG No. 15. *Records of the Veteran's Administration: Civil War Pension Application Files*. File No. C-2, 573248. Pvt. Albert D. J. Cashier, Company G, 95th Illinois Infantry. Washington, D.C.

_____. *Records of the Adjutant General's Office 1780–1917: Compiled Military Service Records*. Pvt. Albert D. J. Cashier, 95th Illinois Infantry. Washington, D.C.

Parker, Tony. "Woman Civil War Vet Honored." *The Pantagraph*. Bloomington, Illinois, January 3, 1996. *Pantagraph*. Bloomington, Illinois, January 3, 1996.

Robertson, James I., Jr., and the editors of Time-Life Books. "Women Who Wore The Blue and the Gray." p. 27. *The Civil War: Tenting Tonight: The Soldier's Life*. Alexandria, Virginia: Time-Life Books, 1984.

Rokker, W. H. *Illinois in the War for the Union*. pp. 530–532. Springfield and Chicago, Illinois: Publishing House of W. H. Rokker, 1887.

Star staff. "Posed as a Man for 60 Years." *Washington Star*. Washington, D. C: March 29, 1913.

Wheelwright, Julie. *Amazons and Military Maids: Women Who Dressed as Men in the Pursuit of Life, Liberty and Happiness*. pp. 140–141. London: Pandora Press, 1989.

Wood, Wales W., Esq. *History of the 95th Regiment Illinois Infantry Volunteers*. p. 226. Chicago: Tribune Company Book and Job Printing Office, 1865.

Sarah Emma Evelyn Edmonds

Botkin, B. A. *A Civil War Treasury of Tales Legends and Folklore*. pp. 130–133. New York: Random House, 1960.

Bowman, John S. *Encyclopedia of the Civil War*. p. 72. Greenwich, Connecticut: Brompton Books Corp., 1992.

Brown, Ida C. "Michigan Men in the Civil War." pp. 70, 74. *Michigan Historical Collections. Bulletin No. 27*. Ann Arbor, Michigan: The University of Michigan, September 1977.

Chang, Ina. *A Separate Battle: Women and*

the Civil War. pp. 51, 54, 56. New York: Lodestar Books, 1991.

Conklin, E. F. *Women at Gettysburg 1863.* pp. 135–136. Gettysburg, Pennsylvania: Thomas Publications, 1993.

Dannett, Sylvia D. L. *She Rode with the Generals: The True and Incredible Story of Sarah Emma Seelye, Alias Franklin Thompson.* New York: Thomas Nelson and Son, 1960.

Davis, Burke. *The Civil War: Strange and Fascinating Facts.* pp. 148–149. New York: The Fairfax Press, 1982.

Dyer, Frederick H. *A Compendium of the War of the Rebellion.* Part 3. p. 1282. Regimental Histories. Michigan Volunteers 2nd Infantry Regiment. The Civil War CD-ROM. Carmel, Indiana: Guild Press of Indiana, Inc., 1997.

Edmonds, Sarah Emma. *Nurse and Spy in the Union Army.* Hartford, Connecticut: W. S. Williams and Co., 1865.

Fladeland, Betty. "Alias Frank Thompson." pp. 435–462. *Michigan History Vol. 42*, 1958.

Hall, Richard. *Patriots in Disguise: Women Warriors of the Civil War.* pp. 46–97. New York: Paragon House, 1993.

Lannan, Charles. *The Red Book of Michigan: A Civil, Military and Biographical History.* pp. 194, 316–317. Detroit, Michigan: E. B. Smith and Co., 1871.

Leonard, Elizabeth D. *All the Daring of the Soldier.* pp. 170–185. New York: W. W. Norton and Company, 1999.

Lowry, Thomas P., M.D. *The Story the Soldiers Wouldn't Tell.* pp. 82,119–120. Mechanicsburg: Stockpole Books, 1994.

Markle, Donald E. *Spies and Spymasters of the Civil War.* pp. 175–179. New York: Hippocrene Books, 1994.

McCracken, Lawrence. "Thrilling Civil War Story of Girl Spy Revealed at Last; Novel Heroine Actually Lived." p. 12. *The Detroit Free Press.* Detroit, Michigan, October 6, 1935.

National Archives. *Official Records of the Union and Confederate Armies (1860–1901)* Series II. Volume 8. p. 992. Washington, D.C.

_____. RG 15. *Records of the Veteran's Administration. Sara Edmonds Seelye Pension File.* Application No. 526889. Certificate No. SC282.136. Washington, D.C.

_____. RG 94. *Records of the Adjutant General's Office.* Compiled Military Service Records. *Pvt. Franklin Thompson.* Washington, D.C.

Robertson, James I., Jr., and the editors of Time-Life Books. "Women Who Wore The Blue and The Gray." p. 27. *The Civil War: Tenting Tonight: The Soldier's Life.* Alexandria, Virginia: Time-Life Books, 1984.

Robertson, John. *Michigan in the War, 1861–1865.* pp. 30–37. Lansing, Michigan: W. S. George and Co., 1883.

Schneider, Frederick, Col. "Sarah Emma Edmonds-Seeley (Alias Franklin Thompson) The Female Soldier; of the Second Michigan Veteran Volunteer Infantry." p. 7. *The State Republican.* Lansing, Michigan: June 19 and 26, 1900.

Stern, Philip Van Doren. *Secret Missions of the Civil War.* pp. 121–129. New York: Bonanza Books, 1990.

Loreta Janeta Velazquez

Bowman, John S. *Encyclopedia of the Civil War.* pp. 107, 171. Greenwich, Connecticut: Brompton Books Corp., 1992.

Chang, Ina. *A Separate Battle: Women and the Civil War.* pp. 49–53. New York: Lodestar Books, 1991.

Conklin, E. F. *Women at Gettysburg 1863.* pp. 135–137. Gettysburg, Pennsylvania: Thomas Publications, 1993.

Davis, Burke. *The Civil War: Strange and Fascinating Facts.* p. 239. New York:The Fairfax Press, 1982.

Hall, Richard. *Patriots in Disguise: Women Warriors of the Civil War.* p. 107. New York: Paragon House, 1993.

Hoffert, Sylvia D. "Madame Loretta [sic] Velazquez; Heroine or Hoaxer." pp. 24–26. *Civil War Times Illustrated.* Vol. XVII. No. 3. Harrisburg, Pennsylvania, June, 1978.

Larson, Rebecca D. *Blue and Gray Roses of Intrigue.* pp. 46–48. Gettysburg, Pennsylvania: Thomas Publications, 1993.

Leonard, Elizabeth D. *All the Daring of the Soldier.* pp. 252–263. New York: W. W. Norton and Co., 1999.

Lowry, Thomas P., M.D. *The Story the Soldiers Wouldn't Tell.* pp. 120–121. Mechanicsburg, Pennsylvania: Stockpole Books, 1944.

Markle, Donald E. *Spies and Spymasters in the Civil War.* p. 213. New York: Hippocrene Books, 1994.

Massey, Mary Elizabeth. *Bonnet Brigades.* pp. 82–84, 195, 310. New York: A.A. Knopf, 1966.

_____. *Women in the Civil War.* pp. 82–84, 195, 310. Lincoln, Nebraska: University of Nebraska Press Bison Books, 1994.

National Archives. *Official Records.* Series II. Vol. 8. p. 936. Washington, D.C.

_____. RG 110. *Provost Marshall General's Bureau List of Scouts, Guides, Spies, and Detectives.* Box 6. Washington, D.C.

Picayune staff. "Venezuela Colonization Program." *New Orleans Daily Picayune.* New Orleans, Louisiana, January 5, 1867.

Schultz, Jane Ellen. *Women at the Front: Gender and Genre in Literature of the American Civil War.* pp. 305–306. Ann Arbor, Michigan: University of Michigan, 1988.

Velazquez, Loreta. *The Woman in Battle: A Narrative of the Exploits, Adventures, and Travels of Madame Loreta Janita Velazquez.* Hartford, Connecticut: T. Belknap, 1876.

Waugh, Charles G., and Martin H. Greenberg. *The Woman's War in the South: Recollections and Reflections of the American Civil War.* pp. 167–210. Nashville, Tennessee: Cumberland House Publishing Inc., 1999.

Worthington, C. J. *The Woman in Battle: A Narrative of the Exploits, Adventures, and Travels of Madame Loreta Janita Velazquez.* Hartford, Connecticut: Belknap 1876. (Reprint) New York: Arno Press, 1972.

Frances Louisa Clayton

Bowman, John S. *The Civil War Day by Day.* pp. 91, 94. Greenwich, Connecticut: Brompton Books, 1991.

_____. *Encyclopedia of the Civil War.* p. 164. Greenwich, Connecticut: Brompton Books, 1992.

Chang, Ina. *A Separate Battle: Women and the Civil War.* p. 46. New York: Lodestar Books, 1991.

Commager, Henry Steele. *Illustrated History of the Civil War.* p. 168. New York: Promontory Press, 1976.

Dyer, Frederick H. *A Compendium of the War of the Rebellion.* Part 3. p. 1295. Regimental Histories. Minnesota Volunteers 2nd Independent Battery Light Artillery. The Civil War CD-ROM. Carmel, Indiana: Guild Press of Indiana, Inc., 1997.

Eagle staff. "Eventful History of a Soldier Woman." *Grand Rapids Eagle.* Grand Rapids, Michigan, November 19, 1863.

Foenander, Terry. "Eventful History of a Soldier Woman." p. 9. *Civil War News.* Toowoomba, QLD, Australia: Harrison Printing Co., 2000.

Hall, Richard. *Patriots in Disguise; Women Warriors of the Civil War.* pp. 27–28, 198. New York: Paragon House, 1993.

Leonard, Elizabeth D. *All the Daring of the Soldier.* pp. 212–214. New York: W.W. Norton and Co., 1999.

Picayune staff. "Eventful History of a Soldier Woman." *New Orleans Daily Picayune.* New Orleans, Louisiana, Sunday, November 22, 1863.

Robertson, James I., Jr., and the editors of Time-Life Books. "Women Who Wore the Blue and the Gray." p. 27. *The Civil War: Tenting Tonight: The Soldier's Life.* Alexandria, Virginia: Time-Life Books, 1984.

Frances Hook

Chronicle staff. "Another Female Soldier." p. 1. *Daily Morning Chronicle.* Washington, D. C, March 1, 1864.

Dyer, Frederick H. *A Compendium of the War of the Rebellion.* Part 3. p. 1048. Regimental Histories. Illinois Volunteers 11th Infantry Regiment. The Civil War CD-ROM. Carmel, Indiana: Guild Press of Indiana, Inc., 1997.

Ibid. p. 1060. 33rd Infantry Regiment.

Ibid. p. 1084. 90th Infantry Regiment.

Foenander, Terry. "Another Female Soldier. p. 11. "*Civil War News.* Toowoomba, QLD, Australia: Harrison Printing Co. Pty. Ltd., 2000.

Ibid. "A Gallant Female Soldier - Romantic Story." p. 12.

Leonard, Elizabeth D. *All the Daring of the Soldier.* pp. 216–217. New York: W. W. Norton and Co., 1999.

Thompson, Charles Willis. "Women Who

Fought as Soldiers." Section 7. *The New York Times*. New York: The New York Times Corp., April 4, 1915.

Tribune staff. "A Gallant Female Soldier — Romantic History." p. 1. *The New York Daily Tribune*. New York, March 18, 1864.

Charlotte Hatfield

Bowman, John S. *The Civil War Day by Day*. p. 182. Greenwich, Connecticut: Brompton Books, 1991.

_____. *Encyclopedia of the Civil War*. p. 180. Greenwich, Connecticut: Brompton Books, 1992.

Brown, D. Alexander. "The Battle of Westport." pp. 4–11, 40–43. Harrisburg, Pennsylvania: Primedia History Group, July 1996.

Dyer, Frederick H. *A Compendium of the War of the Rebellion*. Part 3. p. 1160. Regimental Histories Iowa Volunteers 3rd Cavalry Regiment. The Civil War CD-ROM. Carmel, Indiana: Guild Press of Indiana, 1997.

Hall, Richard. *Patriots in Disguise: Women Warriors of the Civil War*. pp. 167–177. New York: Paragon House, 1993.

Mazzulla, Fred W., and William Kostka. *Mountain Charley or the Adventures of Mrs. E. J. Guerin, who was Thirteen Years in Male Attire*. Norman, Oklahoma: University of Oklahoma Press, 1968.

Sarah Malinda Pritchard Blalock

Hall, Richard. *Patriots in Disguise: Women Warriors of the Civil War*. pp. 102–103, 197, 203. New York: Paragon House, 1993.

Leonard, Elizabeth D. *All the Daring of the Soldier*. pp. 217–219. New York: W. W. Norton and Co., 1999.

Lowry, Thomas P., M.D. *The Story the Soldiers Wouldn't Tell*. p. 122. Mechanicsburg, Pennsylvania: Stockpole Books, 1994.

Massey, Mary Elizabeth. *Bonnet Brigades*. p. 81. New York: A. A. Knopf, 1966.

_____. *Women in the Civil War*. p. 81. Lincoln, Nebraska: University of Nebraska Press Bison Books, 1994.

National Archives. RG 94. *Records of the Adjutant General's Office*. Record and Pension Office Document File #184934. Washington, D.C.

Ibid. RG 109. *War Department Collection of Confederate Records*. Compiled Military Service Records. Washington, D.C.

Stevens, Peter F. *Rebels in Blue: The Story of Keith and Malinda Blalock*. Dallas, Texas: Taylor Publishing Co., 2000.

Waugh, Charles G., and Martin H. Greenberg. *The Women's War in the South: Recollections and Reflections of the American Civil War*. p. x. Nashville, Tennessee: Cumberland House, 1999.

Fannie Wilson and Nellie Graves

Chang, Ina. *A Separate Battle: Women and the Civil War*. p. 49. New York: Lodestar Books, 1991.

Chronicle staff. "Adventures of a Long Island Girl." *Daily Morning Chronicle*. Washington, D.C, Saturday, August 13, 1864.

Dyer, Frederick H. *A Compendium of the War of the Rebellion*. Part 3. p. 1363. Regimental Histories. New Jersey Volunteers 24th Infantry Regiment. The Civil War CD-ROM. Carmel, Indiana: Guild Press of Indiana, Inc., 1997.

Ibid. Part 3. p. 1022. Regimental Histories. Illinois Volunteers 3rd Illinois Cavalry Regiment.

Foenander, Terry. *Civil War News*. pp. 15–16. Toowoomba, QLD, Australia: Harrison Printing Co. Pty. Ltd., 2000.

Hall, Richard. *Patriots in Disguise: Women Warriors of the Civil War*. pp. 161, 200. New York: Paragon House, 1993.

Leonard, Elizabeth D. *All the Daring of the Soldier*. p. 212. New York: W. W. Norton and Co., 1999.

Massey, Mary Elizabeth. *Bonnet Brigades*. p. 81. New York: A. A. Knopf, 1966.

_____. *Women in the Civil War*. p. 81. Lincoln, Nebraska: University of Nebraska Press Bison Books, 1994.

Memphis Times staff. "Adventures of a Long Island Girl." *The Memphis Tennessee Times*. Memphis, Tennessee: August 5, 1864.

Amy Clarke

Chang, Ina. *A Separate Battle*. p. 49. New York: Lodestar Books, 1991.

City Gazette staff. "Woman in the Confederate Ranks." *The Cairo, Illinois, City Gazette*. Cairo, Illinois, December 25, 1862.

Foenander, Terry. *Civil War News*. pp. 4–5. Toowoomba, QLD, Australia: Harrison Printing Co. Pty. Ltd., 2000.

Hall, Richard. *Patriots in Disguise: Women Warriors of the Civil War*. pp. 6–8, 99–100, 197, 203. New York: Paragon House, 1993.

Leonard, Elizabeth D. *All the Daring of the Soldier*. pp. 213–215. New York: W. W. Norton and Co., 1999.

Lowry, Thomas P., M.D. *The Story the Soldiers Wouldn't Tell*. pp. 122. Mechanicsburg, Pennsylvania: Stockpole Books, 1994.

Massey, Mary Elizabeth. *Bonnet Brigades*. pp. 81. New York: A. A. Knopf, 1966.

_____. *Women in the Civil War*. p. 81. Lincoln, Nebraska: University of Nebraska Press Bison Books, 1994.

Mississippian staff. "Woman in the Confederate Ranks, A Strange Eventful Story." *The Jackson Mississippian*. Jackson, Mississippi, December 30, 1862.

Philadelphia Inquirer staff. "Women in the Confederate Ranks, A Strange Eventful Story." *The Philadelphia Inquirer*, Philadelphia, Pennsylvania, January 24, 1863.

Picayune staff. "Woman in the Confederate Ranks." *The New Orleans Daily Picayune*. New Orleans, Louisiana, Sunday, January 25, 1863.

Frank Martin

Brown, Ida C. "Michigan Men in the Civil War." pp. 70, 74. *Michigan Historical Collections. Bulletin No. 27*. Ann Arbor, Michigan: The University of Michigan, September 1977.

Dyer, Frederick H. *A Compendium of the War of the Rebellion*. Part 3. p. 1285. Regimental Histories. Michigan Volunteers 8th Infantry Regiment. The Civil War CD-ROM. Carmel, Indiana: Guild Press of Indiana, Inc., 1997.

Ibid. p. 1292. Regimental Histories. Michigan Volunteers 25th Infantry Regiment.

Ibid. p. 1637. Regimental Histories. Tennessee Volunteers 2nd Cavalry Regiment.

Foenander, Terry. *Civil War News*. pp. 6–7. Toowoomba, QLD, Australia: Harrison Printing Co. Pty. Ltd., 2000.

Hall, Richard. *Patriots in Disguise: Women Warriors of the Civil War*. pp. 26–27. New York: Paragon House, 1993.

Journal staff. "The Story of a Female Soldier: How Women Join the Army." *The Louisville Journal*. Louisville, Kentucky, May 29, 1863.

Picayune staff. "The Story of a Female Soldier: How Women Join the Army." *The New Orleans Daily Picayune*. New Orleans, Louisiana, May 24, 1863.

Woodruff, Charles. "Letter from Charles Woodruff 25th Michigan Infantry." David O. Woodruff Collection. Ann Arbor, Michigan: Bentley Historical Library. University of Michigan, May 1, 1863.

Lizzie Compton

Bowman, John S. *Encyclopedia of the Civil War*. p. 190. Greenwich, Connecticut: Brompton Books Corp., 1992.

Chronicle staff. "Lizzie Compton, the Soldier Girl." p. 1. *Daily Morning Chronicle*. Washington, D.C., Wednesday, February 24, 1864.

Foenander, Terry. *Civil War News*. pp. 9–10. Toowoomba, QLD, Australia: Harrison Printing Co. Pty. Ltd., 2000.

Hall, Richard. *Patriots in Disguise: Women Warriors of the Civil War*. pp. 161, 198, 202. New York: Paragon House, 1993.

Leonard, Elizabeth D. *All the Daring of the Soldier*. p. 224. New York: W. W. Norton and Co., 1999.

Massey, Mary Elizabeth. *Bonnet Brigades*. p. 80. New York: A. A. Knopf, 1966.

_____. *Women in the Civil War*. p. 80. Lincoln, Nebraska: University of Nebraska Press Bison Books, 1994.

Union staff. "Lizzie Compton, the Soldier Girl." *Rochester Union*. Rochester, New York, February 21, 1864.

Charles H. Williams

Dyer, Frederick H. *A Compendium of the*

War of the Rebellion. Part 3. p. 1165. Regimental Histories. Iowa Volunteers 2nd Infantry Regiment. The Civil War CD-ROM. Carmel, Indiana: Guild Press of Indiana, Inc., 1997.

Foenander, Terry. *Civil War News.* pp. 1–2. Toowoomba, QLD, Australia: Harrison Printing Co. Pty. Ltd., 2000.

Hall, Richard. *Patriots in Disguise: Women Warriors of the Civil War.* p. 201. New York: Paragon House, 1993.

Republican staff. "An Iowa Girl Discovered in Soldier's Costume. Romantic Story." *The St. Louis Republican.* St. Louis, Missouri, August 1861.

Tribune staff. "An Iowa Girl Discovered in Soldier's Costume. Romantic Story." *New York Daily Tribune,* New York, September 1, 1861. (Reprint)

Marian McKenzie

Dyer, Frederick H. *A Compendium of the War of the Rebellion.* Part 3. p. 1207. Regimental Histories. Kentucky Volunteers 23rd Infantry Regiment. The Civil War CD-ROM. Carmel, Indiana: Guild Press of Indiana, Inc., 1997.

Ibid. Part 3. p. 1537. Regimental Histories. Ohio Volunteers 92nd Infantry Regiment. The Civil War CD-ROM. Carmel, Indiana: Guild Press of Indiana, Inc., 1997.

Ibid. Part 3. p. 1499. Regimental Histories. Ohio Volunteers 8th Infantry Regiment. The Civil War CD-ROM. Carmel, Indiana: Guild Press of Indiana, Inc., 1997.

Foenander, Terry. *Civil War News.* p. 4. Toowoomba, QLD. Australia: Harrison Printing Co. 2000.

Leonard, Elizabeth D. *All the Daring of the Soldier.* pp. 242–244. New York: W. W. Norton and Co., 1999.

National Archives. *Official Records of the Union and Confederate Armies in the War of the Rebellion.* Series II, Vol.5. pp. 121–122, 155, 166, 547–548. Union correspondence, orders, etc. relating to prisoners of war and state from December 1, 1862 to June 10, 1863. Washington, D.C.

Times staff. Article. p. 3. *New York Times.* New York: The New York Times Corp., Sunday, January 25, 1863.

Molly and Mary Bell

Hall, Richard. *Patriots in Disguise: Women Warriors of the Civil War.* pp. 103, 198, 203. New York: Paragon House, 1993.

Leonard, Elizabeth D. *All the Daring of the Soldier.* pp. 243–245. New York: W. W. Norton and Co., 1999.

Lowry, Thomas P., M.D. *The Story the Soldiers Wouldn't Tell.* p. 33. Mechanicsburg, Pennsylvania: Stockpole Books, 1994.

Massey, Mary Elizabeth. *Bonnet Brigades.* pp. 84–85. New York: A. A. Knopf, 1966.

_____. *Women in the Civil War.* pp. 84–85. Lincoln, Nebraska: University of Nebraska Press Bison Books, 1994.

Richmond Daily Examiner staff. *The Richmond Daily Examiner.* Richmond, Virginia: October 31, 1864 and November 25, 1864.

Waugh, Charles G., and Martin H. Greenberg. *The Woman's War in the South: Recollections and Reflections of the American Civil War.* pp. 299–302. Nashville, Tennessee: Cumberland House, 1999.

Notable Women Soldiers

HENRIETTA SPENCER

Dyer, Frederick H. *A Compendium of the War of the Rebellion.* Part 3. p. 1478. Regimental Histories. Ohio Volunteers 10th Regiment Cavalry. The Civil War CD-ROM. Carmel, Indiana: Guild Press of Indiana, Inc., 1997.

Foenander, Terry. *Civil War News.* p. 4. Toowoomba, QLD, Australia: Harrison Printing Co. Pty. Ltd., 2000.

Times staff. "A Girl Soldier." *The New York Times.* New York: The New York Times Corp., Saturday, January 24, 1863.

HATTY ROBINSON

Dyer, Frederick H. *A Compendium of the War of the Rebellion.* Part 3. p. 1589. Regimental Histories. Pennsylvania Volunteers 46th Infantry Regiment. The Civil War CD-ROM. Carmel, Indiana: Guild Press of Indiana, Inc., 1997.

Foenander, Terry. *Civil War News.* p. 2. Toowoomba, QLD, Australia: Harrison Printing Co. Pty. Ltd., 2000.

Hall, Richard. *Patriots in Disguise: Women Warriors of the Civil War*. p. 203. New York: Paragon House, 1993.

Times staff. "Another Female Soldier." [Our Baltimore Correspondence. Baltimore, Maryland, Sunday, October 6, 1861.] *The New York Times*. New York: The New York Times Corp., October 9, 1861.

LOUISA HOFFMAN

Chronicle staff. "A Woman Soldier." *Daily Morning Chronicle*. Washington, D.C., Saturday, August 26, 1864. (Reprint)

Dyer, Frederick H. *A Compendium of the War of the Rebellion*. Part 3. p. 1496. Regimental Histories. Ohio Volunteers 1st Infantry Regiment. The Civil War CD-ROM. Carmel, Indiana: Guild Press of Indiana, Inc., 1997.

Ibid. A Compendium of the War of the Rebellion. Part 3. p. 1643. Regimental Histories. Tennessee Volunteers 1st Regiment Infantry. The Civil War CD-ROM. Carmel, Indiana: Guild Press of Indiana, Inc., 1997.

Foenander, Terry. *Civil War News*. p. 16. Toowoomba, QLD, Australia: Harrison Printing Co. Pty. Ltd., 2000.

Nashville Press staff. "A Woman Soldier." *The Nashville Press*. Nashville, Tennessee, August 23, 1864.

ELIZABETH A. NILES

Dyer, Frederick H. *A Compendium of the War of the Rebellion*. Part 3. p. 1358. Regimental Histories. New Jersey Volunteers 4th Infantry Regiment. The Civil War CD-ROM. Carmel, Indiana: Guild Press of Indiana, Inc., 1997.

Farmers Advocate staff. *Farmers Advocate*. Charleston, West Virginia, July 30, 1898.

Hall, Richard. *Patriots in Disguise: Women Warriors of the Civil War*. p. 199. New York: Paragon House, 1993.

Leonard, Elizabeth D. *All the Daring of the Soldier*. p. 224. New York: W. W. Norton and Co., 1999.

Lowry, Thomas P., MD. *The Story the Soldiers Wouldn't Tell*. pp. 121–122. Mechanicsburg, Pennsylvania: Stockpole Books, 1994.

National Archives. RG 94. *Administrative Precedent File* #3H36. Washington, D.C.

Schultz, Jane Ellen. *Women at the Front: Gender and Genre in Literature of the American Civil War*. p. 292. Ann Arbor, Michigan: University of Michigan, 1988.

Times staff. "Woman who fought in the Civil War beside Hubby Dies, Age Ninety two." Section 7. *The New York Times*. New York: The New York Times Corp., April 4, 1915.

MARY SEABERRY

Dyer, Frederick H. *A Compendium of the War of the Rebellion*. Part 3. p. 1521. Regimental Histories. Ohio Volunteers 52nd Infantry Regiment. The Civil War CD-ROM. Carmel, Indiana: Guild Press of Indiana, 1997.

Hall, Richard. *Patriots in Disguise: Women Warriors of the Civil War*. pp. 199–203. New York: Paragon House, 1993.

Leonard, Elizabeth D. *All the Daring of the Soldier*. p. 210. New York: W. W. Norton and Co., 1999.

PRIVATE CHARLEY

Bowman, John S. *Encyclopedia of the Civil War*. p. 99. Greenwich, Connecticut: Brompton Books Corp., 1992.

Cairo News staff. "Tragic Finale of a War Romance." *The Cairo News*. Cairo, Illinois, April 15, 1863.

Conklin, E. F. *Women at Gettysburg 1863*. p. 136. Gettysburg, Pennsylvania: Thomas Publications, 1993.

Dyer, Frederick H. *A Compendium of the War of the Rebellion*. Part 3. p. 1171. Regimental Histories, Iowa Volunteers 14th Infantry Regiment. The Civil War CD-ROM. Carmel, Indiana: Guild Press of Indiana, Inc., 1997.

Foenander, Terry. *Civil War News*. pp. 5–6. Toowoomba, QLD, Australia: Harrison Printing Co., 2000.

Picayune staff. "Tragic Finale of a War Romance." *Daily Picayune*. New Orleans, Louisiana, May 8, 1863.

MARY OWENS JENKINS

Dyer, Frederick H. *A Compendium of the War of the Rebellion*. Part 3. p. 1563. Regimental Histories. Pennsylvania Volunteers 9th Regiment Cavalry. (92nd Volunteers) ("Lochiel Cavalry.") The Civil War CD-ROM. Carmel, Indiana: Guild Press of Indiana, Inc., 1997.

Hall, Richard. *Patriots in Disguise: Women Warriors of the Civil War*. pp. 199, 203. New York: Paragon House, 1993.

Ingraham, Betty. "And of Mary Owen(s) Jenkins." p. 7. *Civil War Times Illustrated*. Harrisburg, Pennsylvania: Primedia, Inc., June 1959.

Leonard, Elizabeth D. *All the Daring of the Soldier*. pp. 222–223. New York: W. W. Norton and Co., 1999.

Lowry, Thomas P., M.D. *The Story the Soldiers Wouldn't Tell*. p. 121. Mechanicsburg, Pennsylvania: Stockpole Books, 1994.

Massey, Mary Elizabeth. *Bonnet Brigades*. p. 80. New York: A. A. Knopf, 1966.

_____. *Women in the Civil War*. p. 80. Lincoln, Nebraska: University of Nebraska Press Bison Books, 1994.

National Archives. RG No. 94. "Served by Her Lover's Side." *Administrative Precedent File #3H36*. Washington, D.C.

Schultz, Jane Ellen. *Women at the Front: Gender and Genre in Literature of the Civil War*. p. 290. Ann Arbor, Michigan: University of Michigan, 1988.

Times staff. "Women Who Fought as Soldiers." Section 7. *The New York Times*. New York: The New York Times Corp., April 4, 1915.

FRANCES DAY

Dyer, Frederick H. *A Compendium of the War of the Rebellion*. Part 3. p. 1614. Regimental Histories. Pennsylvania Volunteers 126th Infantry Regiment. The Civil War CD-ROM. Carmel, Indiana: Guild Press of Indiana, Inc., 1997.

Hall, Richard. *Patriots in Disguise: Women Warriors of the Civil War*. pp. 198, 203. New York: Paragon House, 1993.

Leonard, Elizabeth D. *All the Daring of the Soldier*. pp. 220–221. New York: W. W. Norton and Co., 1999.

National Archives. *Records of the Adjutant General's Office 1780–1917: Compiled Military Service Records*. Military Service Record of Sgt. Frank Mayne, 126th Pennsylvania Infantry Regiment. Washington, D.C.

MARY ELLEN WISE

Chronicle staff. "The Brave Soldier." *Daily Morning Chronicle*. Washington, D.C., September 30, 1864.

Dyer, Frederick H. *A Compendium of the War of the Rebellion*. Part 3. p. 1132. Regimental Histories. Indiana Volunteers 34th Regiment Infantry. The Civil War CD-ROM. Carmel, Indiana: Guild Press of Indiana, Inc., 1997.

Foenander, Terry. *Civil War News*. p. 16. Toowoomba, QLD, Australia: Harrison Printing Co. Pty. Ltd., 2000.

Hall, Richard. *Patriots in Disguise: Women Warriors of the Civil War*. pp. 200–201. New York: Paragon House, 1993.

Herald staff. "Female Private." *New York Herald*. New York, August 14, 1864.

Leonard, Elizabeth D. *All the Daring of the Soldier*. p. 212. New York: W. W. Norton and Co., 1999.

Massey, Mary Elizabeth. *Bonnet Brigades*. p. 80. New York: A. A. Knopf, 1966.

_____. *Women in the Civil War*. p. 80. Lincoln, Nebraska: University of Nebraska Press Bison Books, 1994.

Times staff. "Women Who Fought as Soldiers." Section 7. *The New York Times*. New York: The New York Times Corp., April 4, 1915.

Elizabeth Van Lew

Bowman, John S. *Encyclopedia of the Civil War*. p. 171. Greenwich, Connecticut: Brompton Books Corp., 1992.

Chang, Ina. *A Separate Battle: Women and the Civil War*. p. 57. New York:Lodestar Books, 1991.

Civil War Times staff. "Federal Spies in Richmond." *Civil War Times Illustrated*. Harrisburg, Pennsylvania: Primedia Publications, February 4, 1965.

Eicher, David J. *Civil War Battlefields*. p. 136. Dallas, Texas: Taylor Publishing Co., 1995.

Hesseltine, William. *Civil War Prisons*. pp. 60–79. Kent, Ohio: The Kent State University Press, 1997.

Kane, Harnett Thomas. *Spies for the Blue and Gray*. pp. 231–249. New York, New York: Doubleday, 1954.

Larson, Rebecca D. *Blue and Gray Roses of*

Intrigue. pp. 21–27. Gettysburg, Pennsylvania: Thomas Publications, 1993

Leonard, Elizabeth D. *All the Daring of the Soldier.* pp. 50–57. New York: W. W. Norton and Co., 1999.

Markle, Donald E. *Spies and Spymasters of the Civil War.* pp. 18–19, 58,179–186.New York: Hippocrene Books, 1994.

Massey, Mary Elizabeth. *Bonnet Brigades.* pp. 87, 89, 101–102, 343. New York: A. A. Knopf, 1966.

_____. *Women in the Civil War.* pp. 87, 89, 101–102, 343. Lincoln, Nebraska: University of Nebraska Press Bison Books, 1994.

Ryan, David J. *A Yankee Spy in Richmond: The Civil War Diary of "Crazy Bet" Van Lew.* Mechanicsburg, Pennsylvania: Stockpole Books, 1996.

Sun staff. "The Big Breakout from Libby Prison." p. 17. *The Baltimore Sun Magazine.* Baltimore, Maryland: *The Baltimore Sun,* July 1, 1960.

Time-Life Books editors. "The General's Network." pp. 86–89. *The Civil War: Spies, Scouts, and Raiders: Irregular Operations.* Alexandria, Virginia: Time-Life Books, 1985.

Times staff. "Famous Secret Service Agents." Section 7. *The New York Times.* New York: The New York Times Corp., April 4, 1915.

Ibid. "Reported Escape of One Hundred and Nine Union Officers." *The New York Times.* New York: The New York Times Corp., February 15, 1864,

Vandiver, Frank E. *1001 Things Everyone Should Know About the Civil War.* p. 247. New York: Random House, 1999.

Rose O'Neal Greenhow

Bakeless, John. *Spies of the Confederacy.* pp. 28–63. Philadelphia, Pennsylvania: J. B. Lippincott Company, 1970.

Bowman, John S. *Encyclopedia of the Civil War.* pp. 93, 110. Greenwich,Connecticut: Brompton Books, 1992.

Chang, Ina. *A Separate Battle: Women and the Civil War.* pp. 57–59. New York: Lodestar Books, 1991.

Cochran, Hamilton. *Blockade Runners of the Confederacy.* pp. 133–142. New York: The Bobbs-Merrill Co., Inc., 1958.

Davis, Burke. *The Civil War: Strange and Fascinating Facts.* pp. 104, 146–147. New York: The Fairfax Press, 1982.

Duke University Online Archival Collection. "Rose O'Neal Greenhow Papers." Special Collections Library Duke University. *HTTP://scriptiorium.lib.duke.edu/greenhow/.*

Garrison, Webb. *A Treasury of Civil War Tales.* pp. 80–83. New York: Ballantine Books, 1988.

Greenhow, Rose. *My Imprisonment, or the First Year of Abolition Rule in Washington.* London, England: Richard Bentley and Son, 1863.

Kane, Harnett Thomas. *Spies for the Blue and Gray.* pp. 17–67. New York, New York: Doubleday, 1954.

Larson, Rebecca. *Blue and Grey — Roses of Intrigue.* pp. 7–12. Gettysburg,Pennsylvania: Thomas Publications, 1993.

Leonard, Elizabeth D. *All the Daring of the Soldier.* pp. 35–44. New York: W. W. Norton and Co., 1999.

Markle, Donald E. *Spies and Spymasters of the Civil War.* pp. 19–20, 159–164. New York: Hippocrene Books, 1994.

Massey, Mary Elizabeth. *Bonnet Brigades.* pp. 88, 90–93. New York: A. A. Knopf, 1966.

_____, *Women in the Civil War.* pp. 88, 90–93. Lincoln, Nebraska: University of Nebraska Press Bison Books, 1994.

Stern, Philip Van Doren. *Secret Missions of the Civil War.* pp. 54–64. New York: Bonanza Books, 1990.

Time-Life Books editors. "Currents of Conspiracy." pp. 23–32. *The Civil War: Spies, Scouts and Raiders: Irregular Operations.* Alexandria, Virginia: Time-Life Books, 1985.

Times staff. *"Famous Secret Service Agents."* Section 7. *The New York Times.* New York: The New York Times Corp., April 4, 1915.

Vandiver, Frank E. *1001 Things Everyone Should Know About the Civil War.* pp. 230, 256. New York: Random House, 1999.

Waugh, Charles G., and Martin H. Greenberg. *The Woman's War in the South. Recollections and Reflections of the American Civil War.* pp. 31–51. Nashville, Tennessee: Cumberland House Publishing, Inc., 1999.

Maria Isabella Boyd

Bakeless, John. *Spies for the Confederacy.* pp.

141–181. Philadelphia, Pennsylvania: J.B. Lippincott Company, 1970.

Botkin, B. A. *A Civil War Treasury of Tales, Legends and Folklore.* pp. 137–139. New York: Random House, 1960.

Bowman, John S. *The Civil War Almanac.* p. 315. New York: Gallery Books, 1983.

_____. *Encyclopedia of the Civil War.* p. 29. Greenwich, Connecticut: Brompton Press Corp, 1992.

Boyd, Maria Isabella. *Belle Boyd in Camp and Prison.* Baton Rouge, Louisiana: Louisiana State University Press, 1998.

Catton, Bruce, and editors of American Heritage. *The American Heritage Picture History of the Civil War.* p. 494. New York: American Heritage Publishing Co., 1960.

Chang, Ina. *A Separate Battle: Women and the Civil War.* pp. 57–61. New York: Lodestar Books, 1991.

Cochran, Hamilton. *Blockade Runners of the Confederacy.* pp. 142–153. New York: The Bobbs-Merrill Co. Inc., 1958.

Conklin, E. F. *Women at Gettysburg 1863.* pp. 4–5. Gettysburg, Pennsylvania: Thomas Publications, 1993.

Davis, Burke. *The Civil War: Strange and Fascinating Facts.* pp. 147–148. New York: The Fairfax Press, 1982.

Davis, Curtis Carroll. *Belle Boyd: In Camp and Prison.* Cranbury, New Jersey: Thomas Yoseloff Publishing, 1968.

Kane, Harnett Thomas. *Spies for the Blue and Gray.* pp. 129–155. New York, New York: Doubleday, 1954.

Larson, Rebecca D. *Blue and Gray Roses of Intrigue.* pp. 17–20. Gettysburg, Pennsylvania: Thomas Publications, 1993.

Leonard, Elizabeth D. *All the Daring of the Soldier.* pp. 25–35. New York: W. W. Norton and Co., 1999.

Markle, Donald E. *Spies and Spymasters of the Civil War.* pp. 155–159. New York: Hippocrene Books, 1994.

Massey, Mary Elizabeth. *Bonnet Brigades.* pp. 96–98. New York: A. A. Knopf, 1966.

_____. *Women in the Civil War.* pp. 96–98. Lincoln, Nebraska: University of Nebraska Press Bison Books, 1994.

Scarborough, Ruth. *Belle Boyd: Siren of the South.* Macon, Georgia: Mercer University Press, 1983.

Stern, Philip Van Doren. *Secret Missions of the Civil War.* pp. 96–107. New York: Bonanza Books, 1990.

Time-Life Books editors. "The Siren of the Shenandoah." pp. 48–49. *The Civil War: Spies, Scouts and Raiders: Irregular Operations.* Alexandria, Virginia: Time-Life Books, 1985.

Times staff. "Famous Secret Service Agents." Section 7. *The New York Times.* New York: The New York Times Corp., April 4, 1915.

Vandiver, Frank E. *1001 Things Everyone Should Know About the Civil War.* p. 247. New York: Random House, 1999.

Antonia Ford

Bakeless, John. *Spies of the Confederacy.* pp. 24–25, 61–62. Philadelphia, Pennsylvania: J.B. Lippincott Company, 1970.

Baker, L.C. *History of the United States Secret Service.* pp. 168–173, 384. Philadelphia, Pennsylvania: L. C. Baker, 1867.

Davis, Burke. *The Civil War: Strange and Fascinating Facts.* pp. 149–150. New York: The Fairfax Press, 1982.

_____. *JEB Stuart: The Last Cavalier.* pp. 71, 188. New York: Rinehart and Co. Inc., 1957.

Kane, Harnett Thomas. *Spies for the Blue and Gray.* pp. 169–175. New York, New York: Doubleday, 1954.

Larson, Rebecca D. *Blue and Gray Roses of Intrigue.* pp. 13–16. Gettysburg, Pennsylvania: Thomas Publications, 1993.

Leonard, Elizabeth D. *All the Daring of the Soldier.* pp. 45–50, 62, 231–232. New York: W. W. Norton and Co., 1999.

Markle, Donald E. *Spies and Spymasters of the Civil War.* pp. 167–168, 200. New York: Hippocrene Books, 1994.

Massey, Mary Elizabeth. *Bonnet Brigades.* pp. 98–99. New York: A. A. Knopf, 1966.

_____. *Women in the Civil War.* pp. 98–99. Lincoln, Nebraska: University of Nebraska Press Bison Books, 1994.

Ramage, James A. *Grey Ghost.* pp. 67–69. Louisville, Kentucky: The University Press of Kentucky, 1999.

Russell, Charles E. *Memoirs of Colonel John Mosby.* pp. 168–200. Boston, Massachusetts. n.p., 1917.

Times staff. "News of the Day: The Rebellion." *The New York Times*, New York: The New York Times Corp., March 18, 1863.

Charlotte and Virginia Moon

Kane, Harnett Thomas. *Spies for the Blue and Gray*. pp. 263–267. New York, New York: Doubleday, 1954.

Larson, Rebecca D. *Blue and Gray Roses of Intrigue*. pp. 41–45. Gettysburg, Pennsylvania: Thomas Publications, 1993.

Leonard, Elizabeth D. *All the Daring of the Soldier*. pp. 66–67. New York: W. W. Norton, 1999.

Markle, Donald E. *Spies and Spymasters of the Civil War*. pp. 167–170, 207. New York: Hippocrene Books, 1994.

Massey, Mary Elizabeth. *Bonnet Brigades*. p. 29. New York: A. A. Knopf, 1966.

_____. *Women in the Civil War*. p. 29. Lincoln, Nebraska: University of Nebraska Press Bison Books, 1994.

Olivia Floyd

Kinchen, Oscar A. *Women Who Spied for the Blue and the Gray*. p. 27. Philadelphia, Pennsylvania: Dorrance, 1972.

Larson, Rebecca D. *Blue and Gray Roses of Intrigue*. p. 57–58. Gettysburg, Pennsylvania: Thomas Publications, 1993.

Leonard, Elizabeth D. *All the Daring of the Soldier*. pp. 67–68. New York: W. W. Norton and Co., 1999.

National Archives. *Official Records*. Ser. 2. Vol. 4. [S# 117] p. 698. National Archives. Washington, D.C.

Times staff. "Olivia Floyd Dead." *The New York Times*. New York: The New York Times Corp., December 12, 1905.

Mrs. E.H. Baker

Bakeless, John. *Spies of the Confederacy*. pp. 89–125. Philadelphia, Pennsylvania: J.B. Lippincott Company, 1970.

Kane, Harnett Thomas. *Spies for the Blue and Gray*. pp. 71–74. New York, New York: Doubleday, 1954.

Larson, Rebecca D. *Blue and Gray Roses of Intrigue*. p. 61. Gettysburg, Pennsylvania: Thomas Publications, 1993.

Markle, Donald E. *Spies and Spymasters of the Civil War*. pp. 171–173, 193. New York: Hippocrene Books, 1994.

Rebecca Wright

Bakeless, John. *Spies of the Confederacy*. p. 131. Philadelphia, Pennsylvania: J.B. Lippincott Company, 1970.

Bowman, John S. *The Civil War Day by Day*. p. 178. Greenwich, Connecticut: Brompton Books Corp., 1991.

_____. *Encyclopedia of the Civil War*. pp. 184–188. Greenwich, Connecticut: Brompton Books Corp., 1992.

Catton, Bruce, and the editors of American Heritage. *The American Heritage Picture History of the Civil War*. pp. 538–541. New York: American Heritage Publishing Co., 1960.

Civil War Times staff. "The Loyal Girl of Winchester." p. 15. Vol. II, #3. *The Civil War Times*. Gettysburg, Pennsylvania: E. J. Stockpole Publishing, June, 1960.

Larson, Rebecca D. *Blue and Gray Roses of Intrigue*. pp. 53–56. Gettysburg, Pennsylvania: Thomas Publications, 1993

Leonard, Elizabeth D. *All the Daring of the Soldier*. pp. 69–70. New York:W. W. Norton and Co., 1999.

Lewis, Thomas A., and the editors of Time-Life Books. The Civil War: *The Shenandoah in Flames: The Valley Campaign of 1864*. p. 113. Alexandria, Virginia: Time-Life Books, 1987.

Markle, Donald E. *Spies and Spymasters of the Civil War*. p. 189. New York: Hippocrene Books, 1994.

Massey, Mary Elizabeth. *Bonnet Brigades*. pp. 103, 135. New York: A. A. Knopf, 1966.

_____. *Women in the Civil War*. pp. 103, 135. Lincoln, Nebraska: University of Nebraska Press Bison Books, 1994.

Notable Women Spies

HATTIE LAWTON

Baker, Lafayette. *History of the U.S. Secret Service*. p. 617, Philadelphia, Pennsylvania: L.C. Baker, 1867.

Kane, Harnett Thomas. *Spies for the Blue and Gray*. pp. 100–108. New York, New York: Doubleday, 1954.

Larson, Rebecca D. *Blue and Gray Roses of Intrigue*. pp. 59–60. Gettysburg, Pennsylvania: Thomas Publications, 1993.

Markle, Donald E. *Spies and Spymasters of the Civil War*. pp. 187–189. New York: Hippocrene Books, 1994.

Time-Life Books editors. "Currents of Conspiracy." pp. 29. *The Civil War. Spies, Scouts and Raiders: Irregular Operations*. Alexandria, Virginia: Time-Life Books, 1985.

MARY ELIZABETH BOWSER

Chang, Ina. *A Separate Battle: Women and the Civil War*. p. 57. New York: Lodestar Books, 1991.

Kane, Harnett Thomas. *Spies for the Blue and Gray*. p. 239. New York, New York: Doubleday, 1954.

Larson, Rebecca D. *Blue and Gray Roses of Intrigue*. pp. 21–24. Gettysburg, Pennsylvania: Thomas Publications, 1993.

Leonard, Elizabeth D. *All the Daring of the Soldier*. pp. 54–55, 66. New York: W. W. Norton and Co., 1999.

Markle, Donald E. *Spies and Spymasters of the Civil War*. pp. 58, 183, 194. New York: Hippocrene Books, 1994.

Time-Life Books editors. "The General's Network." p. 88. *The Civil War. Spies, Scouts and Raiders: Irregular Operations*. Alexandria, Virginia: Time-Life Books, 1985.

Harriet Tubman

Botkin, B.A. *A Civil War Treasury of Tales, Legends and Folklore*. pp. 149–151. New York: Random House, 1960.

Bowman, John S. *The Civil War Almanac*. p. 387. New York: Gallery Books, 1983.

_____. *Encyclopedia of the Civil War*. p. 168. Greenwich, Connecticut: Brompton Books Corp., 1992.

Bradford, Sarah. *Scenes in the Life of Harriet Tubman*. pp. 38–42. Auburn, New York: W. J. Moses Printer, 1869.

Chang, Ina. *A Separate Battle: Women and the Civil War*. pp. 12–13, 55–57, 74–75. New York: Lodestar Books, 1991.

Davis, William C., and the editors of Time-Life Books. "One Nation, Divisible." p. 68. *The Civil War: Brother Against Brother: The War Begins*. Alexandria, Virginia: Time-Life books, 1983.

Hall, Richard. *Patriots in Disguise: Women Warriors of the Civil War*. pp. 164–166. 200. New York: Paragon House, 1993.

Leonard, Elizabeth D. *All the Daring of the Soldier*. pp. 70–71, 83. New York: W.W. Norton and Co., 1999.

Markle, Donald E. *Spies and Spymasters of the Civil War*. pp. 58–59, 213. New York: Hippocrene Books, 1994.

Massey, Mary Elizabeth. *Bonnet Brigades*. pp. 269–270. New York: A. A. Knopf, 1966.

_____. *Women in the Civil War*. pp. 269–270. Lincoln: Nebraska. University of Nebraska Press Bison Books, 1994.

Stein, Alice P. " The North's Unsung Sisters of Mercy." p. 44. *America's Civil War*. Leesburg Virginia: Primedia Special Interest Publications, September, 1999.

Pauline Cushman

Bowman, John S. *Encyclopedia of the Civil War*. p. 65. Greenwich, Connecticut: Brompton Books Corp., 1992.

Chronicle staff. "The Female Federal Scout." *Daily Morning Chronicle*. Washington, D.C., May 28, 1864. (Reprint)

Detroit Tribune staff. "The Female Federal Scout." *The Detroit Tribune*. Detroit, Michigan: The Detroit Tribune Co., May 25, 1864.

Foenander, Terry. *Civil War News*. pp. 13–14. Toowoomba, QLD, Australia: Harrison Printing Co. Pty. Ltd., 2000.

Kane, Harnett Thomas. *Spies for the Blue and Gray*. pp. 177–191. New York, New York: Doubleday, 1954.

Larson, Rebecca D. *Blue and Gray Roses of Intrigue*. pp. 31–33. Gettysburg, Pennsylvania: Thomas Publications, 1993

Leonard, Elizabeth D. *All the Daring of the Soldier*. pp. 57–63. New York: W. W. Norton and Co., 1999.

Markle, Donald E. *Spies and Spymasters of the Civil War*. pp. 173–175, 198, 215. New York: Hippocrene Books, 1994.

Massey, Mary Elizabeth. *Bonnet Brigades*. pp. 102–103. New York: A. A. Knopf, 1966.

_____. *Women in the Civil War*. pp. 102–103. Lincoln, Nebraska: University of Nebraska Press Bison Books, 1994.

Moore, Frank. *Women of the War*. pp. 170–175. Hartford, Connecticut: S. S. Scranton and Co., 1867.

Times staff. "Famous Secret Service Agents." Section 7. *The New York Times*. New York: The New York Times Corp., April 4, 1915.

Kady Brownell

Botkin, B. A. *A Civil War Treasury of Tales, Legends, and Folklore.* pp. 130–133, 137–139. New York: Random House, 1960.

Bowman, John S. *Encyclopedia of the Civil War.* p. 32. Greenwich, Connecticut: Brompton Books, 1989.

Chang, Ina. *A Separate Battle: Women and the Civil War.* p. 49. New York: Lodestar Books, 1991.

Dyer, Frederick H. *A Compendium of the War of the Rebellion.* Part 3. p. 1634. Regimental Histories. Rhode Island Volunteers 1st Infantry Regiment. The Civil War CD-ROM. Carmel, Indiana: Guild Press of Indiana, Inc., 1997.

Ibid. Part 3. p. 1635. Regimental Histories. Rhode Island Volunteers 5th Infantry Regiment. The Civil War CD-ROM. Carmel, Indiana: Guild Press of Indiana, Inc., 1997.

Hall, Richard. *Patriots in Disguise: Women Warriors of the Civil War.* pp. 4–6. New York: Paragon House, 1993.

Leonard, Elizabeth D. *All the Daring of the Soldier.* pp. 113–121. New York: W. W. Norton and Co., 1999.

_____. *Yankee Women.* p. 173. New York: W. W. Norton and Company, 1994.

Massey, Mary Elizabeth. *Bonnet Brigades.* pp. 69–70. New York: A. A. Knopf, 1966.

_____. *Women in the Civil War.* pp. 69–70. Lincoln, Nebraska: University of Nebraska Press Bison Books, 1994.

Moore. Frank. *Women of the War.* pp. 54–64. Hartford, Connecticut: S. S. Scranton and Co., 1867.

Anna Blair Etheridge

Bowman, John S. *Encyclopedia of the Civil War.* p. 73. Greenwich, Connecticut: Brompton Books Corp., 1992.

Brockett, L.P., and Mary Vaughan. *Woman's Work in the Civil War: A Record of Heroism, Patriotism and Patience.* pp. 749–753. Philadelphia: Ziegler, McCurdy Co., 1867.

Conklin, E. F. *Women at Gettysburg 1863.* pp. 93–104. Gettysburg, Pennsylvania: Thomas Publications, 1993.

Chronicle staff. "The Vivandiere again." *Daily Morning Chronicle.* Washington, D.C., Monday, May 30, 1864.

Dyer, Frederick H. *A Compendium of the War of the Rebellion.* Part 3. p. 1281. Regimental Histories. Michigan Volunteers 2nd Infantry Regiment. The Civil War CD-ROM. Carmel, Indiana: Guild Press of Indiana, 1997.

Ibid. Part 3. p. 1282. Regimental Histories. Michigan Volunteers 3rd Infantry Regiment.

Ibid. Part 3. p. 1283. Regimental Histories. Michigan Volunteers 5th Infantry Regiment.

Foenander, Terry. *Civil War News.* p. 14. Toowoomba, QLD, Australia: Harrison Printing Co. Pty. Ltd., 2000.

Hall, Richard. *Patriots in Disguise: Women Warriors of the Civil War.* pp. 33–45. New York: Paragon House, 1993.

Leonard, Elizabeth D. *All the Daring of the Soldier.* pp. 106–113. New York: W. W. Norton and Co., 1999.

_____. *Yankee Women.* pp. 173–175. New York: W. W. Norton and Co., 1999.

Millbrook, Minnie Dubbs. "Michigan Women Who Went to War." p. 22. *Michigan Women in the Civil War.* Michigan Civil War Centennial Observance Commission, 1963.

Moore, Frank. *Woman of the War.* pp. 513–518. Hartford, Connecticut: S.S. Scranton and Co., 1867.

Marie Tepe

Conklin, E. F. *Women at Gettysburg 1863.* pp. 105–110. Gettysburg, Pennsylvania: Thomas Publications, 1993.

Goolrick, William K., and the editors of Time-Life Books. "French Mary's Wartime Odyssey." p. 70. *The Civil War: Rebels Resurgent: Fredericksburg to Chancellorsville.* Alexandria, Virginia: Time-Life Books, 1985.

Hall, Richard. *Patriots in Disguise: Women Warriors of the Civil War.* pp. 6–8, 199, 203. New York: Paragon House, 1993.

Leonard, Elizabeth D. *All the Daring of the Soldier.* pp. 150–151. New York: W. W. Norton and Co., 1999.

Notable Daughters of the Regiment

BRIDGET DIVERS

Bowman, John S. *Encyclopedia of the Civil*

War. p. 168. Greenwich, Connecticut: Brompton Books Corp., 1992.

Conklin, E. F. *Women at Gettysburg 1863*. pp. 138–144. Gettysburg, Pennsylvania: Thomas Publications, 1993.

Davis, Burke. *The Civil War: Strange and Fascinating Facts*. p. 144. New York: The Fairfax Press, 1982.

Dyer, Frederick H. *A Compendium of the War of the Rebellion*. Part 3. p. 1269. Regimental Histories. Michigan Volunteers 1st Cavalry Regiment. 2nd Infantry Regiment. The Civil War CD-ROM. Carmel, Indiana: Guild Press of Indiana, Inc., 1997.

Hall, Richard. *Patriots in Disguise: Women Warriors of the Civil War*. pp. 28–32, 98, 199, 202. New York: Paragon House, 1993.

Leonard, Elizabeth D. *All the Daring of the Soldier*. pp. 121–125, 130, 132. New York: W. W. Norton and Co., 1999.

_____. *Yankee Women*. pp. 173–175. New York: W. W. Norton and Company, 1994.

Massey, Mary Elizabeth. *Bonnet Brigades*. pp. 70, 78, 85. New York: A. A. Knopf, 1966.

_____. *Women in the Civil War*. pp. 70, 78, 85. Lincoln, Nebraska: University of Nebraska Press Bison Books, 1994.

Moore, Frank. *Women of the War*. pp. 109–112. Hartford, Connecticut: S. S. Scranton and Co., 1867.

BELLE REYNOLDS

Dyer, Frederick H. *A Compendium of the War of the Rebellion*. Part 3. p. 1052. Regimental Histories. Illinois Volunteers 17th Infantry Regiment. The Civil War CD-ROM. Carmel, Indiana: Guild Press of Indiana, Inc., 1997.

Hall, Richard. *Patriots in Disguise: Women Warriors of the Civil War*. pp. 6–8, 8–12, 199. New York: Paragon House, 1993.

Leonard, Elizabeth D. *All the Daring of the Soldier*. pp. 125–131. New York: W. W. Norton and Co., 1999.

Massey, Mary Elizabeth. *Bonnet Brigades*. pp. 69, 353. New York: A. A. Knopf, 1966.

_____. *Women in the Civil War*. pp. 69, 353. Lincoln, Nebraska: University of Nebraska Press Bison Books, 1994.

Moore, Frank. *Women of the War*. pp. 254, 277. Hartford, Connecticut: S. S. Scranton and Co., 1867.

Emma Sansom

Botkin, B. A. *A Civil War Treasury of Tales Legends and Folklore*. p. 255. New York: Random House, 1960.

Bowman, John S. *Encyclopedia of the Civil War*. p. 76. Greenwich, Connecticut: Brompton Books Corp., 1992.

Massey, Mary Elizabeth. *Bonnet Brigades*. p. 104. New York: A. A. Knopf, 1966.

_____. *Women in the Civil War*. p. 104. Lincoln, Nebraska: University of Nebraska Press Bison Books, 1994.

Vandiver, Frank E. *1001 Things Everyone Should Know About the Civil War*. p. 153. New York: Random House, 1999.

Waugh, Charles G., and Martin H. Greenberg. *The Woman's War in the South: Recollections and Reflections of the American Civil War*. pp. 119–126. Nashville, Tennessee: Cumberland House Publications, Inc., 1999.

Anna Ella Carroll

Blackwell, Sarah E. *A Military Genius: The Life of Anna Ella Carroll*. 2 Volumes. Washington, D.C., (1891–1895)

Bowman, John S. *The Civil War Almanac*. pp. 321–322. New York: Gallery Books, 1983.

_____. *Encyclopedia of the Civil War*. pp. 43, 76, 97. Greenwich, Connecticut: Brompton Books Corp., 1992.

Carroll, Anna Ella. "The Tennessee Plan." (Handwritten Document). Maryland Historic Society. Baltimore, Maryland: November 30, 1861.

Greenbie, Marjorie Barstow. *My Dear Lady*. New York: Whittlesey House, 1940.

Larson, Rebecca D. *Blue and Gray Roses of Intrigue*. pp. 34–35. Gettysburg, Pennsylvania: Thomas Publications, 1993.

Massey, Mary Elizabeth. *Bonnet Brigades*. pp. 168–170, 320. New York: A.A. Knopf, 1966.

_____. *Women in the Civil War*. pp. 168–170, 320. Lincoln, Nebraska: University of Nebraska Press Bison Books, 1994.

Barbara Frietchie

Bailey, Ronald H., and the editors of Time-Life Books. "The Making of a Union

Heroine." p. 20. *The Civil War: The Blood-iest Day: The Battle of Antietam.* Alexandria, Virginia: Time-Life Books, 1984.

Bowman, John S. *Encyclopedia of the Civil War.* p. 85. Greenwich, Connecticut: Brompton Books Corp., 1992.

Davis, Burke. *The Civil War: Strange and Fascinating Facts.* pp. 86–89. New York: The Fairfax Press, 1982.

Garrison, Webb. *A Treasury of Civil War Tales.* pp. 80–83, 184–185. New York: Ballantine Books, 1988.

Leonard, Elizabeth D. *All the Daring of the Soldier.* pp. 168–169. New York: W. W. Norton and Co., 1999.

Vandiver, Frank E. *1001 Things Everyone Should Know About the Civil War.* p. 63. New York: Random House, 1999.

Civil War Heroines

LOLA, PANCHITA, AND EUGENIA SANCHEZ

Leonard, Elizabeth D. *All the Daring of the Soldier.* p. 67. New York: W. W. Norton and Co., 1999.

Underwood, J. L. *The Women of the Confederacy.* New York: Neale Publishing, 1906.

ANTOINETTE POLK

Leonard, Elizabeth D. *All the Daring of the Soldier.* p. 68. New York: W. W. Norton and Co., 1999.

Massey, Mary Elizabeth. *Bonnet Brigades.* p. 104. New York: A. A. Knopf, 1966.

_____. *Women in the Civil War.* p. 104. Lincoln, Nebraska: University of Nebraska Press Bison Books, 1994.

Simkins, Francis Butler, and James Welch Patton. *The Women of the Confederacy.* New York: Garret and Massey, 1936. Reprinted — St. Clair Shores, Michigan: Scholarly Press, 1976.

LAURA RATCLIFFE

Bakeless, John. *Spies of the Confederacy.* pp. 62–63. Philadelphia, Pennsylvania: J.B. Lippincott Company, 1970.

Larson, Rebecca D. *Blue and Gray Roses of Intrigue.* pp. 37–38. Gettysburg, Pennsylvania: Thomas Publications, 1993.

Markle, Donald E. *Spies and Spymasters of the Civil War.* pp. 168, 201. New York: Hippocrene Books, 1994.

Russell, Charles E. *Memoirs of Colonel John Mosby.* pp. 21, 46, 93. Boston, Massachusetts, 1917. n.p.

NANCY HART

Hall, Richard. *Patriots in Disguise: Women Warriors of the Civil War.* pp. 104, 198, 203. New York: Paragon House, 1993.

Larson, Rebecca D. *Blue and Gray Roses of Intrigue.* p. 49. Gettysburg, Pennsylvania: Thomas Publications, 1993.

Leonard, Elizabeth D. *All the Daring of the Soldier.* p. 91. New York: W. W. Norton and Co., 1999.

Markle, Donald E. *Spies and Spymasters of the Civil War.* pp. 168, 201. New York: Hippocrene Books, 1994.

CLARA JUDD

Bakeless, John. *Spies for the Confederacy.* pp. 214–215. Philadelphia, Pennsylvania: J.B. Lippincott Company, 1970.

Larson, Rebecca D. *Blue and Gray Roses of Intrigue.* p. 39. Gettysburg, Pennsylvania: Thomas Publications, 1993.

Sarah E. Thompson

Bowman, John S. *The Civil War Almanac.* pp. 360–361. New York: Gallery Books, 1983.

_____. *The Civil War Day by Day.* p. 176. Greenwich, Connecticut: Brompton Books Corp., 1989.

_____. *Encyclopedia of the Civil War.* pp. 122–123. Greenwich, Connecticut: Brompton Books Corp., 1992.

Hoehling, A.A. *Women Who Spied.* pp. 26–40. New York: Dodd, Mead and Company, 1967.

Leonard, Elizabeth D. *All the Daring of the Soldier.* p. 69. New York: W. W. Norton and Co., 1999.

"Sarah E. Thompson Papers." Special Collections Library. Duke University. Durham, North Carolina.

Schutzer, A. I. *Great Civil War Escapes.* pp. 77–119. New York: G. P. Putnam, 1967.

Stern, Philip Van Doren. *Secret Missions of the Civil War.* pp. 155–167. New York: Bonanza Books, 1990.

Mary Ann Ball Bickerdyke

Bailey, Ronald H., and the editors of Time-Life Books. "Sherman on the March." pp. 24–26. *The Civil War. Battles for Atlanta: Sherman Moves East.* Alexandria, Virginia: Time-Life Books, 1985.

Baker, Nina Brown. *Cyclone in Calico: The Story of Mary Ann Bickerdyke.* Boston, Massachusetts. Little, Brown and Company, 1952.

Botkin, B. A. *A Civil War Treasury of Tales Legends and Folklore.* pp. 140–141. New York: Random House, 1960.

Bowman, John S. *Encyclopedia of the Civil War.* p. 26. Greenwich, Connecticut: Brompton Books Corp., 1992.

Brocket, L.P., and Mary Vaughan. *Woman's Work in the Civil War: A Record of Heroism, Patriotism and Patience.* pp. 165–170, 172–186. Philadelphia: Ziegler, McCurdy and Co., 1867.

Chang, Ina. *A Separate Battle: Women and the Civil War.* pp. 41–43. New York: Lodestar Books, 1991.

Jackson, Donald Dale, and the editors of Time-Life Books. "An Artery of Love." pp. 128–130. *The Civil War. Twenty Million Yankees: The Northern Home Front.* Alexandria, Virginia: Time-Life Books, 1985.

Leonard, Elizabeth D. *All the Daring of the Soldier.* p. xx. New York: W. W. Norton and Co., 1999.

Massey, Mary Elizabeth. *Bonnet Brigades.* pp. 48–49. New York: A. A. Knopf, 1966.

_____. *Women in the Civil War.* pp. 48–49. Lincoln, Nebraska: University of Nebraska Press Bison Books, 1994.

Moore, Frank. *Women of the War.* pp. 465–471. Hartford, Connecticut: S. S. Scranton and Co., 1867.

O'Brien, Jean Getman. "Mrs. Mary Ann (Mother) Bickerdyke: The Brigadier Commanding Hospitals." p. 21. *Civil War Times Illustrated.* Vol. 1, Number 9. Gettysburg, Pennsylvania: Historical Times, Inc., January 1963.

Stein, Alice P. "The North's Unsung Sisters of Mercy." pp. 39–44. *America's Civil War.*

Leesburg, Virginia: Primedia Special Interest Publications, September 1999.

Clara Barton

Bailey, Ronald H., and the editors of Time-Life Books. *The Civil War: The Bloodiest Day: The Battle of Antietam.* p. 136. Alexandria, Virginia: Time-Life Books, 1984.

Bowman, John S. *The Civil War Almanac.* p. 313. New York: Gallery Books, 1983.

_____. *Encyclopedia of the Civil War.* p. 22. Greenwich, Connecticut: Brompton Books Corp., 1992.

Brocket, L.P., and Mary Vaughan. *Woman's Work in the Civil War: A Record of Heroism, Patriotism and Patience.* pp. 111–132. Philadelphia: Ziegler, McCurdy Co., 1867.

Burgess, Lauren Cook. *An Uncommon Soldier.* p. 4. New York: Oxford University Press, 1994.

Burnett, William G. *Clara Barton at Andersonville.* Pamphlet. Andersonville, Georgia, undated.

Catton, Bruce, and the editors of American Heritage. *The American Heritage Picture History of the Civil War.* p. 371. New York: American Heritage Publishing Co., 1960.

_____. *The Army of the Potomac: Mr. Lincoln's Army.* p. 316. Garden City, New York: Doubleday and Co. Inc., 1962.

Chang, Ina. *A Separate Battle: Women and the Civil War.* pp. 24–25, 43, 86–87. New York: Lodestar Books, 1991.

Commager, Henry Steele. *The Blue and the Gray.* pp. 779–780. New York: The Fairfax Press, 1982.

_____. *Illustrated History of the Civil War.* p. 166. New York: Promontory Press, 1976.

Garrison, Webb. *A Treasury of Civil War Tales.* pp. 64–68. New York: Ballantine Books, 1988.

Hubble, John T. "Clara Barton, Soldier or Pacifist?" pp. 152–160. *Civil War History, A Journal of the Middle Period.* Vol. XXIV. Kent, Ohio: Kent State University Press, 1978.

Jackson, Donald Dale, and the editors of Time-Life Books. "An Artery of Love." p. 128. *The Civil War. Twenty Million Yankees: The Northern Home Front.* Alexandria, Virginia: Time-Life Books, 1985.

Leonard, Elizabeth D. *Yankee Women.* p. xx.

New York: W. W. Norton and Company, 1994.

Massey, Mary Elizabeth. *Bonnet Brigades.* pp. 44, 46, 51–52, 132, 337. New York: A. A. Knopf, 1966.

_____. *Women in the Civil War.* pp. 44, 46, 51–52, 132, 337. Lincoln, Nebraska: University of Nebraska Press Bison Books, 1994.

Oats, Stephen B. *A Woman of Valor: Clara Barton and the Civil War.* New York: The Free Press, 1994.

O'Brien, Jean Getman. "Clara Barton Brought Mercy to Antietam." p. 38. *Civil War Times Illustrated.* Vol. 1, Number 5. Gettysburg, Pennsylvania: Historical Times Inc., August 1962.

Robertson, James I., Jr., and the editors of Time-Life Books. "The Wasted Legions." pp. 94, 98. *The Civil War: Tenting Tonight: The Soldier's Life.* Alexandria, Virginia: Time-Life Books, 1984.

Rose, Isabella. *Angel of the Battlefield.* New York: Harper and Brothers Publishers, 1956.

Sheppard, Peggy. *Andersonville, Georgia U.S.A.* pp. 4, 45–57. Andersonville, Georgia: Sheppard Publications, 1998.

Stein, Alice P. "The North's Unsung Sisters of Mercy." pp. 38–44. *America's Civil War.* Leesburg, Virginia: Primedia Special Interest Publications, September 1999.

Civil War Nurses

LOUISA MAY ALCOTT

Chang, Ina. *A Separate Battle: Women and the Civil War.* pp. 32–35, 37–39, 41. New York: Lodestar Books, 1991.

Davis, Burke. *The Civil War: Strange and Fascinating Facts.* p. 77. New York: The Fairfax Press, 1982.

Massey, Mary Elizabeth. *Bonnet Brigades.* pp. 63, 178. New York: A. A. Knopf, 1966.

_____. *Women in the Civil War.* pp. 63, 178. Lincoln, Nebraska: University of Nebraska Press Bison Books, 1994.

Robertson, James I., Jr., and the editors of Time-Life Books. "The Wasted Legions." pp. 94, 98. *The Civil War: Tenting Tonight: The Soldier's Life.* Alexandria, Virginia: Time-Life Books, 1984.

Stein, Alice P. "The North's Unsung Sisters of Mercy." pp. 42–43. *America's Civil War.* Leesburg, Virginia: Primedia Special Interest Publications, September 1999.

Vandiver, Frank E. *1001 Things Everyone Should Know About the Civil War.* p. 34. New York: Random House, 1999.

MARY ASHTON RICE LIVERMORE

Bowman, John S. *Encyclopedia of the Civil War.* p. 112. Greenwich, Connecticut: Brompton Books Corp., 1992.

Brocket, L.P., and Mary Vaughan. *Woman's Work in the Civil War: A Record of Heroism, Patriotism and Patience.* pp. 577–589. Philadelphia, Pennsylvania: Ziegler, McCurdy and Co., 1867.

Chang, Ina. *A Separate Battle: Women and the Civil War.* pp. 26–31. New York: Lodestar Books, 1991.

Conklin, E. F. *Women at Gettysburg 1863.* p. 135. Gettysburg, Pennsylvania: Thomas Publications, 1993.

Hall, Richard. *Patriots in Disguise: Women Warriors of the Civil War.* pp. 28, 157. New York: Paragon House, 1993.

Jackson, Donald Dale, and the editors of Time-Life Books. "An Artery of Love." pp. 116, 119–120, 122–124, 127, 133. *The Civil War: Twenty Million Yankees: The Northern Home Front.* Alexandria, Virginia: Time-Life Books, 1985.

Leonard, Elizabeth D. *All the Daring of the Soldier.* pp. 111, 120, 209–210. New York: W. W. Norton and Co., 1999.

_____. *Yankee Women.* pp. xvii, xix, 8. New York: W. W. Norton and Company, 1994.

Massey, Mary Elizabeth. *Bonnet Brigades.* pp. 11, 38, 49–50, 79. New York: A. A. Knopf, 1966.

_____. *Women in the Civil War.* pp. 11, 38, 49–50, 79. Lincoln, Nebraska: University of Nebraska Press Bison Books, 1994.

SALLY LOUISE TOMPKINS

Chang, Ina. *A Separate Battle: Women and the Civil War.* p. 37. New York: Lodestar Books, 1991.

Channing, Steven A., and the editors of Time-Life Books. p. 59. *The Civil War. Confederate Ordeal: The Southern Homefront.* Alexandria, Virginia: Time-Life Books, 1984.

Massey, Mary Elizabeth. *Bonnet Brigades*. pp. 47–48. New York: A. A. Knopf, 1966.

_____. *Women in the Civil War*. pp. 47–48. Lincoln, Nebraska: University of Nebraska Press Bison Books, 1994.

Stein, Alice P. "The North's Unsung Sisters of Mercy." pp. 42–43. *America's Civil War*. Leesburg, Virginia: Primedia Special Interest Publications, September 1999.

Waugh, Charles G., and Martin H. Greenberg. *The Woman's War in the South: Recollections and Reflections of the American Civil War*. pp. 303–306. Nashville, Tennessee: Cumberland House Publications, Inc., 1999.

Women Doctors in the Civil War

MARY EDWARDS WALKER

Bowman, John S. *Encyclopedia of the Civil War*. p. 179. Greenwich, Connecticut: Brompton Books Corp., 1992

Leonard, Elizabeth D. *Yankee Women*. pp. 104–157, 193–194. New York: W. W. Norton and Co., 1994.

Markle, Donald E. *Spies and Spymasters of the Civil War*. pp. 188, 214. New York: Hippocrene Books, 1994.

Massey, Mary Elizabeth. *Bonnet Brigades*. pp. 360–361. New York: A. A. Knopf, 1966.

_____. *Women in the Civil War*. pp. 360–361. Lincoln, Nebraska: University of Nebraska Press Bison Books, 1994.

ELIZABETH BLACKWELL

Bowman, John S. *Encyclopedia of the Civil War*. p. 27. Greenwich, Connecticut: Brompton Books Corp., 1992

Brocket, L.P., and Mary Vaughan. *Woman's Work in the Civil War: A Record of Heroism, Patriotism and Patience*. pp. 111–132, 165–170, 172–186, 527–529, 749–753. Philadelphia: Ziegler, McCurdy and Co., 1867.

Chang, Ina. *A Separate Battle: Women and the Civil War*. pp. 20–23. New York: Lodestar Books, 1991.

Jackson, Donald Dale, and the editors of Time-Life Books. "An Artery of Love." p. 120. *The Civil War: Twenty Million Yankees: The Northern Home Front*. Alexandria, Virginia: Time-Life Books, 1985.

Leonard, Elizabeth D. *Yankee Women*. pp. xx. 10–11, 106. New York: W. W. Norton and Company, 1994.

Massey, Mary Elizabeth. *Bonnet Brigades*. pp. 9, 33, 46, 334–335. New York: A. A. Knopf, 1966.

_____. *Women in the Civil War*. pp. 9, 33, 46, 334–335. Lincoln, Nebraska: University of Nebraska Press Bison Books, 1994.

Women Crusaders

DOROTHEA DIX

Bowman, John S. *Encyclopedia of the Civil War*. p. 69. Greenwich, Connecticut: Brompton Books Corp., 1992.

Brocket, L.P., and Mary Vaughan. *Woman's Work in the Civil War: A Record of Heroism, Patriotism and Patience*. pp. 97–108. Philadelphia, Pennsylvania: Ziegler, McCurdy and Co., 1867.

Chang, Ina. *A Separate Battle: Women and the Civil War*. pp. 36–37. New York: Lodestar Books, 1991.

Jackson, Donald Dale, and the editors of Time-Life Books. "An Artery of Love." pp. 127–128. *The Civil War. Twenty Million Yankees: The Northern Home Front*. Alexandria, Virginia: Time-Life Books, 1985.

Leonard, Elizabeth D. *Yankee Women*. pp. xix, 11, 14, 29, 36, 93. New York: W. W. Norton and Company, 1994.

Massey, Mary Elizabeth. *Bonnet Brigades*. pp. 23, 46–47, 51, 61, 74, 330, 351. New York: A. A. Knopf, 1966.

_____. *Women in the Civil War*. pp. 23, 46–47, 51, 61, 74, 330, 351. Lincoln, Nebraska: University of Nebraska Press Bison Books, 1994.

Millbrook, Minnie Dubbs. "Michigan Women Who Went to War." p. 22. *Michigan Women in the Civil War*. Michigan Civil War Centennial Observance Commission, 1963.

Robertson, James I., Jr., and the editors of Time-Life Books. The Wasted Legions." pp. 95, 98. *The Civil War: Tenting Tonight: The Soldier's Life*. Alexandria, Virginia: Time-Life Books, 1984.

Stein, Alice P. "The North's Unsung Sisters of Mercy." pp. 40–42. *America's Civil War.* Leesburg, Virginia: Primedia Special Interest Publications, September 1999.

HARRIET BEECHER STOWE

Bowman, John S. *The Civil War Day by Day.* p. 16. Greenwich, Connecticut: Brompton Books Corp., 1991.

_____. *Encyclopedia of the Civil War.* pp. 165, 169. Greenwich, Connecticut: Brompton Books Corp., 1992.

Chang, Ina. *A Separate Battle: Women and the Civil War.* pp. 8–17. New York: Lodestar Books, 1991.

Davis, William C., and the editors of Time-Life Books. "One Nation, Divisible." pp. 47, 66. *The Civil War: Brother Against Brother: The War Begins.* Alexandria, Virginia: Time-Life books, 1983.

Garrison, Webb. *A Treasury of Civil War Tales.* pp. 3–5. New York: Ballantine Books, 1988.

Jackson, Donald Dale, and the editors of Time-Life Books. "Fissures of Dissent." p. 39. *The Civil War: Twenty Million Yankees: The Northern Home Front.* Alexandria, Virginia: Time-Life Books, 1985.

Massey, Mary Elizabeth. *Bonnet Brigades.* pp. 15, 253, 306. New York: A. A. Knopf, 1966.

_____. *Women in the Civil War.* pp. 15, 253, 306. Lincoln, Nebraska: University of Nebraska Press Bison Books, 1994.

JULIA WARD HOWE

Bowman, John S. *Encyclopedia of the Civil War.* p. 99. Greenwich, Connecticut: Brompton Books Corp., 1992.

Commager, Henry Steele. *The Blue and the Gray.* pp. 571–573. New York: The Fairfax Press, 1982.

Davis, Burke. *The Civil War: Strange and Fascinating Facts.* p. 73. New York: The Fairfax Press, 1982.

Garrison, Webb. *A Treasury of Civil War Tales.* pp. 100–102. New York: Ballantine Books, 1988.

Massey, Mary Elizabeth. *Bonnet Brigades.* p. 177. New York: A. A. Knopf, 1966.

_____. *Women in the Civil War.* p. 177. Lincoln, Nebraska: University of Nebraska Press Bison Books, 1994.

Vandiver, Frank E. *1001 Things Everyone Should Know About the Civil War.* pp. 235–236. New York: Random House, 1999.

Index

Index

Index